Rick Steves ®

SNAPSHOT

Hill Towns
of
Central Italy

P9-DML-677

CONTENTS

INTRODUCTION

This Snapshot guide, excerpted from my guidebook *Rick Steves Italy*, introduces you to the hill towns of central Italy. Here in Italy's heartland, you'll enjoy an idyllic landscape, time-passed medieval hill towns, and tree-lined meandering backcountry roads. Dine on Italy's heartiest food in an atmospheric farmhouse, and taste a glass of wine poured by a proud vintner whose family's name has been on the bottle for generations.

I've included a mix of towns and cities, some undiscovered, some deservedly popular. Choose among the back-door towns of Volterra and Civita, the wine lovers' towns of Montepulciano and Montalcino, touristy towered San Gimignano, manicured Pienza, classic Orvieto, tradition-steeped Siena, and spiritual, artsy Assisi—or even better, visit them all.

To help you have the best trip possible, I've included the following topics in this book:

• **Planning Your Time,** with advice on how to make the most of your limited time

• **Orientation,** including tourist information (abbreviated as TI), tips on public transportation, local tour options, and helpful hints

• **Sights** with ratings:

    ▲▲▲—Don't miss

    ▲▲—Try hard to see

    ▲—Worthwhile if you can make it

    No rating—Worth knowing about

• **Sleeping** and **Eating,** with good-value recommendations in every price range

• **Connections,** with tips on trains, buses, and driving

Practicalities, near the end of this book, has information on money, staying connected, hotel reservations, transportation, and more, plus Italian survival phrases.

   To travel smartly, read this little book in its entirety before you go. It's my hope that this guide will make your trip more meaningful and rewarding. Traveling like a temporary local, you'll get the absolute most out of every mile, minute, and dollar.

Buon viaggio!

Rick Steves

HILL TOWNS
OF CENTRAL ITALY

The sun-soaked hill towns of central Italy offer what to many is the quintessential Italian experience: sun-dried tomatoes, homemade pasta, wispy cypress-lined drive-ways following desolate ridges to fortified 16th-century farmhouses, atmospheric *enoteche* serving famously tasty wines, and dusty old-timers warming the same bench day after day while soccer balls buzz around them like innocuous flies. Hill towns are best enjoyed by adapting to the pace of the countryside. So, slow...down...and savor the delights that this region offers. Spend the night if you can, as many hill towns are mobbed by day-trippers.

PLANNING YOUR TIME

How in Dante's name does a traveler choose from Italy's hundreds of hill towns? The one(s) you visit will depend on your interests, time, and mode of transportation.

For me, **Volterra**—with its rustic vitality—is a clear winner, and its out-of-the-way location keeps it from being trampled by tourist crowds. Multitowered **San Gimignano** is a classic, but because it's such an easy hill town to visit (about 1.5 hours by bus from Florence), peak-season crowds can overwhelm its charms.

Wine aficionados head for **Montepulciano** (my favorite of the two towns) and **Montalcino**—each a happy gauntlet of wine shops and art galleries. Fans of architecture and urban design appreciate **Pienza**'s well-planned streets and squares.

Assisi, Siena, and Orvieto—while technically hill towns—are in a category by themselves: Bigger and with more major ar-

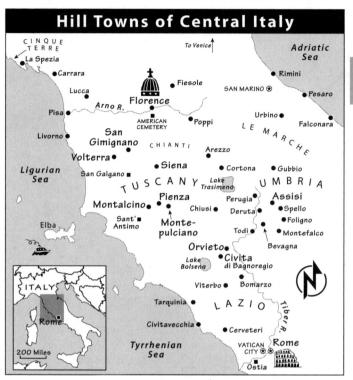

Hill Towns of Central Italy

tistic and historic sights, they each get their own chapter. (The Orvieto chapter also includes my all-around favorite hill town, the stranded-on-a-hilltop Civita di Bagnoregio.)

GETTING AROUND THE HILL TOWNS

While you can reach just about any place with public buses, taxis, and patience, most hill towns are easier and more efficient to visit by car. For more on all of these topics, see the Practicalities chapter.

By Bus or Train

Buses are often the only public-transportation choice to get between small hill towns. While trains link some towns, hill towns—being on hills—don't quite fit the railroad plan. Stations are likely to be in the valley a couple of miles from the town center, connected by a local bus. Buses don't always drive up into

HILL TOWNS

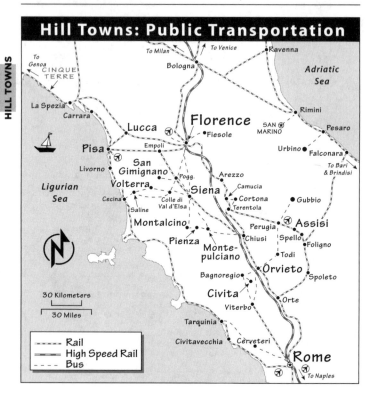

Hill Towns: Public Transportation

To Genoa · CINQUE TERRE

To Milan · To Venice · Ravenna

Bologna

Adriatic Sea

La Spezia · Carrara

Lucca · Florence · SAN MARINO · Rimini · Pesaro

Fiesole

Pisa · Empoli · Urbino · Falconara

Livorno · San Gimignano · Pogg. · Arezzo · To Bari & Brindisi

Ligurian Sea

Volterra · Siena · Camucia

Cecina · Colle di Val d'Elsa · Cortona · Gubbio

Saline · Terentola

Montalcino · Perugia · Assisi

Pienza · Chiusi · Spello · Foligno

Monte-pulciano · Todi

Bagnoregio · Orvieto · Spoleto

30 Kilometers

30 Miles

Civita · Orte

Viterbo

Tarquinia

Civitavecchia · Cerveteri

Rome

To Naples

---- Rail
──── High Speed Rail
- - - Bus

the town itself. Fortunately, stations are sometimes connected to the town by escalator or elevator. (For more on traveling by train and bus in Italy, see the appendix.) If you're pinched for time, it makes sense to narrow your focus to one or two hill towns, or rent a car.

By Car

Exploring the hill towns by car can be a great experience. Wait to pick up your car until the last sizable town you visit (or at the nearest airport to avoid big-city traffic), and carry a good, detailed road map in addition to any digital navigation systems. Freeways (such as the toll autostrada and the non-toll *superstrada*) are the fastest way to connect two points, but smaller roads, including the super-scenic

Driving in Tuscany

S-222, which runs through the heart of the Chianti region (connecting Florence and Siena), are more rewarding.

Parking can be challenging. Some towns don't allow visitors to park in the city center: Leave your car outside the walls and walk into town. Signs reading *ZTL (Zona Traffico Limitato)*—often above a red circle—indicate no driving or parking is allowed. Parking lots, identified by blue *P* signs, are usually free and plentiful outside city walls (and sometimes linked to the town center by elevators or escalators). If street parking is available, nearby kiosks sell "pay and display" tickets. White lines indicate free parking, blue lines are pay parking, and yellow lines are spaces for local residents. To reduce theft, choose a parking lot instead of street parking if possible. Your hotelier can also recommend parking options.

HILL TOWNS

SLEEPING IN A HILL TOWN

For a relaxing break from big-city Italy, settle down in an *agri-turismo*—a farmhouse that rents out rooms to travelers (usually for a minimum of a week in high season). These rural B&Bs—almost by definition in the middle of nowhere—provide a good home base from which to find the magic of Italy's hill towns. I've listed several good options throughout these chapters.

SIENA

Siena was medieval Florence's archrival. And while Florence ultimately won the battle for political and economic superiority, Siena still competes for the tourists. Sure, Florence has the heavyweight sights. But Siena seems to be every Italy connoisseur's favorite town. In my office, whenever Siena is mentioned, someone exclaims, "Siena? I looove Siena!"

Once upon a time (about 1260-1348), Siena was a major banking and trade center, and a military power in a class with Florence, Venice, and Genoa. With a population of about 50,000, it was even bigger than Paris. Situated on the north-south road to Rome (Via Francigena), Siena traded with all of Europe. Then, in 1348, the Black Death—an epidemic of bubonic plague—swept through Europe, hitting Siena and cutting the population by more than a third. Siena never recovered. In the 1550s, Florence, with the help of Philip II's Spanish army, conquered the flailing city-state, forever rendering Siena a nonthreatening backwater. Siena's loss became our sightseeing gain, as its political and economic irrelevance pickled the city in a purely medieval brine. Today, Siena's population is still at its medieval level of 50,000, although only 18,000 of those live within the walls.

Situated atop three hills, Siena qualifies as Italy's ultimate "hill town." Its thriving historic center, with red-brick lanes cascading every which way, offers Italy's best medieval city experience. Most people visit Siena, just 35 miles south of Florence, as a day trip, but it's best experienced at twilight. While Florence has the blockbuster museums, Siena has an easy-to-enjoy soul: Courtyards sport flower-decked wells, alleys dead-end at rooftop views, and the sky is a rich blue dome.

For those who dream of a Fiat-free Italy, Siena is a haven. Pedestrians rule in the old center of town, as the only drivers allowed are residents and cabbies. Sit at a café on the main square. Wander narrow streets lined with colorful flags and studded with iron rings to tether horses. Take time to savor the first European city to eliminate automobile traffic from its main square (1966) and then, just to be silly, wonder what would happen if they did it in your hometown.

PLANNING YOUR TIME

On a quick trip, consider spending two nights in Siena (or three nights with a whole-day side-trip into Florence). Whatever you do, be sure to enjoy a sleepy medieval evening in Siena. The next morning, you can see the city's major sights in half a day.

Orientation to Siena

Siena lounges atop a hill, stretching its three legs out from Il Campo. This pedestrianized main square is the historic meeting point of Siena's neighborhoods.

Just about everything mentioned in this chapter is within a 15-minute walk of the square. Navigate by three major landmarks (Il Campo, Duomo, and Church of San Domenico), following the excellent system of street-corner signs. The typical visitor sticks to the Il Campo-San Domenico axis. Make it a point to stray from this main artery. Sienese streets go in anything but a straight line, so it's easy to get lost—  but equally easy to get found. Don't be afraid to explore.

Siena itself is one big sight. Its individual attractions come in two little clusters: the square (Civic Museum and City Tower) and the cathedral (Baptistery and Duomo Museum, with its surprise viewpoint), plus the Pinacoteca for art lovers. Check these sights off, and then you're free to wander.

TOURIST INFORMATION

The TI is just across from the cathedral (daily April-Oct 9:30-18:30; Nov-March Mon-Sat 10:00-17:00, Sun 10:00-13:00; Piazza del Duomo 1, tel. 0577-280-551, www.terresiena.it). They hand out a few pretty booklets (including the regional *Terre di Siena* guide) and a free map. The bookshop next to the information desk sells more detailed Siena maps.

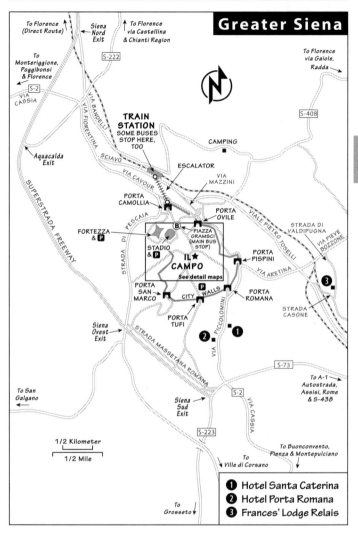

SIENA

Greater Siena

To Florence (Direct Route)

Siena Nord Exit

To Florence via Castellina & Chianti Region

To Florence via Gaiole, Radda

To Monteriggione, Poggibonsi & Florence

S-222

S-2

VIA CASSIA

S-408

VIA BANDELLI

VIA FIORENTINA

SCIAVO

VIA CAVOUR

TRAIN STATION
SOME BUSES STOP HERE, TOO

ESCALATOR

CAMPING

VIA MAZZINI

Aquacalda Exit

SUPERSTRADA FREEWAY

STRADA DI PESCAIA

PORTA CAMOLLIA

PORTA OVILE

VIALE PIETRO TOSELLI

STRADA DI VALDIPUGNA

VIA PIEVE BOZZONE

FORTEZZA & P

B

PIAZZA GRAMSCI (MAIN BUS STOP)

STADIO & P

IL CAMPO
See detail maps

PORTA PISPINI

VIA ARETINA

3

PORTA SAN MARCO

CITY WALLS

P

VIA PICCOLOMINI

PORTA ROMANA

STRADA CASONE

PORTA TUFI

Siena Ovest Exit

STRADA MASSETANA ROMANA

2

1

S-73

To A-1 Autostrada, Assisi, Rome & S-438

To San Galgano

Siena Sud Exit

S-2

VIA CASSIA

S-223

To Buonconvento, Pienza & Montepulciano

1/2 Kilometer

1/2 Mile

To Ville di Corsano

To Grosseto

1 Hotel Santa Caterina
2 Hotel Porta Romana
3 Frances' Lodge Relais

ARRIVAL IN SIENA
By Train

The small train station at the base of the hill, on the edge of town, has a bar/tobacco shop, a bus office (Mon-Fri 7:15-19:30, Sat 7:15-17:45, Sun 7:15-12:00 & 15:15-18:30, opens later in winter), and a newsstand (which sells local bus tickets—buy one now if you're taking the city bus into town), but no baggage check or lockers (stow bags at Piazza Gramsci—see "By Intercity Bus," later). A shopping mall with a Pam supermarket (handy for picnic supplies) is across the plaza right in front of the station. WCs are at the far north on track 1, past the pharmacy to the left.

Getting from the Train Station to the City Center: To reach central Siena, you can hop aboard the city bus, ride a long series of escalators, or take a taxi.

By Bus or Escalator: To reach either the bus or the escalators, head for the shopping mall across the square. From the tracks, go down the stairs into the tunnel that connects the platforms; this leads (with escalators) right up into the mall. Alternatively, you can exit the station out the front door, bear left across the square, and use the corner entrance marked "Galleria Porta Siena" (near the Pam supermarket).

To ride the **city bus,** go through the shopping mall's right-hand door at the corner entrance and take the elevator down to the subterranean bus stop. If you didn't buy bus tickets in the train station, you can get them from the blue machine (press "F" to toggle to English, then select "A" for type of ticket). Buses leave frequently (6/hour, fewer on Sun and after 22:00, €1.20, about a 10-minute ride into town). Smaller shuttle buses go up to Piazza del Sale, while bigger city buses head to nearby Piazza Gramsci (both at the north end of town, walkable to most of my recommended hotels). Before boarding, double-check the destination with the driver by asking *"Centro?"* Validate your ticket in the machine onboard.

Riding the **escalator** into town takes a few minutes longer and requires more walking than the bus. From the station, enter the mall at the far-left end as described above. Once inside, go straight ahead and ride the escalators up two floors to the food court. Continue directly through the glass doors to another escalator (marked *Porta Camollia/Centro*) that takes you gradually, up, up, up into town. Exiting the escalator, turn left down the big street, bear left at the fork, then continue straight through the town gate. From here, landmarks are well-signed (go up Via Camollia).

By Taxi: The taxi stand is to your left as you exit the train station, but as the city is chronically short on cabs, getting one here can take a while (about €10 to Il Campo, taxi tel. 0577-49222).

Getting to the Train Station from the City Center: You can ride a smaller shuttle bus directly to the station from Piazza del Sale, or catch an orange or red-and-silver city bus from Piazza Gramsci (which may take a more roundabout route). Multiple bus routes make this trip—look for *Ferrovia* or *Stazione* on schedules and marked on the bus, and confirm with the driver that the bus is going to the *stazione* (staht-see-OH-nay).

By Intercity Bus

Most buses arrive in Siena at Piazza Gramsci, a few blocks north of the city center. (Some buses only go to the train station; others go first to the train station, then continue to Piazza Gramsci—to find out, ask your driver, "pee-aht-sah GRAHM-chee?") The main bus companies are Sena/Baltour and Tiemme/Siena Mobilità. Day-trippers can store baggage in the Sottopassaggio la Lizza passage-way underneath Piazza Gramsci at the Tiemme/Siena Mobilità office (daily 7:00-19:00, carry-on-sized luggage no more than 33 pounds, no overnight storage). From Piazza Gramsci, it's an easy walk into the town center—just head in the opposite direction of the tree-filled park.

SIENA

By Car

Siena is not a good place to drive. Plan on parking in a big lot or garage and walking into town.

Drivers coming from the autostrada take the *Siena Ovest* exit and follow signs for *Centro,* then *Stadio* (stadium). The soccer-ball signs take you to the stadium lot (Parcheggio Stadio, €2/hour, pay when you leave) near Piazza Gramsci and the huge, bare-brick Church of San Domenico. The nearby Fortezza lot charges the same amount.

Another good option is the underground Santa Caterina garage (you'll see signs on the way to the stadium lot, same price). From the garage, hike 150 yards uphill through a gate to an escala-tor on the right, which carries you up into the city. If you're staying in the south end of town, try the Il Campo lot, near Porta Tufi.

On parking spots, blue stripes mean pay and display; white stripes mean free parking. You can park for free in the lot west of the Fortezza; in white-striped spots behind the Hotel Villa Liberty (south of the Fortezza); and overnight in most city lots (20:00-8:00). Signs showing a street cleaner and a day of the week indicate when the street is closed to cars for cleaning.

Driving within Siena's city center is restricted to local cars and is policed by automatic cameras. If you drive or park anywhere marked *Zona Traffico Limitato (ZTL),* you'll likely have a hefty ticket waiting for you in the mail back home. Check with your hotel in advance if you plan to drop off your bags before parking.

HELPFUL HINTS

Combo-Tickets: Siena always seems to be experimenting with different combo-tickets, but in general, only three are worth considering: the €12 Opa Si combo-ticket that includes the Duomo, Duomo Museum, Crypt, and Baptistery (valid three days; sold only at ticket office near Duomo Museum entrance); the €13 combo-ticket covering the Civic Museum and Santa Maria della Scala; and the €20 combo-ticket covering the Civic Museum, Santa Maria della Scala, and City Tower (valid two days).

SIENA

Wednesday Morning Market: The weekly market (clothes, knick-knacks, and food) sprawls between the Fortezza and Piazza Gramsci along Viale Cesare Maccari and the adjacent Viale XXV Aprile.

Internet Access: Cheap Phone Center is hidden in a small shopping corridor near Il Campo (daily 10:00-20:00; coming from Il Campo, go uphill past recommended Albergo Tre Donzelle, then turn left and go 20 yards along Via Cecco Angiolieri).

Post Office: It's on Piazza Matteotti (Mon-Fri 8:15-19:00, Sat 8:15-12:30, closed Sun).

Bookstores: For books and magazines in English, try **Libreria Senese** (daily 9:00-20:00, Via di Città 62, tel. 0577-280-845) and the **Feltrinelli** bookstore at Banchi di Sopra 52 (Mon-Sat 9:00-19:45, closed Sun, tel. 0577-271-104).

Laundry: Onda Blu is a modern, self-service launderette just 50 yards from Il Campo (about €6 wash and dry, daily 8:00-21:15, Via del Casato di Sotto 17).

Travel Agency: Carroccio Viaggi sells train, plane, and some bus tickets for a small fee (Mon-Fri 9:00-12:30 & 15:30-19:00, Sat 9:30-12:00, closed Sun, Via Montanini 20, tel. 0577-226-964, www.carroccioviaggi.com, info@carroccioviaggi.com).

Wine Classes: The **Tuscan Wine School** gives two-hour classes on Italian wine and food. The midday class (12:00) focuses on the local food culture and has tastings at vendors around town. Afternoon classes (16:00) teach Tuscan wines and stay in the classroom (€40/person, 20 percent discount for afternoon class with this book, classes Mon-Sat, closed Sun, Via di Stalloreggi 26, 30 yards from recommended Hotel Duomo, tel. 0577-221-704, mobile 333-722-9716, www.tuscanwineschool.com, tuscanwineschool@gmail.com, Rebecca).

Tours in Siena

Tours by Roberto: Tuscany Minibus and Siena Walking Tours

Tours by Roberto, led by Roberto Bechi, offers off-the-beaten-path minibus tours of the surrounding countryside (up to eight passengers, convenient pickup at hotel) and also arranges Siena city walks. Regardless of the size of your group, they charge per person, so these minibus tours are very economical. The first participants to book choose an itinerary—then others can join until the van fills. Roberto's passions are Sienese culture, Tuscan history, and local cuisine (tour options explained on website, full-day minibus tours-€90/person, 4-hour off-season tours-€60/person, entry fees extra; if Roberto is booked, his assistant, Fiorenza, or wife, Patti, can schedule the same tours with a good alternative guide; booking mobile 320-147-6590, Roberto's mobile 328-425-5648, www. toursbyroberto.com, toursbyroberto@gmail.com, multiday tours also offered).

Other Local Guides

Federica Olla, who leads walking tours of Siena, is a smart, youthful guide with a knack for creative teaching (€55/hour, mobile 338-133-9525, www.ollaeventi.com, info@ollaeventi.com).

GSO Guides Co-op is a group of 10 young professional guides who offer good tours covering Siena and all of Tuscany and Umbria (€140/half-day, €260/full day, they don't drive but can join you in your car, 10 percent discount for Rick Steves readers, www.guidesienaeoltre.com, mobile 338-611-0127, Silvia does the booking). Among them, Stefania Fabrizi stands out (mobile 338-640-7796, stefaniafabrizi@katamail.com).

Walking Tours

The **TI** offers walking tours of the old town. Guides usually conduct their walks in both English and Italian (€20—pay guide directly, daily April-Nov at 11:00, 2 hours, no interiors except for the Duomo, depart from TI, Piazza del Duomo 1, tel. 0577-280-551).

Bus Tours

Aggressively utilizing commissions, a company called **My Tour** has a lock on all hotel tour-promotion space. Every hotel has a rack of their brochures, which advertise a variety of five-hour countryside tours by bus (www.mytours.it, depart from Piazza Gramsci).

Siena City Walk

It's easy to get to know Siena on foot, and this short self-guided walk laces together its most important sights. You can do this walk as a quick orientation, or you can use it to lace together visits to the major sights (breaking the narration to tour City Hall, the Duomo, the Duomo Museum, and Santa Maria della Scala—all described in more detail under "Sights in Siena"). If you do the walk without entering the sights, it works great at night when the city is peaceful.
• *Start in the center of the main square, Il Campo, standing just below the fountain.*

Il Campo

This square is the heart of Siena, both geographically and metaphorically. It fans out from City Hall as if to create an amphitheater. Twice each summer, all eyes are on Il Campo when it hosts the famous Palio horse races.

Originally, this area was just a field *(campo)* located outside the city walls (which encircled the cathedral). Bits of those original

Siena at a Glance

▲▲▲Il Campo Best square in Italy. **Hours:** Always open. See page 13.

▲▲▲Duomo Art-packed cathedral with mosaic floors and statues by Michelangelo and Bernini. **Hours:** March-Oct Mon-Sat 10:30-19:00, Sun 13:30-18:00; Nov-Feb closes daily at 17:30. See page 26.

▲▲Civic Museum City museum in City Hall with Sienese frescoes, the *Effects of Good and Bad Government*. **Hours:** Daily mid-March-Oct 10:00-19:00, Nov-mid-March until 18:00. See page 23.

▲▲Duomo Museum Siena's best museum, displaying cathedral art (including Duccio's *Maestà*) and offering sweeping Tuscan views. **Hours:** Daily March-Oct 10:30-19:00, Nov-Feb 10:30-17:30. See page 30.

▲City Tower 330-foot tower climb. **Hours:** Daily March-mid-Oct 10:00-19:00, mid-Oct-Feb until 16:00. See page 25.

▲Pinacoteca Fine Sienese paintings. **Hours:** Tue-Sat 8:15-19:15, Sun-Mon 9:00-13:00. See page 25.

▲Baptistery Cave-like building with baptismal font decorated by Ghiberti and Donatello. **Hours:** Daily March-Oct 10:30-19:00, Nov-Feb until 17:30. See page 32.

▲Santa Maria della Scala Museum with much of the original *Fountain of Joy*, Byzantine reliquaries, and vibrant ceiling and wall frescoes depicting day-to-day life in a medieval hospital. **Hours:** March-Oct Mon and Wed 10:30-16:30, Thu-Sun 10:30-18:30, closed Tue; Nov-Feb closes at 16:00. See page 32.

Crypt Site of 12th-century church, housing some of Siena's oldest frescoes. **Hours:** Daily March-Oct 10:30-19:00, Nov-Feb 10:30-17:30. See page 32.

Church of San Domenico Huge brick church with St. Catherine's head and thumb. **Hours:** Daily 7:00-18:30, shorter hours Nov-Feb. See page 33.

Sanctuary of St. Catherine Home of St. Catherine. **Hours:** Daily 9:00-18:00, Chapel of the Crucifixion closed 12:30-15:00. See page 34.

walls, which curved against today's square, can be seen above the pharmacy (the black-and-white stones, third story up, to the right as you face City Hall). In the 1200s, with the advent of the Sienese republic, the city expanded. Il Campo became its marketplace and the historic junction of Siena's various competing *contrade* (neighborhood districts). The square and its buildings are the color of the soil upon which they stand—a color known to artists and Crayola users as "Burnt Sienna."

City Hall (Palazzo Pubblico), with its looming tower, dominates the square. In medieval Siena, this was the center of the city, and the whole focus of Il Campo still flows down to it.

The **City Tower** was built around 1340. At 330 feet, it's one of Italy's tallest secular towers. Medieval Siena was a proud repub-

lic, and this tower stands like an exclamation point—an architectural declaration of independence from papacy and empire. The tower's Italian nickname, Torre del Mangia, comes from a hedonistic bell-ringer who consumed his earnings like a glutton consumes food. (His chewed-up statue is just inside City Hall's courtyard, to the left as you enter.) The open **chapel** located at the base of the tower was built in 1348 as thanks to God for ending the Black Death (after it killed more than a third of the population). These days, the chapel is used to bless Palio contestants (and to provide an open space for EMTs who stand by during the race).

You can visit the Civic Museum inside City Hall and climb the tower.

• *Now turn around and take a closer look at the fountain in the top center of the square.*

Fountain of Joy (Fonte Gaia)

This fountain—a copy of an early 15th-century work by Jacopo della Quercia—marks the square's high point. The joy is all about how the Sienese republic blessed its people with water. Find Lady Justice with her scales and sword (right of center), overseeing the free distribution

of water to all. Imagine residents gathering here in the 1400s to fill their jugs. The Fountain of Joy still reminds locals that life in Siena is good. Notice the pigeons politely waiting their turn to tightrope gingerly down slippery spouts to slurp a drink from wolves' snouts. The relief panel on the left shows God creating Adam by helping him to his feet. It's said that this reclining Adam (carved a century before Michelangelo's day) influenced Michelangelo when he painted his Sistine Chapel ceiling. The original fountain is exhibited indoors at Santa Maria della Scala.

• Leave Il Campo uphill on the widest ramp. With your back to the tower, it's at 10:00. After a few steps you reach Via di Città. Turn left and walk 100 yards uphill toward the white, neo-Gothic palace. Halfway there, at the first corner, notice small plaques high on the building facades—these mark the neighborhood, or contrade. *You are stepping from the Forest into the Eagle. Notice also the once mighty and foreboding medieval tower house. Towers once soared all around town, but they're now truncated and no longer add to the skyline—look for their bases as you walk the city.*

On the left, you reach the big . . .

Chigi-Saracini Palace (Palazzo Chigi-Saracini)

This old fortified noble palace is today home to a prestigious music academy, the Accademia Musicale Chigiana. If open, step into the courtyard with its photogenic well (powerful medieval families enjoyed direct connections to the city aqueduct). The walls of the loggia are decorated with the busts of Chigi-Saracini patriarchs, and the vaults are painted in the "grotesque" style popular during the Renaissance. What look like pigeonholes in the other walls are actually for scaffolding, for both construction and ongoing maintenance. The palace hosts a festival each July and August with popular concerts almost nightly, international talent, and affordable tickets (box office just off courtyard; one-hour tours of the palace's library, art, and musical instruments cost €5 and run 2/day; Via di Città 89, www.chigiana.it).

• Continue up the hill on Via di Città to the next intersection. As you walk, notice how strict rules protect the look of exteriors. Many families live in each building, but all shutters are the same color. Inside, apartments can be modern, and expensive—some of the priciest in Italy.

Quattro Cantoni

The intersection known as Quattro Cantoni (the four corners) offers a delightful perch from which to study the city. The modern column (from 1996) with a Carrara marble she-wolf on top functions as a flag holder for the *contrada*. You are still in the Eagle district (see the fountain and the corner plaque)—but beware. Just one block up the street, a ready-to-pounce panther—from the rival neighboring district—awaits.

Only the very rich could afford stone residences. The fancy buildings here hide their economical brick construction behind a stucco veneer. The stone tower on this corner had only one door—30 feet above street level and reached by ladder, which could be pulled up as necessary. Within a few doors, you'll find a classy bar, an elegant grocery store, and a *gelateria.*

Take a little side-trip, venturing up Via di San Pietro. Interesting stops include the window with Palio video clips playing (at #1), Simon and Paula's art shop with delightful Palio and *contrade* knickknacks (#5), a weaver's shop (#7), a gelato purveyor (#10), an art gallery (#11), and four enticing little *osterias.* After a block you'll reach the best art museum in town, the **Pinacoteca**. From there to the former town gate (Porta all'Arco), the street becomes more workaday, with local shops and no tourists.

• *Back at the Four Corners, head up Via del Capitano, passing another massive Chigi family palace (bankers sure know how to get their hands on people's money) to the cathedral and Piazza del Duomo. Find a shady seat against the wall of the old hospital facing the church.*

Piazza del Duomo and the Duomo

The pair of she-wolves atop columns flanking the cathedral's facade says it all: The church was built and paid for not by the pope but by the people and the republic of Siena.

This 13th-century Gothic cathedral, with its six-story striped bell tower—Siena's ultimate tribute to the Virgin Mary—is heaped with statues, plastered with frescoes, and paved with

art. Study the richly ornamented facade. The interior is a Renaissance riot of striped columns, remarkably intricate inlaid-marble floors, a Michelangelo statue, evocative Bernini sculptures, and the amazing Piccolomini Library. (If you want to enter now, you'll need a ticket from the booth around to the right.)

Facing the cathedral is Santa Maria della Scala, a huge building that housed pilgrims and, until the 1990s, was used as a hospital. Its labyrinthine 12th-century cellars—carved out of volcanic tuff and finished with brick—go down several floors, and during medieval times were used to store supplies for the hospital upstairs. Today, the exhibit-filled hospital and cellars can be a welcome refuge from the hot streets.

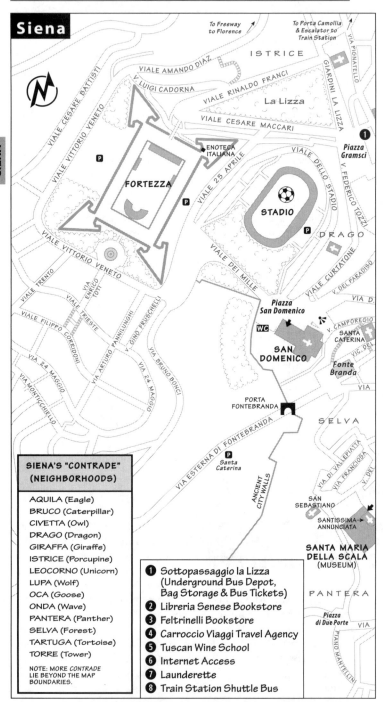

Siena

SIENA

SIENA'S "CONTRADE" (NEIGHBORHOODS)

AQUILA (Eagle)
BRUCO (Caterpillar)
CIVETTA (Owl)
DRAGO (Dragon)
GIRAFFA (Giraffe)
ISTRICE (Porcupine)
LEOCORNO (Unicorn)
LUPA (Wolf)
OCA (Goose)
ONDA (Wave)
PANTERA (Panther)
SELVA (Forest)
TARTUGA (Tortoise)
TORRE (Tower)

NOTE: MORE *CONTRADE* LIE BEYOND THE MAP BOUNDARIES.

1 Sottopassaggio la Lizza (Underground Bus Depot, Bag Storage & Bus Tickets)
2 Libreria Senese Bookstore
3 Feltrinelli Bookstore
4 Carroccio Viaggi Travel Agency
5 Tuscan Wine School
6 Internet Access
7 Launderette
8 Train Station Shuttle Bus

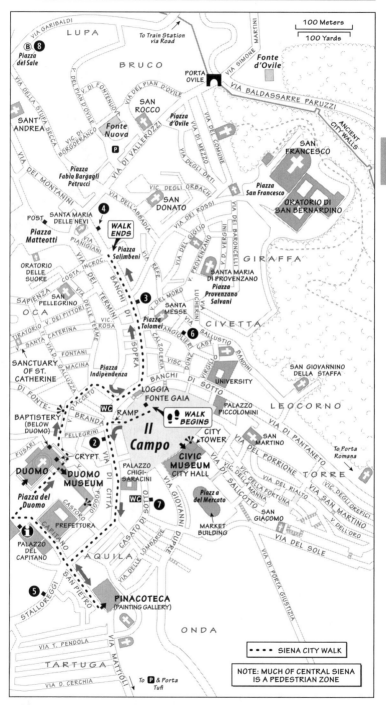

Siena's *Contrade* and the Palio

Siena's 17 historic neighborhoods, or *contrade*, each with a parish church, well or fountain, and square, still play an active role in the life of the city. Each is represented by a mascot (porcupine, unicorn, wolf, etc.) and unique colors worn proudly by residents.

Contrada pride is evident year-round in Siena's parades and colorful banners, lamps, and wall plaques. If you hear the thunder of distant drumming, run to it for some medieval action—there's a good chance it'll feature flag throwers. Buy a scarf in *contrada* colors, and join in the merriment of these lively neighborhood festivals.

Contrade rivalries are most visible twice a year—on July 2 and August 16—during the city's world-famous horse race, the **Palio di Siena.** Ten of the 17 neighborhoods compete (chosen by rotation and lot), hurling themselves with medieval abandon into several days of trial races and traditional revelry. Jockeys—usually from out of town—are considered hired guns, no better than paid mercenaries. Bets are placed on which *contrada* will win...and lose. Despite the shady behind-the-scenes dealing, on the big day the horses are taken into their *contrada*'s church to be blessed. ("Go and return victorious," says the priest.) It's considered a sign of luck if a horse leaves droppings in the church.

On the evening of the race, Il Campo is stuffed to the brim with locals and tourists. Dirt is brought in and packed down to create the track's surface, while mattresses pad the walls of surrounding buildings. The most treacherous spots are the sharp corners, where many a rider has bitten the dust.

Picture the scene: Ten snorting horses and their nervous rid-

---

Grand as Siena's cathedral is, it's actually the rump of a failed vision. After rival republic Florence began its grand cathedral (1296), proud Siena planned to build an even bigger one, the biggest in all Christendom. But Siena is so hilly that there wasn't enough flat ground upon which to build a church of that size. What to do? Build a big church anyway, and prop up the overhanging edge with the Baptistery (which we'll pass shortly).

Walk around to the right of the church and find the unfinished wall with see-through windows (circa 1330). From here you can envision the audacity of this vision—today's cathedral would have been just a transept. But the vision underestimated the complexity of constructing such a building without enough land. That, coupled with the devastating effects of the 1348 plague, killed the

ers line up near the pharmacy (on the west side of the square) to await the starting signal. Then they race like crazy while spectators wave the scarves of their neighborhoods.

Every possible vantage point and perch is packed with people straining to see the action. One lap around the course is about a third of a mile (350 meters); three laps make a full circuit. In this no-holds-barred race—which lasts just over a minute—a horse can win even without its rider (jockeys ride precariously without saddles and often fall off the horses' sweaty backs).

SIENA

When the winner crosses the line, 1/17th of Siena—the prevailing neighborhood—goes berserk. Winners receive a *palio* (banner), typically painted by a local artist and always featuring the Virgin Mary (the race is dedicated to her). But the true prizes are proving that your *contrada* is *numero uno*, and mocking your losing rivals.

All over town, sketches and posters depict the Palio. This is not some folkloric event—it's a real medieval moment. If you're packed onto the square with 60,000 people, all hungry for victory, you may not see much, but you'll feel it. Bleacher and balcony seats are expensive, but it's free to join the masses in the square. Go with an empty bladder as there are no WCs, and be prepared to surrender any sense of personal space.

While the actual Palio packs the city, you can more easily see the horse-race trials—called *prove*—on any of the three days before the main event (usually at 9:00 and after 19:00, free seats in bleachers). For more information, visit www.ilpalio.org.

city's ability and will to finish the project. Many Sienese saw the Black Death as a sign from God, punishing them for their pride. They canceled their plans and humbly faded into the background of Tuscan history.

• *Walk to the rear of the church (past the ticket office for the church complex and the Duomo Museum) and pause at the top of the marble stairs leading down. The Duomo Museum (to your right) houses the church's art.*

Supporting an Oversized Church

From here, look down the stairs leading behind the church and see the architect's quandary. The church sticks out high above the lower street level. Partway down the stairs is the Crypt, and below that is the Baptistery. Each is an integral part of the foundation for the oversized structure. (Both the Crypt and the Baptistery are worth entering.)

• *Descend the stairs, nicknamed "The Steps of St. Catherine," as she would have climbed them each day on her walk from home to the hospital. Below the Baptistery, jog right, then left, and through a tunnel down Via di Diaceto. Pause for a beautiful view of the towering brick Dominican church in the distance on the left. Then continue straight up the lane until you reach the next big square.*

Piazza Indipendenza

This square celebrates the creation of a unified Italy (1860) with a 19th-century loggia sporting busts of the first two Italian kings. Stacking history on history, the neo-Renaissance loggia is backed by a Gothic palace and an older medieval tower.

• *Head right downhill one block (on Via delle Terme), back to the grand Via di Città, and take a few steps to the left to see another fancier loggia.*

Loggia della Mercanzia

This Gothic-Renaissance loggia was built about 1420 as a kind of headquarters for the union of merchants (it's just above Il Campo). Siena's nobility purchased it, and eventually it became the clubhouse of the local elites. To this day, it's a private, ritzy, and no-toriously   out-of-step-with-the-times men's club. The "Gli Uniti" above the door is a "let's stick together" declaration.

• *From here, steep steps lead down to Il Campo, but we'll go left and uphill on Via Banchi di Sopra. Pause at the intersection of...*

Via Banchi di Sopra and Via Banchi di Sotto

These main drags are named "upper row of banks" and "lower row of banks." They were once lined with market tables *(banchi)*, and vendors paid rent to the city for a table's position along the street. If the owner of a *banco* neglected to pay up, thugs came along and literally broke *(rotto)* his table. It is from this practice—*banco rotto*, broken table—that we get the English word "bankrupt."

In medieval times, these streets were part of the Via Fran-cigena, the main thoroughfare linking Rome with northern Europe. Today, strollers—out each evening for their *passeggiata*—fill Via Banchi di Sopra. Join the crowd, strolling past Siena's finest shops. You could nip into Nannini, a venerable café and *pasticceria* famous for its local sweets. The traditional Sienese taste treats (*cantucci, ricciarelli,* and various kinds of fruity and nutty *panforte*) are around the far end of the counter in the back (sold by weight, small amounts are fine, a little slice of panforte costs about €3).

A block or so farther up the street, Piazza Tolomei faces the imposing Tolomei family palace. This is a center for the Owl *contrada.* The column in the square is for *contrada* announcements of births, deaths, parties, festivals, and so on.

• *Continue on Via Banchi di Sopra to Piazza Salimbeni; this gets my vote for Siena's finest stretch of palaces.*

Piazza Salimbeni

The next square, Piazza Salimbeni, is dominated by Monte dei Paschi, the head office of a bank founded in 1472. It's amazing to think this bank has been in business on this square for over 500 years. Originally a kind of community bank for common people, in this generation, Monte dei Paschi's image has sunk to become the poster child for Italian bank scandals. Notice the Fort Knox-style base of the building. The statue in the center honors Sallustio Antonio Bandini. His claim to fame: He invented the concept of collateral.

Directly across from Piazza Salimbeni, the steep little lane called Costa dell'Incrociata leads straight (down and then up) to the Church of San Dominico (it's worth the hike). Also nearby (behind the cute green newsstand) is the most elegant grocery store in town, Consorzio Agrario di Siena. It's like a museum of local edibles (for more on this store).

• *With this walk under your belt, you've got the lay of the land. The city is ready for further exploration—the sights associated with City Hall and the Duomo are all just a few minutes away. Enjoy delving deeper into Siena.*

Sights in Siena

IL CAMPO AND NEARBY

The gorgeous red-brick square known as Il Campo is itself worth ▲▲▲. First laid out in the 12th century, today it's the only town square I've seen where people stretch out as if at the beach. At the flat end of its clam-shell shape is City Hall, where you can tour the Civic Museum and climb the City Tower.

▲▲Civic Museum (Museo Civico)

Siena's City Hall is the spot where secular government got its start in early Renaissance Europe. There you'll find city government still at work, along with a sampling of local art, including Siena's first fresco (with a groundbreaking down-to-earth depiction of the

Madonna). It's worth strolling through the dramatic halls to see fascinating frescoes and portraits extolling Siena's greats, saints, and the city-as-utopia.

Cost and Hours: Museum-€9, €13 combo-ticket with Santa Maria della Scala, €20 combo-ticket includes City Tower and Santa Maria della Scala (valid two days), ticket office is straight ahead as you enter City Hall courtyard, daily mid-March-Oct 10:00-19:00, Nov-mid March until 18:00, last entry 45 minutes before closing, audioguide-€5, tel. 0577-292-342, www.comune.siena.it.

Visiting the Museum: Start in the Sala del Risorgimento, with dramatic scenes of Victor Emmanuel II's unification of Italy (surrounded by statues that don't seem to care).

Passing through the chapel, where the city's governors and bureaucrats prayed, enter the Sala del Mappamondo. On opposite walls are two large frescoes. The beautiful *Maestà* (*Enthroned Virgin*, 1315), by Siena's great Simone Martini (c. 1280-1344), is groundbreaking as Siena's first fresco showing a Madonna not in a faraway, gold-leaf heaven, but under the blue sky of a real space that we inhabit. Facing the *Maestà* is the famous *Equestrian Por-*

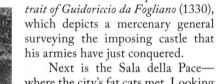

trait of Guidoriccio da Fogliano (1330), which depicts a mercenary general surveying the imposing castle that his armies have just conquered.

Next is the Sala della Pace— where the city's fat cats met. Looking down on the oligarchy during their meetings was a fascinating fresco series showing the *Effects of Good and Bad Government,* by Sienese painter Ambrogio Lorenzetti. Compare the whistle-while-you-work happiness of the utopian community ruled by the utopian government (in the better-preserved fresco) against the crime, devastation, and societal mayhem of a community ruled by politicians with more typical values. The message: Without justice, there can be no prosperity.

On your way out, climb up to the loggia (using the stairs just before the Sala del Risorgimento) for a sweeping view of the city and its surroundings. (For a less impressive version of this view, you could skip the stairs and simply peek behind the curtains in the Sala della Pace.)

▲City Tower (Torre del Mangia)

The tower's nearly 400 steps get pretty skinny at the top, but the reward is one of Italy's best views. For more on the tower, see my "Siena City Walk," earlier.

Cost and Hours: €10, €20 combo-ticket with Civic Museum and Santa Maria della Scala, daily March-mid-Oct 10:00-19:00, mid-Oct-Feb until 16:00, last entry 45 minutes before closing, closed in rain, free and mandatory bag check.

Crowd Alert: Admission is limited to 50 people at a time. Wait at the bottom of the stairs for the green *Avanti* light. Try to avoid midday crowds (up to an hour wait at peak times).

▲Pinacoteca

If you're into medieval art, you'll likely find this quiet, uncrowded, colorful museum delightful. The museum walks you through Siena's art chronologically, from the 12th through the 16th century, when a revolution in realism was percolating in Tuscany.

Cost and Hours: €4, Tue-Sat 8:15-19:15, Sun-Mon 9:00-13:00, free and mandatory bag check (must leave ID). From Il Campo, walk out Via di Città and go left on Via San Pietro to #29; tel. 0577-281-161 or 0577-286-143, www.pinacotecanazionale.siena.it.

Visiting the Museum: In general, the collection lets you follow the evolution of painting styles from Byzantine to Gothic, then to International Gothic, and finally to Renaissance.

Long after Florentine art went realistic, the Sienese embraced a timeless, otherworldly style glittering with lots of gold. But Sienese art features more than just paintings. In this city of proud craftsmen, the gilding and carpentry of the frames almost compete with the actual paintings. The exquisite attention to detail gives a glimpse into the wealth of the 13th and 14th centuries, Siena's Golden Age. The woven silk and gold clothing you'll see was worn by the very people who once walked these halls, when this was a private mansion (appreciate the colonnaded courtyard).

The core of the collection is on the second floor, in Rooms 1-19. Works by Duccio di Buoninsegna (the artist of the *Maestà* in the Duomo Museum) feature groundbreaking innovations that are subtle: less gold-leaf background, fewer gold creases in robes, translucent garments, inlaid-marble thrones, and a more human Mary and Jesus. Notice that the Madonna-and-Bambino pose is eerily identical in each version. *St. Augustine of Siena*, by Duccio's assistant, Simone Martini (who did the *Maestà* and possibly the

Guidoriccio frescoes in the Civic Museum), sets the saint's life in realistic Sienese streets, buildings, and landscapes. In each panel, the saint pops out at the oddest (difficult to draw) angles to save the day.

Also look for religious works by the hometown Lorenzetti brothers (Ambrogio is best known for the secular masterpiece, the *Effects of Good and Bad Government,* in the Civic Museum). *Città sul Mare (City by the Sea)* and *Castello in Riva al Lago (Castle on the Lakeshore)* feature a strange, medieval landscape Cubism. Notice the weird, melancholy light that captures the sense of the Dark Ages.

Several colorful rooms on the first floor are dedicated to Domenico Beccafumi (1486-1551), who designed many of the Duomo's inlaid pavement panels (including *Slaughter of the Innocents*). With strong bodies, twisting poses, and dramatic gestures, Beccafumi's works epitomize the Mannerist style.

CATHEDRAL AREA

The cathedral-related sights (Duomo, Duomo Museum, Crypt, and Baptistery) can be visited with separate tickets, or with the €12 Opa Si combo-ticket (worthwhile only if you'll visit all four sights). The €20 Opa Si Plus combo-ticket adds a guided visit to the Duomo rooftop. All tickets are sold only at the office near the entrance to the Duomo Museum—to the right as you face the cathedral facade—no tickets are sold at sight entrances.

▲▲▲Duomo

Siena's 13th-century cathedral and striped bell tower are one of the most illustrious examples of Romanesque-Gothic style in Italy. The interior showcases the work of the greatest sculptors of every era— Pisano, Donatello, Michelangelo, and Bernini—and the Piccolomini Library features a series of 15th-century frescoes chronicling the adventures of Siena's philanderer-turned-pope, Aeneas Piccolomini.

Cost: €4 includes cathedral and Piccolomini Library, buy ticket at Duomo Museum entrance (facing the cathedral entry, the museum is 100 yards to the right, near the south transept). To add the Duomo Museum, Crypt, and Baptistery, consider the €12 Opa Si combo-ticket; to add an escorted visit into the dome and rooftop (described below), pay €20 for the Opa Si Plus combo-ticket.

Check the line to get into the Duomo before buying tickets— if there's a long wait, you can pay an extra €1 for a "reservation" that lets you skip the line (available at the "reserved/fast entrance" queue).

Hours: March-Oct Mon-Sat 10:30-19:00, Sun 13:30-18:00; Nov-Feb closes daily at 17:30.

Dress Code: Modest dress is required, but stylish paper ponchos are provided for the inappropriately clothed.

Information: Tel. 0577-286-300, www.operaduomo.siena.it.

Tours: The **videoguide** (rent in the nave, €6) is informative but dry. I'd stick with the commentary in this section.

Cathedral Roof Visit: The Opa Si Plus combo-ticket includes all of the cathedral sights plus a 30-minute accompanied Porta del Cielo ("Heaven's Gate") visit to the dome's cupola and roof (timed-entry ticket, escorted visits of 18 people go each half-hour, March-Oct Mon-Sat from 10:30-18:00, Sun 13:30-17:00, less frequent off-season, tel. 0577-286-300 for advance reservations).

❷ Self-Guided Tour: Grab a spot on a stone bench opposite the entry to take in this architectural festival of green, white, pink, and gold.

Exterior View: Like a medieval altarpiece, the facade is divided into sections, each frame filled with patriarchs and prophets, studded with roaring gargoyles, and topped with prickly pinnacles.

The current structure dates back to 1215, with the major decoration done during Siena's heyday (1250-1350). The lower story, by Giovanni Pisano (who worked from 1284 to 1297), features remnants of the fading Romanesque style (round arches over the doors), topped with the pointed arches of the new Gothic style that was seeping in from France. The upper half, in full-blown frilly Gothic, was designed and built a century later.

• *Step inside, putting yourself in the mindset of a pilgrim as you take in this trove of religious art.*

Nave: The heads of 172 popes—who reigned from the time of St. Peter to the 12th century—peer down from above, looking over the fine inlaid art on the floor. With a forest of striped columns, a coffered dome, a large stained-glass window at the far end (described later), and an art gallery's worth of early Renaissance art, this is one busy interior. If you look closely at the popes, you'll see the same four faces repeated over and over.

For almost two centuries (1373-1547), 40 artists paved the marble floor with scenes from the Old Testament, allegories, and intricate patterns. The series starts near the entrance with historical allegories; the larger, more elaborate scenes surrounding the altar are mostly stories from the Old Testament. Many of the floor panels are roped off—and occasionally even covered—to prevent further wear and tear. The second pavement panel from the entrance depicts Siena as a **she-wolf** at the center of the Italian universe, orbited by such lesser lights as Roma, Florentia (Florence), and Pisa. The fourth pavement panel from the entrance is the **Fortune Panel,** with Lady Luck (lower right) parachuting down to earth, where she teeters back and forth on a ball and a tipsy boat. The lesson? Fortune is an unstable foundation for life. On the right wall hangs a dim **painting of St. Catherine** (fourth from entrance), Siena's homegrown saint who had a vision in which she mystically married Christ.

• *Look for the marble altarpiece decorated with statues.*

Piccolomini Altar: This was designed for the tomb of the Sienese-born Pope Pius III (born Francesco Piccolomini), but was never used. The altar is most interesting for its statues: one by Michelangelo, and three by his students. Michelangelo was originally contracted to do 15 statues, but another sculptor had started the marble blocks, and Michelangelo's heart was never in the project. He personally finished only one—the figure of St. Paul (lower right, clearly more interesting than the bland, bored popes above him).

• *Now grab a seat under the...*

Dome: The dome sits on a 12-sided base, but its "coffered" ceiling is actually a painted illusion. Get oriented to the array of sights we'll see by thinking of the church floor as a big 12-hour clock. You're the middle, and the altar is high noon: You'll find the *Slaughter of the Innocents* roped off on the floor at 10 o'clock, Pisano's pulpit between two pillars at 11 o'clock,

a copy of Duccio's round stained-glass window at 12 o'clock, Bernini's chapel at 3 o'clock, the Piccolomini Altar at 7 o'clock, the Piccolomini Library at 8 o'clock, and a Donatello statue at 9 o'clock.

Pisano's Pulpit: The octagonal Carrara marble pulpit (1268) rests on the backs of lions, symbols of Christianity triumphant. Like the lions, the Church eats its catch (devouring paganism) and nurses its cubs. The seven relief panels tell the life of Christ in rich detail. The pulpit is the work of Nicola Pisano (c. 1220-1278), the "Giotto of sculpture," whose revival of classical forms (columns, sarcophagus-like relief panels) signaled the coming Renaissance. His son Giovanni (c. 1240-1319) carved many of the panels, mixing his dad's classicism and realism with the decorative detail and curvy lines of French Gothic.

Duccio's Stained-Glass Rose Window: This is a copy of the original window, (now in the Duomo Museum). The famous rose window was created in 1288 and dedicated to the Virgin Mary.

Slaughter of the Innocents: This pavement panel shows Herod (left), sitting enthroned amid Renaissance arches, as he orders the massacre of all babies to prevent the coming of the promised Messiah. It's a chaotic scene of angry soldiers, grieving mothers, and dead babies, reminding locals that a republic ruled by a tyrant will experience misery.

• *Step into the chapel just behind you (next to the Piccolomini Library), to see the...*

St. John the Baptist Statue: The statue of the rugged saint in his famous rags was created by Donatello. The aging Florentine sculptor, whose style was now considered passé in Florence, came here to build bronze doors for the church (similar to Ghiberti's in Florence). He didn't complete the door project, but he did finish this bronze statue (1457). Notice the cherubs high above it, playfully dangling their feet.

• *Cross the church. Directly opposite find the Chigi Chapel, also known as the...*

Chapel of the Madonna del Voto: To understand why Gian Lorenzo Bernini (1598-1680) is considered the greatest Baroque sculptor, step into this sumptuous chapel (designed in the early 1660s for Fabio Chigi, a.k.a. Pope Alexander VII). Move up to the altar and look back at the two Bernini statues: Mary Magdalene in a state of spiritual ecstasy, and St. Jerome playing the crucifix like a violinist lost in beautiful music.

The painting over the altar is the *Madonna del Voto,* a Madonna and Child adorned with a real crown of gold and jewels (painted by a Sienese master in the mid-13th century). In typical medieval fashion, the scene is set in the golden light of heaven. Mary has the almond eyes, long fingers, and golden folds in her robe that are found in orthodox icons of the time. Still, this Mary tilts her head and looks out sympathetically, ready to listen to the prayers of the faithful. This is the Mary to whom the Palio is dedicated, dear to the hearts of the Sienese. In thanks, they give **offerings** of silver hearts and medallions, many of which now hang on the wall just to the left as you exit the chapel.

• *Cross back to the other side of the church to find the...*

Piccolomini Library: Brilliantly frescoed, the library captures the exuberant, optimistic spirit of the 1400s, when humanism and the Renaissance were born. The never-restored frescoes look nearly as vivid now as the day they were finished 550 years ago. The painter Pinturicchio (c. 1454-1513) was hired to celebrate the life of one of Siena's hometown boys—a man many call "the first humanist," Aeneas Piccolomini (1405-1464), who became Pope Pius II. Each of the 10 scenes is framed with an arch, as if Pinturicchio were opening a window onto the spacious 3-D world we inhabit.

The library also contains intricately decorated, illuminated music scores and a statue (a Roman copy of a Greek original) of the Three Graces, who almost seem to dance to the beat. The oddly huge sheepskin sheets of music are from the days before individual hymnals—they had to be big so that many singers could

read the music from a distance. Appreciate the fine painted decorations on the music—the gold-leaf highlights, the blue tones from ultramarine (made from precious lapis lazuli), and the miniature figures. All of this exquisite detail was lovingly crafted by Benedictine monks for the glory of God.

• *Exit the Duomo and make a U-turn to the left, walking alongside the church to Piazza Jacopo della Quercia.*

Unfinished Church: Construction began in the 1330s on an extension off the right side of the existing Duomo (today's cathedral would have been used as a transept). The nave of the Duomo was supposed to be where the piazza is today. Worshippers would have entered the church from the far end of the piazza through the unfinished wall. (Look way up at the highest part of the wall. That viewpoint is accessible from inside the Duomo Museum.) Some of the nave's green-and-white-striped columns were built, and are now filled in with a brick wall. White stones in the pavement mark where a row of pillars would have been.

The vision was grand, but reality—and the plague—intervened. Look through the unfinished entrance facade, note blue sky where the stained-glass windows would have been, and ponder the struggles, triumphs, and failures of the human spirit.

▲▲Duomo Museum
(Museo dell'Opera e Panorama)

Located in a corner of the Duomo's grand but unfinished extension (to the right as you face the main facade), Siena's most enjoyable museum was built to house the cathedral's art. Here you stand eye-to-eye with the saints and angels who once languished, unknown, in the church's upper reaches (where copies are found today).

Cost and Hours: €7, daily March-Oct 10:30-19:00, Nov-Feb until 17:30, next to the

Duomo, in the skeleton of the unfinished part of the church on the Il Campo side, tel. 0577-286-300, www.operaduomo.siena.it.

Tours: You can rent a **videoguide** for €4, but you'll do fine with just the commentary in this section.

○ Self-Guided Tour: Start your tour at the bottom and work your way up.

Ground Floor: This floor is filled with the cathedral's original Gothic sculptures by Giovanni Pisano, who spent 10 years in the late 1200s carving and orchestrating the decoration of the cathedral with saints, prophets, sibyls, animals, and the original she-wolf with Romulus and Remus.

On the ground floor you'll also find Donatello's fine, round *Madonna and Child* carved relief. A slender, tender Mary gazes down at her chubby-cheeked baby, as her sad eyes say that she knows the eventual fate of her son.

On the opposite side of the room is Duccio's original stained-glass window, which until recently was located above and behind the Duomo's altar. Now the church has a copy, and art lovers can enjoy a close-up look at this masterpiece. The rose window—20 feet across, made in 1288—is dedicated (like the church and the city itself) to the Virgin Mary. The work is by Siena's most famous artist, Duccio di Buoninsegna (c. 1255-1319), and combines elements from rigid Byzantine icons (Mary's almond-shaped bubble, called a *mandorla,* and the full-frontal saints that flank her) with a budding sense of 3-D realism (the throne turned at a three-quarter angle to simulate depth, with angels behind).

Duccio's *Maestà:* Upstairs awaits a private audience with the *Maestà* (*Enthroned Virgin,* 1311), whose panels were once part of the Duomo's main altarpiece. Although the former altarpiece was disassembled (and the frame was lost), most of the pieces are displayed here, with the front side (*Maestà,* with Mary and saints) at one end of the room, and the back side (26 Passion panels) at the other.

The *Maestà* was revolutionary for the time in its sheer size and opulence, and in Duccio's budding realism, which broke standard conventions. Duccio, at the height of his powers, used every innovative arrow in his quiver. He replaced the standard gold-leaf background (symbolizing heaven) with a gold, intricately patterned curtain draped over the throne. Mary's blue robe opens to reveal her body, and the curve of her knee suggests real anatomy beneath the robe. Baby Jesus wears a delicately transparent garment. Their faces are modeled with light—a patchwork of bright flesh and shadowy valleys, as if lit from the left (a technique he likely learned from his contemporary Giotto during a visit to Florence).

The flip side of the *Maestà* featured 26 smaller panels—the medieval equivalent of pages—showing colorful scenes from the Passion of Christ.

Panorama dal Facciatone: About 40 claustrophobic spiral stairs take you to the first viewpoint. You can continue up another 100 steps of a similar spiral staircase to reach the very top. Standing on the wall from this high point in the city, you're rewarded with a stunning view of Siena...and an interesting perspective. Look toward the Duomo and consider this: If Siena's grandiose plans to expand the cathedral had come to fruition, you'd be looking straight down the nave toward the altar.

▲Baptistery *(Battistero)*

This richly adorned and quietly tucked-away cave of art is worth a look for its cool tranquility and exquisite art, including an ornately painted vaulted ceiling. The highlight is the baptismal font designed by Jacopo della Quercia and adorned with bronze panels and angels by Quercia, Ghiberti, and Donatello. It dates from the 1420s, the start of the Renaissance.

Cost and Hours: €4, daily March-Oct 10:30-19:00, Nov-Feb until 17:30.

Crypt (Cripta)

The cathedral "crypt" is archaeologically important. The site of a small 12th-century Romanesque church, it was filled in with dirt a century after its creation to provide a foundation for the huge church that sits atop it today. Recently excavated (with modern metal supports from the 1990s), the several rediscovered rooms show off what are likely the oldest frescoes in town (well-described in English).

Cost and Hours: €6, €8 during special exhibitions, daily March-Oct 10:30-19:00, Nov-Feb until 17:30, entrance near the top of the stairs between the Baptistery and Duomo Museum.

OTHER CATHEDRAL-AREA SIGHTS

▲Santa Maria della Scala

This museum, opposite the Duomo, operated for centuries as a hospital, foundling home, and pilgrim lodging. Many of those activities are visible in the 15th-century frescoes of its main hall, the Pellegrinaio. Today, the hospital and its cellars are filled with fascinating exhibits (well-described in English).

Cost and Hours: €9, €13 combo-ticket with Civic Museum, €20 combo-ticket includes the Civic Museum and Tower (valid two days); March-Oct Mon and Wed 10:30-16:30, Thu-Sun 10:30-18:30, closed Tue; Nov-Feb closes at 16:00; tel. 0577-534-571, www.santamariadellascala.com.

Visiting the Museum: It's easy to get lost in this gigantic complex, so stay focused on the main attractions—the fancily frescoed

Pellegrinaio Hall (ground floor), most of the original *Fountain of Joy* and some of the most ancient Byzantine reliquaries in existence (first basement), and the Etruscan collection in the Archaeological Museum (second basement), where the Sienese took refuge during WWII bombing.

From the entrance, follow signs to the Pellegrinaio—the long room with the colorful frescoes.

The sumptuously frescoed walls of **Pellegrinaio Hall**—originally a reception hall for visiting pilgrims, then a hospital—show medieval Siena's innovative health care and social welfare system in action (by Sienese painters, c. 1442, wonderfully described in English). Starting in the 11th century, the hospital nursed the sick and cared for abandoned children, as is vividly portrayed in these frescoes. The good works paid off, as bequests and donations poured in, creating the wealth that's evident throughout this building.

Head down the stairs, then continue straight into the darkened rooms with pieces of Siena's landmark fountain—follow signs to Fonte Gaia.

An engaging exhibit explains Jacopo della Quercia's early 15th-century *Fountain of Joy (Fonte Gaia)*—and displays the disassembled pieces of the original fountain itself. In the 19th century, after serious deterioration, the ornate fountain was dismantled and plaster casts were made. (These casts formed the replica that graces Il Campo today.) Here you'll see the eroded original panels paired with their restored casts, along with the actual statues that once stood on the edges of the fountain.

To visit the reliquaries, retrace your steps and follow the signs for *Il Tesoro*. Many of these **Byzantine reliquaries** are made of gold, silver, and precious stones. Legend has it that some were owned by Helen, Constantine's mother. They were "donated" (around 1350) to the hospital shortly after the plague that decimated the city (and the rest of Europe), since the sale of reliquaries was forbidden.

Now, descend into the cavernous second basement. Under the groin vaults of the **Archaeological Museum,** you're alone with piles of ancient Etruscan stuff excavated from tombs dating centuries before Christ (displayed in another labyrinthine exhibit). You'll see terra-cotta funeral urns for ashes (the design was often a standard body with the heads personalized) and piles of domestic artifacts from the 8th to the 5th century B.C.

SAN DOMENICO AREA
Church of San Domenico

This huge brick church is worth a quick look. Spacious and plain (except for the colorful flags of the city's 17 *contrade*), the Gothic interior fits the austere philosophy of the Dominicans and invites meditation on the thoughts and deeds of St. Catherine (1347-1380). Walk up the steps in the rear to see paintings from her life. Halfway up the church on the right, find a copper bust of St. Catherine (for four centuries it contained her skull), a small case housing her thumb (on the right), and a page from her personal devotional book (12th century, on the left). In the chapel (15 feet to the left) surrounded with candles, you'll see Catherine's head (a clay mask around her skull with her actual teeth showing through) atop the altar. Through the door just beyond are the sacristy and the bookstore.

Cost and Hours: Free, daily 7:00-18:30, shorter hours off-season, www.basilicacateriniana.com.

Sanctuary of St. Catherine (Santuario di Santa Caterina)

Step into the cool and peaceful site of Catherine's home. Siena remembers its favorite hometown gal, a simple, unschooled, but mystically devout soul who, helped convince the pope to return from France to Rome. Pilgrims have visited this place since 1464, and architects and artists have greatly embellished what was probably once a humble home (her family worked as wool dyers). You'll see paintings throughout showing scenes from her life.

Enter through the courtyard, and walk down the stairs at the far end. The church on your right contains the wooden crucifix upon which Catherine was meditating when she received the stigmata (the wounds of Christ) in 1375. Take a pew, and try to imagine the scene. Back outside, the oratory across the courtyard stands where the kitchen once was. Go down the stairs (left of the gift shop) to reach the saint's room. Catherine's bare cell is behind wrought-iron doors.

Cost and Hours: Free, daily 9:00-18:00, Chapel of the Crucifixion closed from 12:30-15:00 but church stays open, a few downhill blocks toward the center from San Domenico—follow signs to *Santuario di Santa Caterina*—at Costa di Sant'Antonio 6.

Sleeping in Siena

Finding a room in Siena is tough during Easter (March 27 in 2016) or the Palio (July 2 and Aug 16). Many hotels won't take reservations until the end of May for the Palio, and even then they might require a four-night stay. While day-tripping tour groups turn the town into a Gothic amusement park in midsummer, Siena is basically yours in the evenings and off-season.

Part of Siena's charm is its lively, festive character—this means that all hotels can be plagued with noise, even (and sometimes especially) the hotels in the pedestrian-only zone. If tranquility is

Sleep Code

Abbreviations   (€1=about $1.10, country code: 39)
S=Single, **D**=Double/Twin, **T**=Triple, **Q**=Quad, **b**=bathroom
Price Rankings
  $$$ **Higher Priced**—Most rooms €130 or more
   $$ **Moderately Priced**—Most rooms €90-130
    $ **Lower Priced**—Most rooms €90 or less
Unless otherwise noted, credit cards are accepted, breakfast is included, free Wi-Fi and/or a guest computer is generally available, and English is spoken. Many towns in Italy levy a hotel tax of €1.50-5 per person, per night (often collected in cash; usually not included in the rates I've quoted). Prices change; verify current rates online or by email. For the best prices, always book directly with the hotel.

important for your sanity, ask for a room that's off the street, or consider staying at one of the recommended places outside the center. If your hotel doesn't provide breakfast, eat at a bar on Il Campo or near your hotel.

FANCY SLEEPS NEAR IL CAMPO

These well-run places are a 10-minute walk from Il Campo. If driving, get parking instructions from your hotel in advance. You'll go through Porta San Marco, turn right, and follow signs to your hotel—drop your bags, then park as they instruct.

$$$ Pensione Palazzo Ravizza is elegant and friendly, with 39 rooms and an aristocratic feel—fitting, as it was once the luxurious residence of a noble. Guests enjoy a peaceful garden set on a dramatic bluff, along with a Steinway in the upper lounge (Sb-€180, standard Db-€180, superior Db-€220, Tb-€255, family suites-€300, rooms in back overlook countryside, air-con, elevator, Via Piano dei Mantellini 34, tel. 0577-280-462, www.palazzoravizza.it, bureau@palazzoravizza.it). As parking here is free and the hotel is easily walkable from the center, this is a particularly good value for drivers.

$$$ Hotel Duomo has 20 spacious and tidy but slightly dated rooms, a picnic-friendly roof terrace, and a bizarre floor plan (Sb-€105, Db-€130, Db suite-€180, Tb-€180, Qb-€230, elevator with some stairs, air-con, parking-€20/day; Via di Stalloreggi38, tel. 0577-289-088, www.hotelduomo.it, booking@hotelduomo.it, Alessandro). If you're arriving by train, take a taxi (€12) or ride bus #3 to the Porta Tufi stop, just a few minutes' walk from the hotel.

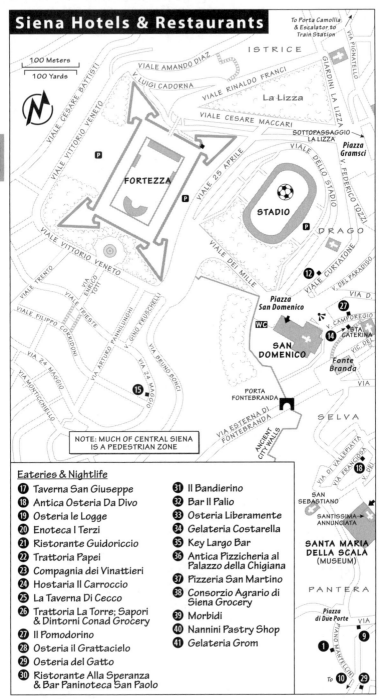

Siena Hotels & Restaurants

SIENA

To Porta Camollia
& Escalator to
Train Station

ISTRICE

VIALE AMANDO DIAZ

V. LUIGI CADORNA

VIALE RINALDO FRANCI

La Lizza

VIALE CESARE MACCARI

SOTTOPASSAGGIO
LA LIZZA

Piazza
Gramsci

VIALE CESARE BATTISTI

VIALE VITTORIO VENETO

100 Meters
100 Yards

FORTEZZA

VIALE 25 APRILE

VIALE DELLO STADIO

STADIO

P

DRAGO

VIALE VITTORIO VENETO

VIALE DEI MILLE

VIALE CURTATONE

VIALE TRENTO

VIA ENRICO TOTI

VIALE TRIESTE

VIALE FILIPPO CORRIDONI

VIA GINO TRUSCHELLI

VIA ARTURO PANNILUNGHI

VIA GINO BONCI

❷ ◆ 12

V. DEL PARADISO

VIA D.

Piazza
San Domenico

❷ 27

V. CAMPOREGIO

WC

❷ 14

STA.
CATERINA

SAN
DOMENICO

Fonte
Branda

VIA

VIA 24 MAGGIO

VIA MONTICCHIELLO

VIA 24 MAGGIO

❷ 15

PORTA
FONTEBRANDA

SELVA

NOTE: MUCH OF CENTRAL SIENA
IS A PEDESTRIAN ZONE

VIA ESTERNA DI
FONTEBRANDA

ANCIENT
CITY WALLS

VIA DI VALLEPIATTA

VIA FRANCIOSA

V. DEL

❷ 18

SAN
SEBASTIANO

SANTISSIMA
ANNUNCIATA

SANTA MARIA
DELLA SCALA
(MUSEUM)

PANTERA

Piazza
di Due Porte

PIANO MANTELLINI

VIA

❷ 9

❶

To ❿

❷ 29

Eateries & Nightlife

17 Taverna San Giuseppe
18 Antica Osteria Da Divo
19 Osteria le Logge
20 Enoteca I Terzi
21 Ristorante Guidoriccio
22 Trattoria Papei
23 Compagnia dei Vinattieri
24 Hostaria Il Carroccio
25 La Taverna Di Cecco
26 Trattoria La Torre; Sapori
   & Dintorni Conad Grocery
27 Il Pomodorino
28 Osteria il Grattacielo
29 Osteria del Gatto
30 Ristorante Alla Speranza
   & Bar Paninoteca San Paolo

31 Il Bandierino
32 Bar Il Palio
33 Osteria Liberamente
34 Gelateria Costarella
35 Key Largo Bar
36 Antica Pizzicheria al
   Palazzo della Chigiana
37 Pizzeria San Martino
38 Consorzio Agrario di
   Siena Grocery
39 Morbidi
40 Nannini Pastry Shop
41 Gelateria Grom

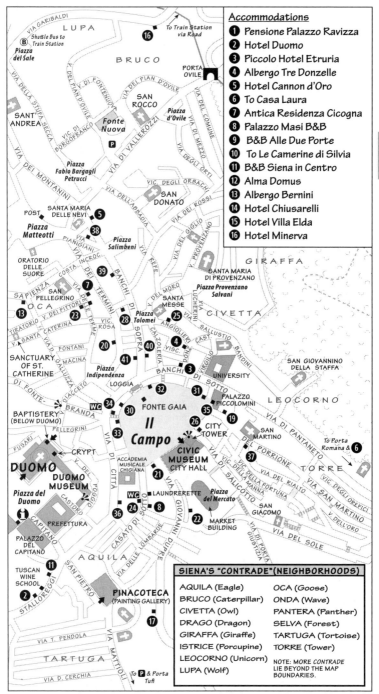

SIENA

To Train Station via Road

Accommodations

1. Pensione Palazzo Ravizza
2. Hotel Duomo
3. Piccolo Hotel Etruria
4. Albergo Tre Donzelle
5. Hotel Cannon d'Oro
6. To Casa Laura
7. Antica Residenza Cicogna
8. Palazzo Masi B&B
9. B&B Alle Due Porte
10. To Le Camerine di Silvia
11. B&B Siena in Centro
12. Alma Domus
13. Albergo Bernini
14. Hotel Chiusarelli
15. Hotel Villa Elda
16. Hotel Minerva

SIENA'S "CONTRADE" (NEIGHBORHOODS)

AQUILA (Eagle)
BRUCO (Caterpillar)
CIVETTA (Owl)
DRAGO (Dragon)
GIRAFFA (Giraffe)
ISTRICE (Porcupine)
LEOCORNO (Unicorn)
LUPA (Wolf)

OCA (Goose)
ONDA (Wave)
PANTERA (Panther)
SELVA (Forest)
TARTUGA (Tortoise)
TORRE (Tower)

NOTE: MORE CONTRADE LIE BEYOND THE MAP BOUNDARIES.

SIMPLE PLACES NEAR IL CAMPO

Most of these listings are forgettable but well-priced, and just a horse wreck away from one of Italy's most wonderful civic spaces.

$$ Piccolo Hotel Etruria, with 20 simple, recently redecorated rooms, is well located and restful (S-€50, Sb-€60, Db-€110, Tb-€138, Qb-€156, use discount code "RSITA" for best rates, breakfast-€6.50, air-con May-Oct only, elevator, at Via delle Donzelle 1, tel. 0577-288-088, www.hoteletruria.com, info@ hoteletruria.com).

$ Albergo Tre Donzelle is a fine budget value with welcoming hosts and 20 homey rooms—these may be the best-value rooms in the center. Il Campo, a block away, is your terrace (S-€38, D-€49, Db-€75, T-€70, Tb-€95, breakfast-€6.50, fans, no elevator; with your back to the tower, head away from Il Campo toward 2 o'clock to Via delle Donzelle 5; tel. 0577-270-390, www.tredonzelle.com, info@tredonzelle.com).

$ Hotel Cannon d'Oro, a few blocks up Via Banchi di Sopra, is a labyrinthine slumbermill renting 30 institutional, overpriced rooms (Sb-€71, Db-€90, Tb-€115, Qb-€136, these discounted prices good with this book through 2016, fans, Via dei Montanini 28, tel. 0577-44-321, www.cannondoro.com, info@cannondoro. com; Maurizio, Tommaso, Serge, and Rodrigo).

$ Casa Laura has eight clean, charming, well-maintained rooms, some of which have brick-and-beam ceilings (Db-€65, Db with air-con-€75, these prices through 2016 when you mention Rick Steves and book directly with the hotel, no elevator, Via Roma 3, about a 10-minute walk from Il Campo toward Porta Romana, tel. 0577-226-061, www.casalaurasiena.com, info@casalaurasiena. com).

B&BS IN THE OLD CENTER

$$ Antica Residenza Cicogna is a seven-room guesthouse with a homey elegance and an ideal location. It's warmly run by the young and charming Elisa and her friend Ilaria, who set out biscotti, Vin Santo, and tea for their guests in the afternoon. With artfully frescoed walls and ceilings, this is remarkably genteel for the price (Db-€98, suite Db-€120, third bed-€15, air-con, no elevator, Via delle Terme 76, tel. 0577-285-613, mobile 347-007-2888, www. anticaresidenzacicogna.it, info@anticaresidenzacicogna.it).

$$ Palazzo Masi B&B, run by friendly Alizzardo and Daniela, is just below Il Campo. They rent six pleasant, spacious, antique-furnished rooms with shared common areas on the second and third floors of a restored 13th-century building (D-€70, Db-€110 with this book in 2016 when you book directly and pay in cash, no breakfast, no elevator; from City Hall, walk 50 yards down Via del Casato di Sotto to #29; mobile 349-600-9155, www.

palazzomasi.com, info@palazzomasi.it). The place is sometimes unstaffed, so confirm arrival time in advance.

$ B&B Alle Due Porte is a charming little establishment renting four big rooms with sweet furniture under big medieval beams. The shared breakfast room is delightful. The manager, Egisto, is a phone call and 10-minute scooter ride away (Db-€85, windowless Db with small bed-€65, Tb-€110, air-con in three rooms, Via di Stalloreggi 51, tel. 0577-287-670, mobile 368-352-3530, www.sienatur.it, soldatini@interfree.it).

$ Le Camerine di Silvia, a romantic hideaway perched near a sweeping, grassy olive grove, rents five simple but cozy rooms in a converted 16th-century building. A small breakfast terrace with fruit trees and a private hedged garden lends itself to contemplation (Db-€50-€80, cash only, view room on request, no breakfast, fans, shared microwave and small fridge, free parking nearby, Via Ettore Bastianini 1, just below recommended Pensione Palazzo Ravizza, mobile 338-761-5052 or 339-123-7687, www.lecamerinedisilvia.com, info@lecamerinedisilvia.com, Conti family).

$ B&B Siena in Centro is a clearinghouse managing 15 rooms and five apartments. Their handy office functions as a reception area; stop by here to pick up your key and be escorted. The rooms are generally spacious, quiet, and comfortable, but with no air-conditioning or Wi-Fi. Their website lets you visualize your options (Sb-€45-60, Db-€70-90, Tb-€90-120, reception open 9:00-13:30 & 15:00-19:00, other times by phone request, Wi-Fi in office, Via di Stalloreggi 16, tel. 0577-43041, mobile 331-281-0136 or 347-465-9753, www.bbsienaincentro.com, info@bbsienaincentro.com, Gioia or Michela).

NEAR SAN DOMENICO CHURCH

These hotels are within a 10- to 15-minute walk northwest of Il Campo. Both Albergo Bernini and Alma Domus are in the old town with fine views and reasonable prices. The other two are farther out in the modern world.

$ Alma Domus is a church-run hotel featuring 28 tidy rooms with quaint balconies, some fantastic views (ask for a room *con vista*), stately public rooms, and a pleasant atmosphere. However, the thin doors, echoey halls, and nearby church bells can be drawbacks, particularly on upper floors. Consider upgrading to a snazzy superior room for slightly more (Sb-€51, Db-€87, Tb-€125, book directly with the hotel and mention Rick Steves for the best price, air-con, elevator; from San Domenico, walk downhill toward the view with the church on your right, turn left down Via Camporegio, make a U-turn down the brick steps to Via Camporegio 37; tel. 0577-44-177, www.hotelalmadomus.it, info@hotelalmadomus.it, Luigi).

$ Albergo Bernini makes you part of a Sienese family in a modest, clean home with 10 traditional rooms. Giovanni, charming wife Daniela, and their daughters welcome you to their spectacular view terrace for breakfast and picnic lunches and dinners (S-€55, D-€80, Db-€100, T-€105, Tb-€125, family room available, breakfast-€5, fans, on the main Il Campo-San Domenico drag at Via della Sapienza 15, tel. 0577-289-047, www.albergobernini.com, hbernin@tin.it).

$$$ Hotel Chiusarelli, with 48 classy rooms in a beautiful frescoed Neoclassical villa, is outside the medieval town center on a busy street. Expect traffic noise at night—ask for a quieter room in the back (which can be guaranteed with reservation, Sb-€105, Db-€160, Tb-€190, ask for 10 percent Rick Steves discount when you book directly with hotel, air-con, across from San Domenico at Viale Curtatone 15, tel. 0577-280-562, www.chiusarelli.com, info@chiusarelli.com).

$$$ Hotel Villa Elda rents 11 bright and light rooms in a recently renovated villa. It's classy, stately, pricey, and run with a feminine charm (Db-€129-159, view Db-about €20 more, extra person-€30, air-con, no elevator, garden and view terrace, closed Nov-March, Viale Ventiquattro Maggio 10, tel. 0577-247-927, www.villaeldasiena.it, info@villaeldasiena.it).

FARTHER FROM THE CENTER

These options, a 10- to 20-minute walk from the center, are convenient for drivers. These first two are about 200 yards outside the Porta Romana. To get to the historic center from here, catch minibus line A uphill to Piazza al Mercato, just behind Il Campo (€1.20). To reach the bus and train stations, take bus #2 (which becomes #17 at Piazza del Sale; when arriving, catch #17 from the station). If driving, from the freeway, take the Siena Sud exit, continue in direction *Romana*, then *Pta Romana/Centro* signs until you see the big city gate.

$$$ Hotel Santa Caterina is a three-star, 18th-century place renting 22 comfy rooms. It's professionally run with real attention to quality. While it's on a big city street, it has a delightful garden terrace with views over the countryside (Sb or small Db-€115, Db-€165, Tb-€195, Qb-€205, book directly with hotel and ask for Rick Steves rate, garden side is quieter, air-con, elevator, parking-€10/day—request when you reserve, Via E.S. Piccolomini 7, tel. 0577-221-105, www.hotelsantacaterinasiena.it, info@hotelsantacaterinasiena.it, Lorenza).

$$ Hotel Porta Romana is at the edge of town, off a busy road. Some of its 15 rooms face the open countryside (request one of these), and breakfast is served in the garden (Sb-€90, Db-€110, extra person-€20, 10 percent Rick Steves discount if you book di-

SIENA

rectly with hotel and pay cash, air-con in most rooms, free parking, inviting sun terrace, outdoor hot tub open April-Oct free to guests with this book, Via E.S. Piccolomini 35, tel. 0577-42299, www. hotelportaromana.com, info@hotelportaromana.com, Marco and Evelia).

$$ Hotel Minerva is your big, professional, plain, efficient option. It's impersonal, with zero personality, but offers predictable comfort in its 56 rooms. It works best for those with cars—parking is reasonable (€12/day), and it's only a 10-minute walk from the action (Sb-€90, Db-€122, Tb-€168, bigger suites available at higher price, view room-€20 extra, air-con, elevator, just inside Porta Ovile at the north end of town at Via Garibaldi 72, tel. 0577-284-474, www.albergominerva.it, info@albergominerva.it).

OUTSIDE SIENA

$$$ Frances' Lodge Relais is a tranquil and delightfully managed farmhouse B&B. Each of its six rooms is bursting with character (well-described on their website). Franca and Franco run this rustic-yet-elegant old place, which features a 19th-century orangery that's been made into a "better homes and palaces" living room, as well as a peaceful garden, eight acres of olive trees and vineyards, and great views of Siena and its countryside—even from the swimming pool (small Db-€170, Db-€190, Db suite-€220, Tb-€250, Tb suite-€300, Qb suite-€380, these prices through 2016 when you book directly with B&B and mention this book, possibly cheaper for longer stays, air-con, free parking, Strada di Valdipugna 2, tel. 0577-42379, mobile 337-671-608, www.franceslodge.it). To the center, it's a five-minute bus ride (€1.60, they'll call to arrange) plus a five-minute walk, or €12 by taxi. Consider having an al fresco dinner in the gazebo, complete with view (make your own picnic, or have your hosts assemble a very fancy one for €20-25/person).

Eating in Siena

Sienese restaurants are reasonable by Florentine and Venetian standards. You can enjoy ordering high on the menu here without going broke. For pasta, a good option is *pici* (PEE-chee), a thick Sienese spaghetti that seems to be at the top of every menu.

IN THE OLD TOWN
Fine Dining

These places deliver an upscale ambience, interesting menus, and generally finer food than my less dressy recommendations. The first two have no outside seating.

Taverna San Giuseppe offers modern Tuscan cuisine with a chic grotto atmosphere. Under a fine old medieval vault, you'll enjoy beautifully presented dishes from a creative and enticing menu. Attentive Matteo and his wonderful wait staff enjoy showing off their Etruscan wine cellar (be sure to venture down). Reserve ahead or arrive early (€10 pastas, €15-20 *secondi,* Mon-Sat 12:00-14:30 & 19:00-22:00, closed Sun, air-con, 7-minute climb up street to the right of City Hall at Via Giovanni Dupre 132, tel. 0577-42286, www.tavernasangiuseppe.it).

Antica Osteria Da Divo is a great splurge. The kitchen is inventive, the ambience is flowery and candlelit, some of the seating fills old Etruscan tombs, and the food is delicate and top-notch. Chef Pino is fanatic for fresh ingredients and gives traditional dishes a creative spin; he and his wife, Claudia, will make you feel at home. Reservations are smart (€12 pastas, €20-26 *secondi,* wine by the glass on request, Wed-Mon 12:00-14:30 & 19:00-22:30, closed Tue; facing Baptistery door, take the far right street to Via Franciosa 29; tel. 0577-284-381, www.osteriadadivo.it). Show this book to finish with a complimentary biscotti and Vin Santo or coffee.

Osteria le Logge caters to a fancy crowd and offers great Mediterranean cuisine with seasonal local ingredients. Inside you'll enjoy a gorgeous living-room setting (books, wood, and wine bottles), and outside there's fine seating on a pedestrian street. This is an excellent choice for dining al fresco (€14 pastas, €24 *secondi,* Mon-Sat 12:00-15:00 & 19:00-23:00, closed Sun, two blocks off Il Campo at Via del Porrione 33, tel. 0577-48013).

Enoteca I Terzi is dressy and modern under medieval vaults with a simple yet enticing menu of creative gourmet dishes and a fine wine selection. They have a few tables on a quiet square out front and an elegant main dining area, but I'd avoid the back room (€10 *primi,* €18 *secondi,* Mon-Sat 11:00-24:00, closed Sun, Via dei Termini 7, tel. 0577-44329).

More Dining Options

Ristorante Guidoriccio, just a few steps below Il Campo, feels warm and welcoming. You'll get smiling service from Ercole and Flora—the place has charm—especially if you let gentle Ercole explore the menu with you and follow his suggestions (€9 pastas, €14-15 *secondi,* Mon-Sat 12:30-14:30 & 19:00-22:30, closed Sun, air-con, no outdoor seating, Via Giovanni Dupre 2, tel. 0577-44350).

Trattoria Papei has a casual, rollicking family atmosphere and friendly servers dishing out generous portions of rib-stickin' Tuscan specialties and grilled meats. This big, sprawling place under brown tents in a parking lot is often jammed—so call to reserve (€8 pastas, €9-13 *secondi,* daily 12:00-15:00 & 19:00-22:30, on the market square behind City Hall at Piazza del Mercato 6, tel. 0577-280-894; Amedeo and Eduardo speak English).

Compagnia dei Vinattieri serves modern Tuscan dishes with a creative twist. In this elegant space, you can enjoy a romantic meal under graceful brick arches. The menu is small and accessible. Owners Marco and Gianfranco are happy to take you down to the marvelous wine cellar (€10 pastas, €16-18 *secondi,* beef is big here, leave this book on the table for a complimentary *aperitivo* or *digestivo,* daily 12:30-15:00 & 19:30-23:00, enter at Via dei Pittori 1 or Via delle Terme 79, tel. 0577-236-568).

Hostaria Il Carroccio, artsy and convivial, seats guests in a tight, sea-foam green dining room and serves elegantly presented, traditional "slow food" recipes with innovative flair at affordable prices (€8 pastas, €14-18 *secondi,* €30 tasting *menu*—minimum two people, cash only, reservations wise, Thu-Tue 12:30-15:00 & 19:30-22:00, closed Wed, Via del Casato di Sotto 32, tel. 0577-41165, sweet Renata and Mauro).

Traditional and Rustic Places

La Taverna Di Cecco is a simple, comfortable little eatery on an uncrowded back lane where earnest Luca and Gianni serve tasty salads and Sienese specialties made with fresh ingredients (€10 pastas and big salads, €12-16 *secondi,* daily 12:00-16:00 & 19:00-23:00, Via Cecco Angiolieri 19, tel. 0577-288-518).

Trattoria La Torre is an unfussy family-run *casalinga* (home-cooking) place, popular for its homemade pasta, a table of which entices customers as they enter. Its open kitchen and ten tables are packed under one medieval brick arch. Service is brisk and casual—because the only menu is posted outside, they'll explain your options individually. Still, come here more for the fun atmosphere than the cuisine. Even with its priceless position below the namesake tower, it feels more like a local hangout than a tourist trap (€8-10 pastas, €8-11 *secondi,* Fri-Wed 12:00-15:00 & 19:00-22:00, closed Thu, just steps below Il Campo at Via di Salicotto 7, tel. 0577-287-548).

Il Pomodorino is a lively restaurant serving meal-size salads and some of the best pizza in town and a wide selection of beer—unusual in wine-crazy Tuscany. The intimate modern interior is covered by brick vaulting, but the real appeal is the outdoor terrace with a great view of the Duomo (€7-10 pizza and salads, daily April-Oct 12:00-late, Nov-March 19:00-late, a few steps from the recommended Alma Domus hotel at Via Camporegio 13, tel. 0577-286-811, mobile 345-026-5865).

Osteria il Grattacielo is a funky hole-in-the-wall with a tight and homey interior and three tables under a tunnel-like arch outside, perfect for a cheap, hearty, memorable-yet-no-frills meal. Luca has no menu and just one solid house wine. You'll eat what he's cooking and pay €6 to €12 for dinner. Lunch is usually a two-course €11 affair with good salads and vegetables (Tue-Sat from 12:00 and from 19:30, closed Sun-Mon, Via dei Pontani 8, mobile 334-631-1458).

Osteria del Gatto is another classic little hole-in-the-wall, thriving with townspeople and powered by a passion for good Sienese cuisine. Friendly Marco Coradeschi and his staff cook and serve daily specials with attitude. As it's so small and popular, it can get loud (€8 pastas, €8-10 *secondi,* Mon-Fri 12:30-15:00 & 19:30-22:00, Sat 19:30-22:00 only, closed Sun, reservations recommended, 5-minute walk from the center at Via San Marco 8, tel. 0577-287-133).

ON IL CAMPO

If you choose to eat on perhaps the finest town square in Italy, you'll pay a premium, meet waiters who don't need to hustle, and get mediocre food. And yet I highly recommend it. The clamshell-shaped Il Campo is lined with venerable cafés, bars, restaurants, and pizzerias. Consider surveying the scene during your sightseeing day and reserving a table of your choice at the place that feels best to you.

Dining and Drinks on the Square

Ristorante Alla Speranza, with perhaps the best view in all of Italy, is a good option on the square (€9-12 pastas and pizzas, €17-19 *secondi,* daily 9:00-late, Piazza Il Campo 32, tel. 0577-280-190, www.allasperanza.it).

Il Bandierino is another decent option for drinks or food, with an angled view of City Hall (€10-12 salads and pizzas, €14-15 pastas; no cover but a 20 percent service charge, daily 11:00-23:00, Piazza Il Campo 64, tel. 0577-275-894).

Bar Il Palio is the best bar on Il Campo for a before- or after-dinner drink: It has straightforward prices, no cover, decent waiters, and a fantastic perspective out over the square (daily 8:30-late, Piazza Il Campo 47, tel. 0577-282-055).

Osteria Liberamente, a dynamic little bar with a trendy vibe, is popular with young locals (fine wines by the glass and €7 cocktails, daily 9:00-late, Piazza Il Campo 27, tel. 0577-274-733, Pino).

Drinks or Snacks Overlooking Il Campo

Gelateria Costarella, on the corner of Via di Città and Costarella dei Barbieri, has good drinks, pastries, sandwiches, and light meals (I'd skip their gelato). The real attraction is upstairs—its simple benches perched over Il Campo. To enjoy these, order your drink or snack from the menu rather than the cheaper bar (daily 8:00-late, Via di Città 33).

Bar Paninoteca San Paolo has a youthful English pub ambience and a row of stools overlooking the square. They have 50 kinds of €5 sandwiches, big €8 salads, and several beers on tap—it's not traditional Italian, but it's quick and filling (order and pay at the counter, food served daily 12:00-late, live music on Fri night, on Vicolo di San Paolo, tel. 0577-226-622).

Key Largo Bar has a nondescript interior, but two long, upper-story benches in the corner offer a wonderful secret perch. Buy your drink or snack at the bar, climb upstairs, and slide the ancient bar to open the door (no cover and no extra charge to sit on the balcony). Enjoy stretching out, and try to imagine how, during the Palio, three layers of spectators cram into this space—notice the iron railing used to plaster the top row of sardines up against the wall. Suddenly you're picturing Palio ponies zipping wildly around the square's notoriously dangerous corner (€4 cocktails, Mon-Fri 7:30-late, Sat-Sun 9:00-late, on the corner of Via Rinaldini).

EATING CHEAPLY IN THE CENTER

Antica Pizzicheria al Palazzo della Chigiana (a.k.a. *Pizzicheria de Miccoli*) may be the official name, but I bet locals just call it Antonio's. For most of his life, frenzied Antonio has carved salami and cheese for the neighborhood. Locals line up here for their €5-7 sandwiches—meat and cheese sold by weight—with a good €10 bottle of Chianti (Italian law dictates that he can't sell *vino* by the glass, only bottles, but he's got a number to choose from and will lend you the glasses). Antonio sells an enticing cheese and meat platter (starting at €15 per person)—but be careful...he's tricky and it can end up costing a fortune (Mon-Sat 8:00-20:00, Sun 10:00-18:00, Via di Città 95, tel. 0577-289-164).

Pizza: Budget eaters look for *pizza al taglio* shops, scattered throughout Siena, selling pizza by the slice. One good bet, **San Martino,** a couple of blocks behind Il Campo, is a local-feeling spot with €2-3 slices and sandwiches to-go or eat in (Mon-Sat 10:00-21:00, closed Sun, Via del Porrione 64).

Gourmet Tuscan Supermarkets/Rosticcerie: **Consorzio Agrario di Siena** is a great place to browse, buy edible gifts, or assemble a cheap yet top quality local meal. Wander through the entire place (salad and smoothie bar at the front, bakery/*rosticcerie*/hot stand-up meals at the back) and enjoy a parade of artisanal Tuscan foods. While office workers pack the eatery in the rear, I create the ultimate salad, choose a smoothie, and enjoy it on the big comfy stone bench across the way on Piazza Salimbeni (daily 8:00-20:30, just off Piazza Matteotti, facing Piazza Salimbeni at Via Pianigiani 9).

Morbidi is a modern upscale take on the same artisanal grocery idea. It's a good choice for breakfast, a quick lunch, or an *aperitivo*—a predinner, light buffet is included with a price of a drink

(Mon-Thu 8:00-20:00, Fri-Sat until 22:00, closed Sun, Via Banchi di Sopra 75, tel. 0577-280-268).

Sapori & Dintorni Conad, at the bottom of Il Campo next to the City Tower, is a classy bakery/supermarket/*rosticceria* serving fresh food to-go or at its bar. This is a good spot to put together a picnic to enjoy on the square (daily 8:30-20:00, Piazza Il Campo 80).

DESSERTS AND TREATS

Siena's claim to caloric fame is its *panforte*, a rich, chewy concoction of nuts, honey, and candied fruits that impresses even fruitcake haters. There are a few varieties: *Margherita*, dusted in powdered sugar, is fruitier, while *panpepato* has a spicy, peppery crust. Locals prefer a chewy, white macaroon-and-almond cookie called *ricciarelli*.

Nannini—ideally located in the center of the evening strolling scene a few blocks off the Campo—is Siena's venerable, top-end pastry shop/café. For a special dessert or a sweet treat any time of day, stop by. The local specialties are around back at the far end of the bar (Mon-Sat 7:30-21:00, Sun 8:00-24:00, *aperitivo* happy hour 18:00 until closing, Banchi di Sopra 24).

Siena Connections

Siena has sparse train connections but is a great hub for buses to the hill towns, though frequency drops on Sundays and holidays. For most, Florence is the gateway to Siena. Even if you're a rail-pass user, connect these two cities by bus—it's faster than the train, and Siena's bus station is more convenient and central than its train station.

BY TRAIN

Siena's train station is at the edge of town.

From Siena by Train to: Florence (direct trains hourly, 1.5-2 hours; bus is better), **Pisa** (2/hour, 2 hours, change at Empoli), **Assisi** (10/day, about 4 hours, most involve 2 changes, bus is faster), **Rome** (1-2/hour, 3-4 hours, change in Florence or Chiusi), **Orvieto** (12/day, 2.5 hours, change in Chiusi). For more information, visit www.trenitalia.com.

BY BUS

The main bus companies are **Tiemme/Siena Mobilità** (mostly regional destinations, tel. 0577-204-111, www.sienamobilita.it) and **Sena/Baltour** (long-distance connections, tel. 0861-199-1900, www.baltour.it). On schedules, the fastest buses are marked *rapida*. Most buses depart Siena from Piazza Gramsci; others leave from the train station (confirm when you buy your ticket).

Tickets and Information: You can buy tickets in the underground passageway (called Sottopassaggio la Lizza) beneath Piazza Gramsci—look for stairwells in front of NH Excelsior Hotel. The larger office handles Tiemme/Siena Mobilità buses (Mon-Fri 6:30-19:30, Sat-Sun 7:00-19:30). The smaller one is for Sena/Baltour buses (Mon-Fri 7:30-20:00, Sat 7:30-12:30 & 13:45-16:15, Sun 10:15-13:15 & 14:00-18:45; Sena/Baltour office also has a desk selling *Eurolines* tickets for bus connections to other countries). Tiemme/Siena Mobilità is cash-only; Sena/Baltour accepts credit cards. You can also get tickets for both Tiemme/Siena Mobilità buses and Sena/Baltour buses at the train station (look for bus-ticket kiosk just inside main door). If necessary, you can buy tickets from the driver, but it costs €3-5 extra.

SIENA

Services: Sottopassaggio la Lizza also has luggage storage, posted bus schedules, and pay WCs.

Tiemme/Siena Mobilità Buses to: Florence (roughly 2/hour, 1.5-hour *rapida/via superstrada* buses are faster than the train, avoid the 2-hour *ordinaria* buses unless you have time to enjoy the beautiful scenery en route; tickets also available at tobacco shops/*tabacchi*; generally leaves from Piazza Gramsci as well as train station), **San Gimignano** (8/day direct, on Sun must change in Poggibonsi, 1.5 hours, from Piazza Gramsci), **Volterra** (4/day Mon-Sat, no buses on Sun, 2 hours, change in Colle di Val d'Elsa, leaves from Piazza Gramsci), **Montepulciano** (6-8/day, none on Sun, 1.5 hours, from train station), **Pienza** (6/day, none on Sun, 1.5 hours, from train station), **Montalcino** (6/day Mon-Sat, 4/day Sun, 1.5 hours, from train station or Piazza del Sale), **Pisa's Galileo Galilei Airport** (3/day, 2 hours, one direct, two via Poggibonsi), **Rome's Fiumicino Airport** (3/day, 3.5 hours, from Piazza Gramsci).

Sena/Baltour Buses to: Rome (9/day, 3 hours, from Piazza Gramsci, arrives at Rome's Tiburtina station on Metro line B with easy connections to the central Termini train station), **Naples** (2/day, 6.5 hours, one at 17:00 and an overnight bus that departs at 00:20), **Milan** (2/day direct, 4.5 hours, more with change in Bologna, departs from Piazza Gramsci, arrives at Milan's Cadorna Station with Metro access and direct trains to Malpensa Airport), **Assisi** (daily at 17:30, 2 hours, departs from Siena train station, arrives at Assisi Santa Maria degli Angeli; from there it's a 10-minute taxi/bus ride uphill to city center). To reach the town center of **Pisa,** the train is better (described earlier).

VOLTERRA
AND SAN GIMIGNANO

This fine duo of hill towns—perhaps Italy's most underrated and most overrated, respectively—sit just a half-hour drive apart in the middle of the triangle formed by three major destinations: Florence, Siena, and Pisa. San Gimignano is the region's glamour girl, getting all of the fawning attention from passing tour buses. And a quick stroll through its core, in the shadows of its 14 surviving medieval towers, is a delight. But once you've seen it, you've seen it...and that's when you head for Volterra. Volterra isn't as eye-catching as San Gimignano, but has an unmistakable authenticity and a surprising depth, richly rewarding travelers adventurous enough to break out of the San Gimignano rut. With its many engaging museums, Volterra offers the best sightseeing of all of Italy's small hill towns.

GETTING THERE

These towns work best for drivers, who can easily reach both of them in one go. Volterra is farther off the main Florence-Siena road, but it's near the main coastal highway connecting the north (Pisa, Lucca, and Cinque Terre) and south (Montalcino/Montepulciano and Rome).

If you're relying on public transportation, both towns are reachable—to a point. Visiting either one by bus from Florence or Siena requires a longer-than-it-should-be trek, often with a transfer (in Colle di Val d'Elsa for Volterra, in Poggibonsi for San Gimignano; see each town's "Connections" section for details). San Gimignano is better-connected, but Volterra merits the additional effort. Note that while these towns are only about a 30-minute

Volterra & San Gimignano Area

drive apart, they're poorly connected to each other by public transit (requiring an infrequent two-hour connection).

PLANNING YOUR TIME

Volterra and San Gimignano are a handy yin-and-yang duo. Ideally, you'll overnight in one town, and visit the other either as a side-trip or en route. There are pros and cons to overnighting in either town: Sleeping in Volterra lets you really settle into a charming, real-feeling burg with good restaurants, but forces you to visit San Gimignano when it's busiest (during the day). Sleeping in San Gimignano lets you enjoy that gorgeous town when it's relatively quiet, but some visitors find it *too* quiet—less interesting to linger in than Volterra. Ultimately I'd aim to sleep in Volterra, and try to visit San Gimignano as early or late in the day as is practical (to mitigate crowds there).

Volterra

Encircled by impressive walls and topped with a grand fortress, Volterra perches high above the rich farmland surrounding it. More than 2,000 years ago, Volterra was one of the most important Etruscan cities, and much larger than we see today. Greek-trained Etruscan artists worked here, leaving a significant stash of art, particularly funerary urns. Eventually Volterra was absorbed into the Roman Empire, and for centuries it was an independent city-state. Volterra fought bitterly against the Florentines, but like many Tuscan towns, it lost in the end and was given a Medici fortress atop the city to "protect" its citizens.

Unlike other famous towns in Tuscany, Volterra feels neither cutesy nor touristy...but real, vibrant, and almost oblivious to the allure of the tourist dollar. Millennia past its prime, Volterra seems to have settled into a well-worn groove; locals are resistant to change. At a recent town meeting about whether to run high-speed Internet cable to the town, a local grumbled, "The Etruscans didn't need it—why do we?" This stubbornness helps make Volterra a refreshing change of pace from its more aggressively commercial neighbors. Volterra also boasts some interesting sights for a small town, from an ancient Roman theater, to a finely decorated Pisan Romanesque cathedral, to an excellent museum of Etruscan artifacts. And each evening charming Annie and Claudia give a delightful, one-hour guided town walk to be sure you appreciate their city (see "Tours in Volterra," later). All in all, Volterra is my favorite small town in Tuscany.

Orientation to Volterra

Compact and walkable, Volterra (pop. 11,000—6,000 inside the old wall) stretches out from the pleasant Piazza dei Priori to the old city gates and beyond. Be ready for lots of steep walking; while the main square and main drag are fairly level, nearly everything else involves a climb.

TOURIST INFORMATION

The helpful TI is on the main square, at Piazza dei Priori 19 (daily 9:30-13:00 & 14:00-18:00, tel. 0588-87257, www.volterratur.it). The TI's excellent €5 audioguide narrates 20 stops (2-for-1 discount on audioguides with this book). Check the TI website for details on frequent summer festivals and concerts.

ARRIVAL IN VOLTERRA

By Public Transport: Buses stop at Piazza Martiri della Libertà in the town center. Train travelers can reach the town with a short bus ride (see "Volterra Connections," later).

By Car: Don't drive into the town center; it's prohibited except for locals (and you'll get a huge fine). It's easiest to simply wind to the top where the road ends at Piazza Martiri della Libertà. (Halfway up the hill, there's a confusing hard right—don't take it;

keep going straight uphill under the wall.) Immediately before the Piazza Martiri bus round-about is the entry to an **underground garage** (P1, €2/hour, €15/day, keep ticket and pay as you leave). It's safe, and you pop out within a few blocks of nearly all my recommended hotels and sights.

Numbered **parking lots** ring the town walls (around €2/hour; try the handy-but-small P4 lot near the Roman Theater and Porta Fiorentina gate) and an unnumbered bus parking lot (below the road to San Gimignano). Also behind town, the P3 lot is free, but requires a steep climb from the Porta di Docciola gate up into town.

Wherever you park, be sure it's permitted—stick to parking lots and pay street parking (indicated with blue lines).

HELPFUL HINTS

Market Day: The market is on Saturday morning near the Roman Theater (8:00-13:00, on Piazza dei Priori). The TI hands out a list of other market days in the area.

Festivals: Volterra's Medieval Festival takes place on the third and fourth Sundays of August. Fall is popular for food festivals.

Internet Access: Several cafés offer free Wi-Fi to customers. **Enjoy Café Internet Point,** right by the main bus stop, has public computers (€3/hour, free Wi-Fi with purchase, daily 6:30-24:00, Piazza dei Martiri 3, tel. 0588-80530).

Laundry: The handy self-service **Lavanderia Azzurra** is just off the main square (€4/wash, €4/dry, change machine, daily 7:00-23:00, Via Roma 7, tel. 0588-80030).

Tours in Volterra

▲▲Guided Volterra Walk

Annie Adair (also listed individually, next) and her colleague Claudia Meucci offer a great one-hour, English-only **introductory walking tour** of Volterra for €10. The walk touches on Volterra's Etruscan, Roman, and medieval history, as well as the contemporary cultural scene (daily April-July and Sept-Oct, rain or shine—Thu-Tue at 18:00, Wed at 12:30; meet in front of alabaster shop on Piazza Martiri della Libertà, no need to reserve, tours run with a minimum of 3 people or €30; www.volterrawalkingtour.com or www.tuscantour.com, info@volterrawalkingtour.com). There's no better way to spend €10 and one hour in this city. I mean it. Don't miss this beautiful experience.

Local Guide

American **Annie Adair** is an excellent guide for private, in-depth tours of Volterra (€60/hour, minimum 2 hours). Her husband Francesco, an easy-going sommelier and wine critic, leads a "Wine

Tasting 101" crash course in sampling Tuscan wines (€50/hour per group, plus cost of wine). For a more in-depth wine experience, Annie and Francesco offer excursions into the heart of Chianti (€450/day for 2-3 people in his car) and can even organize Tuscan weddings for Americans (tel. 0588-086-201, mobile 347-143-5004, www.tuscantour.com, info@tuscantour.com).

Sights in Volterra

I've arranged these sights as a handy little town walk, connected by directions on foot.
• *Begin your visit of town at the Etruscan Arch at the bottom of Via Porta all'Arco (about 4 blocks below the main square, Piazza dei Priori).*

▲Etruscan Arch (Porta all'Arco)
Volterra's renowned Etruscan arch was built of massive stones in the fourth century B.C. Volterra's original wall was four miles around—twice the size of the wall that encircles it today. Imagine: This city had 20,000 people four centuries before Christ. Volterra was a key trading center and one of 12 leading towns in the confederation of *Etruria Propria.* The three seriously eroded heads, dating from the first century B.C., show what happens when you leave something outside for 2,000 years. The newer stones are

part of the 13th-century city wall, which incorporated parts of the much older Etruscan wall.

A plaque just outside remembers June 30, 1944. That night, Nazi forces were planning to blow up the arch to slow the Allied advance. To save their treasured landmark, Volterrans ripped up the stones that pave Via Porta all'Arco, plugged up the gate, and managed to convince the Nazi commander that there was no need to blow up the arch. Today, all of the paving stones are back in their places, and like silent heroes, they welcome you through the oldest standing gate into Volterra. Locals claim this as the oldest surviving round arch of the Etruscan age; some experts believe this is where the Romans got the idea for using a keystone in their arches.
• *Go through the arch and head up Via Porta all'Arco, which I like to call...*

"Artisan Lane" (Via Porta all'Arco)
This steep and atmospheric lane is lined with interesting shops featuring the work of artisans and producers. Because of its alabaster heritage, Volterra developed a tradition of craftsmanship and artistry, and today you'll find a rich variety of handiwork (shops gener-

ally open Mon-Sat 10:00-13:00 & 16:00-19:00, closed Sun; the TI produces a free booklet called *Handicraft in Volterra*).

From the Etruscan Arch, browse your way up the hill, checking out these shops and items (listed from bottom to top): alabaster shops (#57 and #45); book bindery and papery (#26); jewelry (#25); etchings (#23); and bronze work (#6).

• *Reaching the top of Via Porta all'Arco, turn left and walk a few steps into Volterra's main square, Piazza dei Priori. It's dominated by the...*

Palazzo dei Priori

Volterra's City Hall, built about 1200, claims to be the oldest of any Tuscan city-state. It clearly inspired the more famous Palazzo Vecchio in Florence. Town halls like this are emblematic of an era when city-states were powerful. They were architectural exclamation points declaring that, around here, no pope or emperor called the shots. Towns such as Volterra were truly city-states—proudly independent and relatively democratic. They had their own armies, taxes, and even weights and measures. Notice the horizontal "cane" cut into the City Hall wall (10 yards to the right of the door). For a thousand years, this square hosted a market, and the "cane" was the local yardstick. You can pay to see the council chambers, and to climb 159 steps to the top of the bell tower.

Cost and Hours: €1.50 for council chambers, €2 tower climb, mid-March-Oct daily 10:30-17:30, Nov-mid-March usually Sat-Sun only 10:00-16:30.

• *Facing the City Hall, notice the black-and-white-striped wall to the right (set back from the square). The little back door in that wall leads into Volterra's cathedral. (For a thousand years the bishop has lived next door, conveniently right above the TI.)*

Duomo

This church is not as elaborate as its cousin in Pisa, but is a beautiful example of the Pisan Romanesque style. The simple 13th-century facade conceals a more intricate interior (rebuilt in the late 16th and 19th centuries), with a central nave flanked by monolithic stucco columns painted to imitate pink granite, and topped by a gilded, coffered ceiling.

Cost and Hours: Free, daily 8:00-12:30 & 15:00-18:00, Nov-March until 17:00, closed Fri 12:30-16:00 for cleaning.

Visiting the Church: The interior was decorated mostly in the late 16th century, during Florentine rule under the Medici family. Their coat of arms, with its distinctive balls, is repeated multiple times throughout the building.

Head down into the nave to face the main altar. Up the stairs just to the right is a dreamy, painted, and gilded-wood ***Deposition*** (Jesus being taken down from the cross, Nicodemus holding a nail), restored to its original form. Carved in 1228, a generation

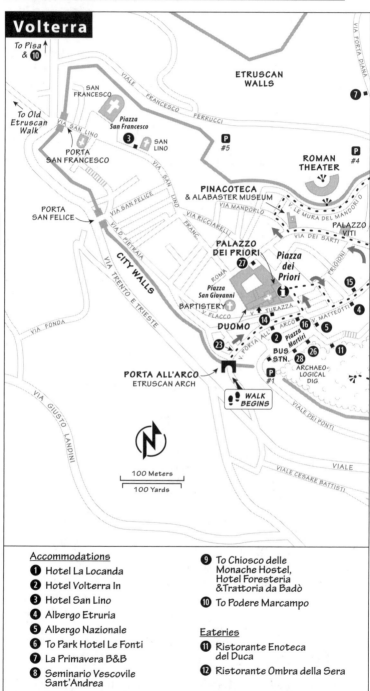

Volterra

VOLTERRA & SAN GIMIGNANO

To Pisa & ⑩

ETRUSCAN WALLS

VIALE FRANCESCO

SAN FRANCESCO

Piazza San Francesco

③

To Old Etruscan Walk

VIA SAN LINO

PORTA SAN FRANCESCO

SAN LINO

VIA SAN LINO

FERRUCCI

P #5

ROMAN THEATER

P #4

VIA SAN FELICE

PINACOTECA & ALABASTER MUSEUM

VIA MANDORLO

V. LE MURA DEL MANDORLO

PORTA SAN FELICE

VIA RICCIARELLI

FRANC.

VIA DEI SARTI

PALAZZO VITI

VIA D. PIETRAIA

PALAZZO DEI PRIORI

Piazza dei Priori

PRIGIONI

CITY WALLS

ROMA

㉗

①

⑮

VIA TRENTO E TRIESTE

Piazza San Giovanni

BAPTISTERY

V. FLACCO

V. TURAZZA

④

VIA FONDA

DUOMO

⑭

V. PORTA ALL' ARCO

②

⑯ V. MATTEOTTI

⑤

㉓

Piazza Martiri

㉖

⑪

BUS STN.

㉘

PORTA ALL'ARCO ETRUSCAN ARCH

P #1

ARCHAEO-LOGICAL DIG

👣 WALK BEGINS

VIA GIUSTO LANDINI

VIALE DEI PONTI

N

100 Meters
100 Yards

VIALE

VIALE CESARE BATTISTI

Accommodations
① Hotel La Locanda
② Hotel Volterra In
③ Hotel San Lino
④ Albergo Etruria
⑤ Albergo Nazionale
⑥ To Park Hotel Le Fonti
⑦ La Primavera B&B
⑧ Seminario Vescovile Sant'Andrea

⑨ To Chiosco delle Monache Hostel, Hotel Foresteria &Trattoria da Badò
⑩ To Podere Marcampo

Eateries
⑪ Ristorante Enoteca del Duca
⑫ Ristorante Ombra della Sera

VIA PORTA DIANA

⑦

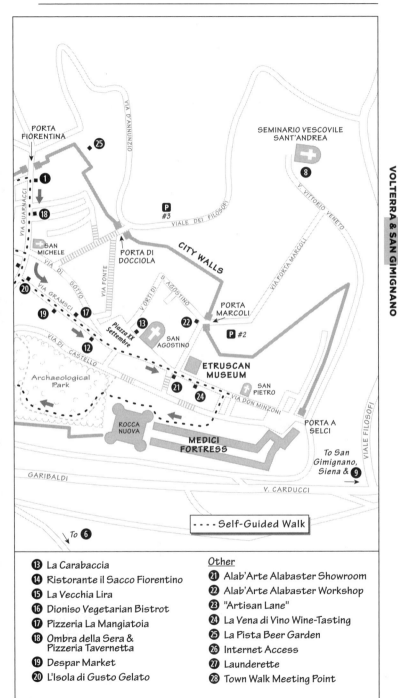

❶ La Carabaccia
❷ Ristorante il Sacco Fiorentino
❸ La Vecchia Lira
❹ Dioniso Vegetarian Bistrot
❺ Pizzeria La Mangiatoia
❻ Ombra della Sera & Pizzeria Tavernetta
❼ Despar Market
❽ L'Isola di Gusto Gelato

Other
㉑ Alab'Arte Alabaster Showroom
㉒ Alab'Arte Alabaster Workshop
㉓ "Artisan Lane"
㉔ La Vena di Vino Wine-Tasting
㉕ La Pista Beer Garden
㉖ Internet Access
㉗ Launderette
㉘ Town Walk Meeting Point

before Giotto, it shows emotion and motion way ahead of its time. Pop a euro into the box to buy some light and stand here as a 13th-century pilgrim would have (their eyes were better in the dark).

The glowing **windows** just to the left (in the transept and behind the altar) are sheets of alabaster. These, along with the recorded Gregorian chants, add to the church's worshipful ambience.

The 12th-century marble **pulpit,** partway down the nave, is also beautifully carved. In the relief panel of the Last Supper, all the apostles are together except Judas, who's under the table with the evil dragon (his name is the only one not carved into the relief). Like most medieval art, the artist remains anonymous.

Just past the pulpit on the right (at the Rosary Chapel), check out the *Annunciation*, painted in 1497 by Mariotto Albertinelli and Fra Bartolomeo (both were students of Fra Angelico). The two, friends since childhood, delicately give worshippers a way to see Mary "conceived by the Holy Spirit." Note the vibrant colors, exaggerated perspective, and Mary's *contrapposto* pose—all attributes of the Renaissance.

At the end of the nave, the large **chapel** to the right of the doors has painted terra-cotta statue groups of the Nativity and the Adoration of the Magi. One is by an anonymous local artist, the other is thought to be the work of master ceramist Andrea della Robbia. Remarkably, no one is certain who did which one—a testament to the skill of local craftsmen. Della Robbia's uncle, Luca, is credited with devising the glazing formula that makes Della Robbia's inventive sculptures shine even in poorly lit interiors. At the end of the chapel, ponder a statue with an unusual but poignant theme: Mary, *Mater Dolorosa* ("mother in pain"), literally pierced by swords as she suffers the agony of seeing her crucified son's dead body.

Step outside the door into Piazza San Giovanni. A common arrangement in the Middle Ages was for the church to face the baptistery (you couldn't enter the church until you were baptized)... and for the hospital to face the cemetery (now the site of an ambulance corps or *misericordia*). These buildings all overlooked a single square. That's how it is in Pisa's famous Field of Miracles (with its Leaning Tower), and that's how it is here. Step into the baptistery and look up into the vast, empty space—plenty of room for the Holy Spirit.

• *Facing the cathedral, circle to the left (passing a 1960 carving of St. Linus, the second pope and friend of St. Peter, who was born here) and go back into the main square, Piazza dei Priori. Face the City Hall, and go down the street to the left; after one short block, you're standing at the head (on the left) of...*

▲Via Matteotti

The town's main drag, named after the popular Socialist leader Giacomo Matteotti (killed by the Fascists in 1924), provides a good cultural scavenger hunt.

At **#1,** on the left, is a typical Italian bank security door. (Step in and say, "Beam me up, Scotty.") Back outside, stand at the corner, and look up and all around. Find the medieval griffin torch holder—symbol of Volterra, looking down Via Matteotti—and imagine it holding a flaming torch. The pharmacy sports the symbol of its medieval guild. Across the street from the bank, **#2** is the base of what was a San Gimignano-style fortified Tuscan tower. Look up and imagine heavy beams cantilevered out, supporting extra wooden rooms and balconies crowding out over the street. Throughout Tuscany, today's stark and stony old building fronts once supported a tangle of wooden extensions.

As you head down Via Matteotti, notice how the doors show centuries of refitting work. Doors that once led to these extra rooms are now partially bricked up to make windows. Contemplate urban density in the 14th century, before the plague thinned out the population. Be careful: A wild boar (a local delicacy) awaits you at **#10.**

At **#12,** on the right, notice the line of doorbells: This typical palace, once the home of a single rich family, is now occupied by many middle-class families. After the social revolution in the 18th century and the rise of the middle class, former palaces were condominium-ized. Even so, like in *Dr. Zhivago,* the original family still lives here. Apartment #1 is the home of Count Guidi.

On the right at **#16,** pop in to the alabaster showroom. Alabaster, mined nearby, has long been a big industry here. Volterra alabaster—softer and more translucent than marble—was sliced thin to serve as windows for Italy's medieval churches.

At **#19,** the recommended La Vecchia Lira is a lively cafeteria. The Bar L'Incontro across the street is a favorite for pastries; in the summer, they sell homemade gelato, while in the winter they make chocolates.

Across the way, side-trip 10 steps up Vicolo delle Prigioni to a fun bakery (Panificio Rosetti). They're happy to sell small quantities if you want to try the local *cantuccini* (almond biscotti) or another treat.

Continue on Via Matteotti to the end of the block. At **#51,** on the left, a bit of Etruscan wall is artfully used to display more alabaster art. And **#56A** is the alabaster art gallery of Paolo Sabatini, who specializes in unique, contemporary sculptures.

By the way, you can only buy a package of cigarettes at the machine in the wall just to the right—labeled "*Vietato ai Minori*" (forbidden to minors)—by inserting an Italian national health care card to prove you're over 18.

VOLTERRA & SAN GIMIGNANO

Locals gather early each evening at Osteria dei Poeti (at **#57**) for some of the best cocktails in town—served with free munchies. The cinema is across the street. Movies in Italy are rarely in *versione originale*; Italians are used to getting their movies dubbed into Italian. To bring some culture to this little town, they also show live broadcasts of operas and concerts (advertised in the window).

On the corner, at **#66,** another Tuscan tower marks the end of the street. This noble house had a ground floor with no interior access to the safe upper floors. Rope ladders were used to get upstairs. The tiny door was wide enough to let in your skinny friends...but definitely not anyone wearing armor and carrying big weapons.

Across the little square stands the ancient Church of St. Michael. After long years of barbarian chaos, the Langobards moved in from the north and asserted law and order in places like Volterra. That generally included building a Christian church on the old Roman forum to symbolically claim and tame the center of town. The church standing here today is Romanesque, dating from the 12th century. Around the right side, find the crude little guy and the smiling octopus under its eaves—they've been making faces at the passing crowds for 800 years.

• *From here you have options. Three more sights—Palazzo Viti (fancy old palace), the Pinacoteca (Volterra's main painting gallery), and the Alabaster Museum (within the Pinacoteca building)—are a short stroll down Via dei Sarti: From the end of Via Matteotti, turn left. If you want to skip straight down to the Roman Theater, just head straight from the end of Via Matteotti onto Via Guarnacci, then turn left when you get to the Porta Fiorentina (Florence Gate). To head directly to Volterra's top sight, the Etruscan Museum, just turn around, walk a block back up Via Matteotti, turn left on Via Gramsci, and follow it all the way through Piazza XX Settembre up Via Don Minzoni to the museum.*

▲Palazzo Viti

Palazzo Viti takes you behind the rustic, heavy stone walls of the city to see how the wealthy lived—in this case, rich from 19th-century alabaster trade. This time warp is popular with Italian movie directors. With 12 rooms on one floor open to the public, Palazzo Viti feels remarkably lived in—because it is. Behind the ropes you'll see intimate family photos. You'll often find Signora Viti herself selling admission tickets. Your visit ends in the cellar with a short wine tasting.

Cost and Hours: €5, April-Oct daily 10:00-13:00 & 14:30-18:30, closed Nov-March, Via dei Sarti 41, tel. 0588-84047, www. palazzoviti.it.

Visiting the Palazzo: The elegant interior is compact and well-described by the English descriptions. You'll climb up a stately staircase, buy your ticket, and head into the grand ballroom. From here, you'll tour the blue-hued dining room (with slice-of-life Chinese scenes painted on rice paper); the salon of battles (with warfare paintings on the walls); and the long hall of temporary exhibits. Looping back, you'll see the porcelain hall (decorated with priceless plates) and the inviting library (notice the delicate lamp with a finely carved alabaster lampshade). The Brachettone Salon is named for the local artist responsible for the small sketch of near-nudes hanging just left of the door into the next room. Brachettone (from *brache*, "pants") is the artistic nickname for Volterra-born Daniele Ricciarelli, who owns the dubious distinction of having painted all of those wispy loincloths over the genitalia of Michelangelo's figures in the Sistine Chapel. (In this drawing, notice a similar aversion to showing the full monty...though everything-but is fair game.) On the table, notice the family wedding photo with Pope John Paul II presiding. In the red room, a portrait of Giuseppe Viti (looking like Pavarotti) hangs next to the exit door. He's the man who purchased the place in 1850. Your visit ends with bedrooms and a dressing room, making it easy to imagine how the other half lived...and, from November through March, presumably still does.

Your Palazzo Viti ticket also gets you a fine little cheese, salami, and wine tasting. As you leave the palace, climb down into the cool little cellar (used as a disco on some weekends), where you can pop into a Roman cistern, marvel at an Etruscan well, and enjoy a friendly sit-down snack. Take full advantage of this tasty extra.

• *A block past Palazzo Viti, also on Via dei Sarti, is the...*

Pinacoteca and Alabaster Museum

The Pinacoteca fills a 15th-century palace with fine paintings that feel more Florentine than Sienese—a reminder of whose domain this town was in. You'll see a stunning altarpiece by Taddeo di Bartolo, once displayed in the original residence. You'll also find roomfuls of gilded altarpieces and saintly statues, as well as a trio of striking High Renaissance altar paintings by Signorelli, Fiorentino, and Ghirlandaio.

Cost and Hours: Likely €8, possible €14 combo-ticket includes Etruscan Museum, daily mid-March-Oct 9:00-19:00, Nov-mid-March 10:00-16:00, Via dei Sarti 1, photos permitted without flash, tel. 0588-87580.

• *Exiting the museum, circle right along the side of the museum building into the tunnel-like Passo del Gualduccio passage (which leads to the parking-lot square); turn right and walk along the wall, with fine views of the...*

VOLTERRA & SAN GIMIGNANO

Roman Theater

Built in the first century A.D., this well-preserved theater has good acoustics. With this fine aerial view from the city wall promenade, there's no reason to pay to enter. The 13th-century wall that you're standing on divided the theater from the town center...so, naturally, the theater became the town dump. Over time, the theater was forgotten—covered in the garbage of Volterra. It was rediscovered in the 1950s and excavated.

The stage wall (immediately in front of the theater seats) was standard Roman design—with three levels from which actors would appear: one level for mortals, one for heroes, and the top one for gods. Parts of two levels still stand. Gods leaped out onto the third level for the last time around the third century A.D., which is when the town began to use the theater stones to build fancy baths instead. You can see the scant remains of the baths behind the theater, including the little round sauna in the far corner with brick supports that raise the heated floor.

From this vantage point, you can trace Volterra's vast Etruscan wall. Find the church in the distance, on the left, and notice the stones just below. They are from the Etruscan wall that followed the ridge into the valley and defined Volterra in the fourth century B.C.

• *From the Roman Theater viewpoint, continue along the wall downhill to the T-intersection (the old gate, Porta Fiorentina, with fine wooden medieval doors, is on your left) and turn right making your way uphill on Via Guarnacci back to Via Matteotti. A block up Via Matteotti, you can't miss the wide, pedestrianized shopping street called Via Gramsci. Follow this up to Piazza XX Settembre, walk through that leafy square, and continue uphill on Via Don Minzoni. Watch on your left for the...*

▲▲Etruscan Museum (Museo Etrusco Guarnacci)

Filled top to bottom with rare Etruscan artifacts, this museum—even with few English explanations and its dusty, old-school style—makes it easy to appreciate how advanced this pre-Roman culture was.

Cost and Hours: Likely €8, possible combo-ticket with Pinacoteca and Alabaster Museum; daily mid-March-Oct 9:00-19:00, Nov-mid-March 10:00-16:30; audioguide-€3, Via Don Minzoni 15, tel. 0588-86347, www.comune.volterra.pi.it/english.

Visiting the Museum: The museum's three floors feel dusty and disorganized. As there are scarcely any English explanations, consider the serious but interesting audioguide; the information below hits the highlights. There's an inviting public garden out back.

The collection starts **on the ground floor** with a small gathering of pre-Etruscan Villanovian artifacts (c. 1500 B.C.), with the oldest items to the left as you enter. To the right are an impressive warrior's hat and a remarkable, richly decorated, double-spouted military flask (for wine and water). Look down to see Etruscan foundations and a road (the discovery of which foiled the museum's attempt to build an elevator here). It's mind-boggling to think that 20,000 people lived within the town's Etruscan walls in 400 B.C.

Filling the rest of the ground floor is a vast collection of Etruscan **funerary urns** (dating from the seventh to the first century B.C.). Designed to contain the ashes of cremated loved ones, each urn is tenderly carved with a unique scene, offering a peek into the still-mysterious Etruscan society. Etruscan urns have two parts: The casket on the bottom contained the remains (with elaborately carved panels), while the lid was decorated with a sculpture of the departed.

First pay attention to the people on top. While contemporaries of the Greeks, the Etruscans were more libertine. Their religion was less demanding, and their women were a respected part of both the social and public spheres. Women and men alike are depicted lounging on Etruscan urns. While they seem to be just hanging out, the lounging dead were actually offering the gods a banquet—in order to gain the Etruscan equivalent of salvation. Etruscans really did lounge like this in front of a table, but this banquet had eternal consequences. The dearly departed are often depicted holding blank wax tablets (symbolizing blank new lives in the next world). Men hold containers that would generally be used at banquets, including libation cups for offering wine to the gods. The women are finely dressed, sometimes holding a pomegranate (symbolizing fertility) or a mirror. Look at the faces, and imagine the lives they lived and the loved ones they left behind.

Now tune into the reliefs carved into the fronts of the caskets. The motifs vary widely, from floral patterns to mystical animals (such as a Starbucks-like mermaid) to parades of magistrates. Most show journeys on horseback—appropriate for someone leaving this world and entering the next. Some show the fabled horseback-and-carriage ride to the underworld, where the dead are greeted by Charon, an underworld demon, with his hammer and pointy ears.

While the finer urns are carved of alabaster, most are made of limestone. Originally they were colorfully painted. Many lids are mismatched—casualties of reckless 18th- and 19th-century archaeological digs.

Head upstairs to the **first floor.** You'll enter a room with a circular mosaic in the floor (a Roman original, found in Volterra

Under the Etruscan Sun
(c. 900 B.C.–A.D. 1)

Around 550 B.C.—just before the Golden Age of Greece—the Etruscan people of central Italy had their own Golden Age. Though their origins are mysterious, their mix of Greek-style art with Roman-style customs helped lay a civilized foundation for the rise of the Roman Empire. As you travel through Italy—particularly in Tuscany (from "Etruscan")—you'll find traces of this long-lost people. Etruscan tombs and artifacts are still being discovered, often by farmers in the countryside.

The Etruscans first appeared in the ninth century B.C., when a number of cities sprouted up in sparsely populated Tuscany and Umbria, including today's hill towns of Cortona, Chiusi, and Volterra. Possibly immigrants from Turkey, but more likely local farmers who moved to the city, they became sailors, traders, and craftsmen, and welcomed new ideas from Greece.

More technologically advanced than their neighbors, the Etruscans mined metal, exporting it around the Mediterranean, both as crude ingots and as some of the finest-crafted jewelry in the known world. They drained and irrigated large tracts of land, creating the fertile farmland of central Italy's breadbasket. With their disciplined army, warships, merchant vessels, and (from the Greek perspective) pirate galleys, they ruled central Italy and the major ports along the Tyrrhenian Sea. For nearly two centuries (c. 700-500 B.C.), much of Italy lived a Golden Age of peace and prosperity under the Etruscan sun.

Judging from the frescoes and many luxury items that have survived, the Etruscans enjoyed the good life: They look healthy and vibrant as they play flutes, dance with birds, or play party games. Etruscan artists celebrated individual people, showing their wrinkles, crooked noses, silly smiles, and funny haircuts.

Scholars today have deciphered the Etruscans' Greek-style alphabet and some individual words, but they have yet to fully understand their language, which is unlike any other in Europe. Much of what we know of the Etruscans comes from their tombs. The tomb was a home in the hereafter, complete with all of the deceased's belongings. The funerary urn might have a statue on the lid of the deceased at a banquet—lying across a dining couch, spooning with his wife, smiles on their faces, living the good life for all eternity.

Seven decades of wars with the Greeks (545-474 B.C.) disrupted their trade routes and drained the Etruscan League, just as a new Mediterranean power was emerging: Rome. In 509 B.C., the Romans overthrew their Etruscan king, and Rome expanded, capturing Etruscan cities one by one (the last in 264 B.C.). Etruscan resisters were killed, the survivors intermarried with Romans, and their kids grew up speaking Latin. By Julius Caesar's time, the only remnants of Etruscan culture were its priests, who be-

The Etruscan Empire

came Rome's professional soothsayers. Interestingly, the Etruscan prophets had foreseen their own demise, having predicted that Etruscan civilization would last 10 centuries.

But Etruscan culture lived on in Roman religion (pantheon of gods, household gods, and divination rituals), art (realism), lifestyle (the banquet), and in a taste for Greek styles—the mix that became our "Western civilization."

Etruscan Sights in Italy

Rome: Traces of original Etruscan engineering projects (e.g., Circus Maximus), Vatican Museum artifacts, and Villa Giulia Museum, with the famous "husband and wife sarcophagus."

Orvieto: Archaeological Museum (coins, dinnerware, and a sarcophagus), necropolis, and underground tunnels and caves.

Volterra: Etruscan gate (Porta all'Arco, from fourth century B.C.) and Etruscan Museum (urns, pottery, and devotional figures).

and transplanted here). Explore more treasures in a series of urn-filled rooms.

Fans of Alberto Giacometti will be amazed at how the tall, skinny figure called *The Evening Shadow* (*L'Ombra della Sera,* third century B.C.) looks just like the modern Swiss sculptor's work—but 2,500 years older. This is an example of the *ex-voto* bronze statues that the Etruscans created in thanks to the gods. With his supremely lanky frame, distinctive wavy hairdo, and inscrutable Mona Lisa smirk, this Etruscan lad captures the illusion of a shadow stretching long late in the day. Admire the sheer artistry of the statue; with its right foot shifted slightly forward, it even hints at the *contrapposto* pose that would become common in this same region during the Renaissance, two millennia later.

The museum's other top piece is the *Urn of the Spouses* (*Urna degli Sposi,* first century B.C.). It's unique for various reasons, includ-

ing its material (it's in terra-cotta—a relatively rare material for these funerary urns) and its depiction of two people rather than one. Looking at this elderly couple, it's easy to imagine the long life they spent together and their desire to pass eternity lounging with each other at a banquet for the gods.

Other highlights include alabaster urns with more Greek myths, *ex-voto* water-bearer statues, kraters (vases with handles used for mixing water and wine), bronze hand mirrors, exquisite golden jewelry that would still be fashionable today, a battle helmet ominously dented at the left temple, black glazed pottery, and hundreds of ancient coins.

The **top floor** features a recreated gravesite, with several neatly aligned urns and artifacts that would have been buried with the deceased. Some of these were funeral dowries that the dead would pack along—including mirrors, coins, hardware for vases, votive statues, pots, pans, and jewelry.

• *After your visit, duck across the street to the alabaster showroom and the wine bar (both described next).*

▲Alabaster Workshop

Alab'Arte offers a fun peek into the art of alabaster. Their showroom is across from the Etruscan Museum. Their powdery workshop is directly opposite the shop, a block down a narrow lane, Via Porta Marcoli. Here you can watch Roberto Chiti and Giorgio Finazzo at work. They are delighted to share their art with visitors. (Everything—including Roberto and Giorgio—is covered in a fine white dust.) Lighting shows off the translucent quality of the stone and the expertise of these artists. This is not a touristy guided visit, but something far more special: the chance to see busy artisans practicing their craft. For more such artisans in action, visit "Artisan Lane" (Via Porta all'Arco) described earlier, or ask the TI for their list of the town's many workshops open to the public.

Cost and Hours: Free, showroom—daily 9:30-13:00 & 15:00-19:00, Via Don Minzoni 18; workshop—March-Oct Mon-Sat 9:30-12:30 & 15:00-19:00, closed Sun, limited hours Nov-Feb, Via Orti Sant'Agostino 28, www.alabarte.com.

▲La Vena di Vino (Wine-Tasting with Bruno and Lucio)

La Vena di Vino, also just across from the Etruscan Museum, is a fun *enoteca* where two guys who have devoted themselves to the

wonders of wine share it with a fun-loving passion. Each day Bruno and Lucio open six or eight bottles, serve your choice by the glass, pair it with characteristic munchies, and offer fine music (guitars available for patrons) and an unusual decor (the place is strewn with bras). Hang out here with the local characters. This is your chance to try the Super Tuscan wine—a creative mix of international grapes grown in Tuscany. According to Bruno, the Brunello (€7/glass) is just right with wild boar, and the Super Tuscan (€6-7/glass) is perfect for meditation. Although Volterra is famously quiet late at night, this place is full of action.

Cost and Hours: Pay per glass, open Wed-Mon 11:30-24:00, closed Tue, 3- to 5-glass wine tastings, Via Don Minzoni 30, tel. 0588-81491, www.lavenadivino.com.

• *Volterra's final sight is perched atop the hill just above the wine bar. Climb up one of the lanes nearby, then walk (to the right) along the formidable wall to find the park.*

Medici Fortress and Archaeological Park

The Parco Archeologico marks what was the acropolis of Volterra from 1500 B.C. until A.D. 1472, when Florence conquered the pesky city. The Florentines burned Volterra's political and historic center, turning it into a grassy commons and building the adjacent Medici Fortezza. The old fortress—a symbol of Florentine dominance—now keeps people in rather than out. It's a maximum-security prison housing only about 150 special prisoners. The park sprawling next to the fortress (toward the town center) is a rare, grassy meadow at the top of a rustic hill town—a favorite place for locals to relax and picnic on a sunny day. Nearby are the remains of the acropolis (€3.50 to enter), but these can be viewed through the fence for free.

Cost and Hours: Free to enter park, open until 20:00 in peak of summer, shorter hours off-season.

Evening Scene

La Pista: Volterra is pretty quiet at night. For a little action during summer evenings you can venture just outside the wall to La Pista, a Tuscan family-friendly neighborhood beer-garden kind of hangout (DJ on weekends, snacks and drinks sold, playground). It's outside the Porta Fiorentina (100 yards to the right in the shadow of the wall).

Passegiata: As they have for generations, Volterrans young and old stroll during the cool of the early evening. The main cruising is along Via Gramsci and Via Matteotti to the main square, Piazza dei Priori.

Aperitivo: Each evening several bars put out little buffet spreads free with a drink to attract a crowd. Bars popular for their *aperitivo* include VolaTerra (Via Turazza 5, next to City Hall), L'Incontro (Via Matteotti 19), and Bar dei Poeti (across from the cinema, Via Matteotti 57). And the gang at La Vena di Vino (described earlier, under "Sights in Volterra") always seems to be ready for a good time.

Sleeping in Volterra

Volterra has plenty of places offering a good night's sleep at a fair price. Lodgings outside of the old town are generally a bit cheaper (and easier for drivers). But keep in mind that these places involve not just walking, but steep walking.

INSIDE VOLTERRA'S OLD TOWN

$$$ Hotel La Locanda feels stately and old-fashioned. This well-located place (just inside Porta Fiorentina, near the Roman Theater and parking lot) rents 18 rooms with flowery decor and modern comforts (Db-€104, Tb-€146, Qb-€189, 10 percent Rick Steves discount, air-con, elevator, Via Guarnacci 24, tel. 0588-81547, www.hotel-lalocanda.com, staff@hotel-lalocanda.com, Stefania and Irina).

$$$ Hotel Volterra In, opened in 2015, is fresh, sports quality furnishings, and is in a central-yet-quiet location. Marco rents 10 bright and spacious rooms (Db-€110, 10 percent direct-booking discount with this book, Via Porta all'Arco 37, tel. 0588-86820, www.hotelvolterrain.it, info@hotelvolterrain.it).

Sleep Code

Abbreviations   **(€1=about $1.10, country code: 39)**
S=Single, **D**=Double/Twin, **T**=Triple, **Q**=Quad, **b**=bathroom
Price Rankings
  $$$ Higher Priced—Most rooms €100 or more
   $$ Moderately Priced—Most rooms €70-100
    $ Lower Priced—Most rooms €70 or less
Unless otherwise noted, credit cards are accepted, breakfast
is included, free Wi-Fi and/or a guest computer is generally
available, and English is spoken. Many towns in Italy levy a
hotel tax of €1.50-5 per person, per night (often collected
in cash; usually not included in the rates I've quoted). Prices
change; verify current rates online or by email. For the best
prices, always book directly with the hotel.

$$ Hotel San Lino fills a former convent with 42 modern, nondescript rooms at the sleepy lower end of town—close to the Porta San Francisco gate, and about a five-minute uphill walk to the main drag. Although it's within the town walls, it doesn't feel like it: The hotel has a fine swimming pool and view terrace, and is the only in-town option that's convenient for drivers, who can park at the on-site garage for €11 (Db-€84-94, "superior" room adds slightly newer furnishings and includes parking for €16 more—worthwhile only for drivers, air-con, elevator, Via San Lino 26, tel. 0588-85250, www.hotelsanlino.net, info@hotelsanlino.com).

$$ Albergo Etruria is on Volterra's main drag. They offer a warm welcome, a perfect location, a peaceful rooftop garden, and 18 cheaply furnished rooms (Sb-€65, Db-€80, Tb-€95, 10 percent direct-booking discount with cash and this book, no air-con, Via Matteotti 32, tel. 0588-87377, www.albergoetruria.it, info@albergoetruria.it, Paola, Daniele, and Sveva).

$$ Albergo Nazionale, with 38 big and aging rooms, is simple, a little musty, short on smiles, popular with school groups, and steps from the bus stop. It's a nicely located last resort if you have your heart set on sleeping in the old town (Sb-€65, Db-€88, Tb-€105, 10 percent direct-booking discount with cash and this book, elevator, Via dei Marchesi 11, tel. 0588-86284 or 0588-84097, www.hotelnazionale-volterra.it, info@hotelnazionale-volterra.it).

JUST OUTSIDE THE OLD TOWN

These accommodations are within a 5- to 20-minute walk of the city walls.

$$$ Park Hotel Le Fonti, a dull and steep 10-minute walk downhill from Porta all'Arco, can't decide whether it's a business hotel or a resort. The spacious, imposing building feels old and

VOLTERRA & SAN GIMIGNANO

stately, and has 64 modern, comfortable rooms, many with views. While generally overpriced, it can be a good value if you manage to snag a deal. In addition to the swimming pool, guests can use its small spa (average is about Db-€129 but prices vary wildly with the season, identical "superior" room adds a view for €20 extra, "deluxe" room with terrace costs €30 extra, elevator, on-site restaurant, wine bar, free parking, Via di Fontecorrenti 2, tel. 0588-85219, www.parkhotellefonti.com, info@parkhotellefonti.com).

$ **La Primavera B&B** feels like a British B&B transplanted to Tuscany. It's a great value just a few minutes' walk outside Porta Fiorentina (near the Roman Theater). Silvia rents five charming, neat-as-a-pin rooms that share a cutesy-country lounge. The house is set back from the road in a pleasant courtyard. With free parking and the shortest walk to the old town among my out-of-town listings, this is a handy option for drivers (Sb-€50, Db-€75, Tb-€100, free parking, Via Porta Diana 15, tel. 0588-87295, mobile 328-865-0390, www.affittacamere-laprimavera.com, info@affittacamere-laprimavera.com).

$ **Chiosco delle Monache,** Volterra's youth hostel, fills a wing of the restored Convent of San Girolamo with 68 beds in 23 rooms. It's modern, spacious, and very institutional, with lots of services and a tranquil cloister. Unfortunately, it's about a 20-minute hike out of town, in a boring area near deserted hospital buildings (bed in dorm room-€18, breakfast extra, lockers; Db-€69, Tb-€90, Qb-€105, includes breakfast; reception closed 13:00-15:00 and after 20:00, elevator, free parking, kids' playroom; Via dell Teatro 4, look for hospital sign from main Volterra-San Gimignano road; tel. 0588-86613, www.ostellovolterra.it, info@ostellovolterra.it).

$ **Hotel Foresteria,** near Chiosco delle Monache and run by the same organization, has 35 big, utilitarian, new-feeling rooms with decent prices but the same location woes as the hostel; it's worth considering for a family with a car and a tight budget (Sb-€58, Db-€82, Tb-€103, Qb-€122, includes breakfast, air-con, elevator, restaurant, free parking, Borgo San Lazzaro, tel. 0588-80050, www.foresteriavolterra.it, info@foresteriavolterra.it).

$ **Seminario Vescovile Sant'Andrea** is your cheap and monastic option. This place has been training priests for more than 500 years. Today, the remaining eight priests still train students, but when classes are over, their 40 rooms—separated by vast and holy halls in an echoing old mansion—are rented very cheaply. Look for the 15th-century Ascension ceramic by Giovanni della Robbia, tucked away in a corner upstairs, and ask to see the abandoned, circa-1400 church (S-€20, Sb-€25, D-€40, Db-€50, T-€60, Tb-€75, no breakfast, closed Oct-March, elevator, closes at 24:00, free parking, 10-minute walk from Etruscan Museum, Viale Vittorio

Veneto 2, tel. 0588-86028, seminariosantandre@gmail.com; Sergio and Sergio—*due Sergi*).

NEAR VOLTERRA

$$ Podere Marcampo is a newer *agriturismo* about two miles outside Volterra on the road to Pisa. Run by Genuino (owner of the recommended Ristorante Enoteca del Duca), his wife Ivana, and their English-speaking daughter Claudia, this peaceful spot has three well-appointed rooms and three apartments, plus a swimming pool with panoramic views. Genuino produces his Sangiovese and award-winning Merlot on site and offers €20 wine tastings with cheese, homemade salumi, and grappa. Cooking classes at their restaurant in town are also available (Db-€94-118, Db apartment-€118-145 depending on size, Qb apartment-€195-210, more expensive mid-July-Aug, includes breakfast with this book, air-con, free self-service laundry, free parking, tel. 0588-85393, Claudia's mobile 328-174-4605, www.agriturismo-marcampo. com, info@agriturismo-marcampo.com).

VOLTERRA & SAN GIMIGNANO

Eating in Volterra

Menus feature a Volterran take on regional dishes. *Zuppa alla Volterrana* is a fresh vegetable-and-bread soup, similar to *ribollita*. *Torta di ceci*, also known as *cecina*, is a savory pancake-like dish made with garbanzo beans. Those with more adventurous palates dive into *trippa* (tripe stew, the traditional breakfast of the alabaster carvers). *Fegatelli* are meatballs made with liver.

Ristorante Enoteca del Duca, serving well-presented and creative Tuscan cuisine, offers the best elegant meal in town. You can dine under a medieval arch with walls lined with wine bottles, in a sedate, high-ceilinged dining room (with an Etruscan statuette at each table), on a nice little patio out back, or in their little *enoteca* (wine cellar). Chef Genuino, daughter Claudia, and the friendly staff take good care of diners. The fine wine list includes Genuino's own highly regarded Merlot and Sangiovese. The spacious seating, dressy clientele, and calm atmosphere make this a good choice for a romantic splurge (€49 food-sampler fixed-price meal—comes with a free glass of wine for diners with this book, €12-15 pastas, €15-22 *secondi*, Wed-Mon 12:30-15:00 & 19:30-22:00, closed Tue, near City Hall at Via di Castello 2, tel. 0588-81510, www.enoteca-delduca-ristorante.it).

Ristorante Ombra della Sera is another good fine-dining option. While they have a dressy interior, I'd eat here to be on the street and part of the *passegiata* action (€10 pastas, €15 *secondi*, daily, Via Gramsci 70, tel. 0588-86663).

La Carabaccia is unique: It feels like a local family invited you over for a dinner of classic Tuscan comfort food that's rarely seen on restaurant menus. They serve only two pastas and two *secondi* on any given day (listed on the chalkboard by the door). Committed to tradition, on Fridays they serve only fish. They also whip up €3-4 sandwiches and pricier cheese-and-cold-cut plates. They also have fun, family-friendly outdoor seating on a traffic-free piazza (€7-9 pastas and *secondi*, Tue-Sun 12:30-14:30 & 19:30-22:00, closed Mon, Piazza XX Settembre 4, tel. 0588-86239, Sara).

Ristorante il Sacco Fiorentino is a family-run local favorite for traditional cuisine and seasonal specials. While mostly indoors, the restaurant has a few nice tables on a peaceful street (€8-10 pastas, €14-17 *secondi*, Thu-Tue 12:00-15:00 & 19:00-22:00, closed Wed, Via Giusto Turazza 13, tel. 0588-88537).

Trattoria da Badò, a 10-minute hike out of town (along the main road toward San Gimignano, near the turn-off for the old hospital), is popular for its *tipica cucina Volterrana*. Giacomo and family offer a rustic atmosphere and serve food with no pretense—"the way you wish your mamma cooks." Reserve before you go, as it's often full (€10-12 pastas, €13 *secondi*, Thu-Tue 12:30-14:30 & 19:30-22:00, closed Wed, Borgo San Lazzero 9, tel. 0588-80402).

La Vecchia Lira, bright and cheery, is a classy self-serve eatery that's a hit with locals as a quick and cheap lunch spot by day (with €5-10 meals), and a fancier restaurant at night (€9-10 pastas, €13-16 *secondi;* Fri-Wed 11:30-14:30 & 19:00-22:30, closed Thu, Via Matteotti 19, tel. 0588-86180, Lamberto and Massimo).

Dioniso Vegetarian Bistrot is a good bet for organic and vegetarian dishes, including creative salads and pizza. Choose between charming streetside tables or the modern, stony interior, where the glass floor hovers over an excavated Etruscan archaeological site (closed Thu, Via Porta All'Arco 11, tel. 0588-81531).

Pizzeria La Mangiatoia is a fun and convivial place with a Tuscan cowboy interior and picnic tables outside amid a family-friendly street scene. Enjoy pizzas, huge salads, kebabs, game dishes, and beer (Thu-Tue 12:00-23:00, closed Wed, Via Gramsci 35, tel. 0588-85695).

Side-by-Side Pizzerias: **Ombra della Sera** dishes out what local kids consider the best pizza in town (closed Mon, Via Guarnacci 16, tel. 0588-85274). **Pizzeria Tavernetta,** next door, has a romantically frescoed dining room upstairs for classier pizza eating (closed Tue, Via Guarnacci 14, tel. 0588-88155).

Picnic: You can assemble a picnic at the few *alimentari* around town (try Despar Market at Via Gramsci

12, daily 7:30-13:00 & 16:00-20:00) and eat in the breezy Archae-ological Park.

Gelato: Of the many ice-cream stands in the center, I've found **L'Isola di Gusto** to be reliably high quality, with flavors limited to what's in season (daily 11:00-late, Via Gramsci 3, cheery Georgia will make you happy).

Volterra Connections

In Volterra, buses come and go from Piazza Martiri della Libertà (buy tickets at the tobacco shop right on the piazza or purchase on board for small extra charge). Most connections are with the C.T.T. bus company (www.pisa.cttnord.it) through Colle di Val d'Elsa ("koh-leh" for short), a workaday town in the valley (4/day Mon-Sat, 1/day Sun, 50 minutes); for Pisa you'll change in Pont-edera or Saline di Volterra. The nearest train station is in Saline di Volterra, a 15-minute bus ride away (7/day, 2/day Sun); however, trains from Saline run only to the coast, not to the major bus des-tinations listed here.

From Volterra by Bus to: Florence (4/day Mon-Sat, 1/day Sun, 2 hours, change in Colle di Val d'Elsa), **Siena** (4/day Mon-Sat, no buses on Sun, 2 hours, change in Colle di Val d'Elsa), **San Gimignano** (4/day Mon-Sat, 1/day Sun, 2 hours, change in Colle di Val d'Elsa, one connection also requires change in Poggibonsi), **Pisa** (9/day, 2 hours, change in Pontedera or Saline di Volterra).

San Gimignano

The epitome of a Tuscan hill town, with 14 medieval towers still standing (out of an original 72), San Gimignano (sahn jee-meen-YAH-noh) is a perfectly preserved tourist trap. There are no im-

portant interiors to sightsee, and the town feels greedy and packed with crass commercialism. The locals seem spoiled by the easy money of tourism, and most of the rustic is faux. But San Gimignano is so easy to reach and so visually striking that it re-mains a good stop, especially if you can sidestep some of the hordes. The town is an ideal place to go against the touristic flow—arrive late in the day, enjoy it at twilight, then take off in the morning before the deluge begins. (Or day-trip here from Volterra—a 30-minute drive away—and visit early or late.)

In the 13th century—back in the days of Romeo and Juliet—feuding noble families ran the hill towns. They'd periodically battle things out from the protection of their respective family towers. Pointy skylines, like San Gimignano's, were the norm in medieval Tuscany.

San Gimignano's cuisine is mostly what you might find in Siena—typical Tuscan home cooking. *Cinghiale* (cheeng-GAH-lay, boar) is served in almost every way: stews, soups, cutlets, and, my favorite, salami. The area is well-known for producing some of the best saffron in Italy; you'll find the spice for sale in shops (fairly expensive) and as a flavoring in meals at finer restaurants. Although Tuscany is normally a red-wine region, the most famous Tuscan white wine comes from here: the inexpensive, light, and fruity Vernaccia di San Gimignano.

Orientation to San Gimignano

While the basic ▲▲▲ sight here is the town of San Gimignano itself (pop. 7,000, just 2,000 of whom live within the walls), there are a few worthwhile stops. The wall circles an amazingly preserved stony town, once on the Via Francigena pilgrimage route to Rome. The road, which cut through the middle of San Gimignano, is named for St. Matthew in the north (Via San Matteo) of town and St. John in the south (Via San Giovanni). The town is centered on two delightful squares—Piazza del Duomo and Piazza della Cisterna—where you find the town well, City Hall, and cathedral (along with most of the tourists).

TOURIST INFORMATION

The helpful TI is in the old center on Piazza del Duomo (daily March-Oct 10:00-13:00 & 15:00-19:00, Nov-Feb 10:00-13:00 & 14:00-18:00, bus tickets, VAT refunds, tel. 0577-940-008, www.sangimignano.com). They also offer a two-hour minibus tour to a countryside winery (€20, April-Oct Tue and Thu at 17:00, book one day in advance).

ARRIVAL IN SAN GIMIGNANO

The **bus** stops at the main town gate, Porta San Giovanni. There's no baggage storage in town.

You can't **drive** within the walled town; drive past the "ZTL" red circle and you'll get socked with a big fine. Three numbered pay lots are a short walk outside the walls: The handiest is Parcheggio Montemaggio (P2), at the bottom of town near the bus stop, just outside Porta San Giovanni (€2/hour, €20/day). Least expensive is the lot below the roundabout and Coop supermarket, called Parcheggio Giubileo (P1; €1.50/hour, €6/day), a steeper hike

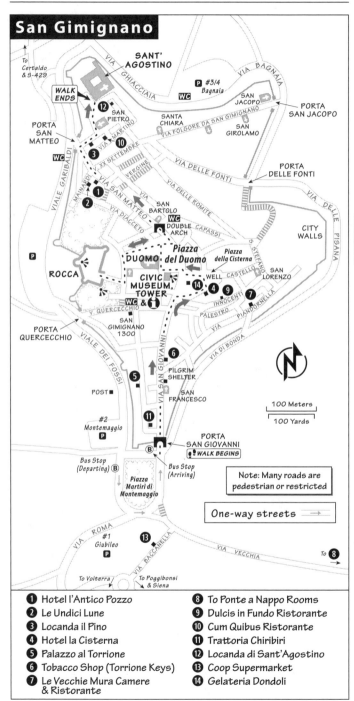

San Gimignano

To Certaldo & S-429

SANT' AGOSTINO

VIA GHIACCIAIA

VIA BAGNAIA

WALK ENDS

P #3/4 Bagnaia

WC

SAN JACOPO

PORTA SAN JACOPO

SAN PIETRO

SANTA CHIARA

SAN GIROLAMO

PORTA SAN MATTEO

VIA MARTINO

VIA FOLGORE DA SAN GIMIGNANO

WC

V. XX SETTEMBRE

VIA DELLE FONTI

PORTA DELLE FONTI

VERGINE

VIALE GARIBALDI

VIA SAN MATTEO

MAINARDI

VIA DELLE ROMITE

VIA DELLE FONTI

VIA PIACCETO

SAN BARTOLO

WC

DOUBLE ARCH

CAPASSI

CITY WALLS

VIA DELLE PISANA

P

ROCCA

Piazza del Duomo

DUOMO

Piazza della Cisterna

WELL

S. STEFANO

SAN LORENZO

CIVIC MUSEUM TOWER & 1

WC

V. QUERCECCHIO

CASTELLO

INNOCENTI

14 4 9 7

PIANDORNELLA

PALESTRO

VIA

SAN GIMIGNANO 1300

PORTA QUERCECCHIO

VIALE DEI FOSSI

VIA SAN GIOVANNI

6

PILGRIM SHELTER

VIA DI BONDA

N

POST

5

SAN FRANCESCO

100 Meters
100 Yards

#2 Montemaggio

P

11

PORTA SAN GIOVANNI

WALK BEGINS

Bus Stop (Departing) B

Piazza Martiri di Montemaggio

B

Bus Stop (Arriving)

Note: Many roads are pedestrian or restricted

One-way streets

VIA ROMA

#1 Giubileo

P

13

VIA BAGNANELLA

VIA VECCHIA

To 8

To Volterra

To Poggibonsi & Siena

❶ Hotel l'Antico Pozzo
❷ Le Undici Lune
❸ Locanda il Pino
❹ Hotel la Cisterna
❺ Palazzo al Torrione
❻ Tobacco Shop (Torrione Keys)
❼ Le Vecchie Mura Camere & Ristorante
❽ To Ponte a Nappo Rooms
❾ Dulcis in Fundo Ristorante
❿ Cum Quibus Ristorante
⓫ Trattoria Chiribiri
⓬ Locanda di Sant'Agostino
⓭ Coop Supermarket
⓮ Gelateria Dondoli

into town. And at the north end of town, by Porta San Jacopo, is Parcheggio Bagnaia (P3/P4, €2/hour, €15/day). Note that some lots—including the one directly in front of Coop and the one just outside Porta San Matteo—are designated for locals and have a one-hour limit for tourists.

HELPFUL HINTS

Market Day: Thursday is market day on Piazza del Duomo (8:00-13:00), but for local merchants, every day is a sales frenzy.

Services: A public **WC** is just off Piazza della Cisterna; you'll also find WCs at the Rocca fortress, near San Bartolo church, just outside Porta San Matteo, and at the Parcheggio Bagnaia parking lot.

Shuttle Bus: A little electric shuttle bus does its laps about hourly all day from Porta San Giovanni to Piazza della Cisterna to Porta San Matteo. Route #1 runs back and forth through town; route #2—which runs only in summer—connects the three parking lots to the town center (€0.75 one-way, €1.50 all-day pass, buy ticket in advance at TI or tobacco shop, possible to buy all-day pass on bus). When pedestrian congestion in the center is greatest (Sat afternoons, all day Sun, and July-Aug), the bus runs along the road skirting the outside of town.

San Gimignano Walk

This quick self-guided walking tour takes you across town, from the bus stop at Porta San Giovanni through the town's main squares to the Duomo, and on to the Sant'Agostino Church.

• *Start at the Porta San Giovanni gate at the bottom (south) end of town.*

Porta San Giovanni

San Gimignano lies about 25 miles from both Siena and Florence, a day's trek for pilgrims en route to those cities, and on a naturally fortified hilltop that encouraged settlement. The town's walls were built in the 13th century, and gates like this helped regulate who came and went. Today, modern posts keep out all but service and emergency vehicles. The small square just outside the gate features a memorial to the town's WWII dead. Follow the pilgrims' route (and flood of modern tourists) through the gate and up the main drag.

About 100 yards up, where the street widens, look right to see a pilgrims' shelter (12th-century, Pisan Romanesque). The eight-pointed Maltese cross on the facade of the church indicates that it was built by the Knights of Malta, whose early mission (before they became a military unit) was to provide hospitality for pilgrims.

It was one of 11 such shelters in town. Today, only the wall of the shelter remains, and the surviving interior of the church houses yet one more shop selling gifty edibles.

• *Carry on past all manner of shops, up to the top of Via San Giovanni. Look up at the formidable inner wall, built 200 years before today's outer wall. Just beyond that is the central Piazza della Cisterna. Sit on the steps of the well.*

Piazza della Cisterna

The piazza is named for the cistern that is served by the old well standing in the center of this square. A clever system of pipes

drained rainwater from the nearby rooftops into the underground cistern. This square has been the center of the town since the ninth century. Turn in a slow circle and observe the commotion of rustic-yet-proud facades crowding in a tight huddle around the well. Imagine this square in pilgrimage times, lined by inns and taverns for the town's guests. Now finger the grooves in the lip of the well and imagine generations of maids and children fetching water. Each Thursday morning, the square fills with a market—as it has for more than a thousand years.

• *Notice San Gimignano's famous towers.*

The Towers

Of the original 72 towers, only 14 survive (and one can be climbed—at the City Hall). Some of the original towers were just

empty, chimney-like structures built to boost noble egos, while others were actually the forts of wealthy families.

Before effective city walls were developed, rich people needed to fortify their own homes. These towers provided a handy refuge when ruffians and rival city-states were sacking the town. If under attack, tower owners would set fire to the external wooden staircase, leaving the sole entrance unreachable a story up; inside, fleeing nobles pulled up behind them the ladders that connected each level, leaving invaders no way to reach the stronghold at the tower's top. These towers became a standard part of medieval skylines. Even after town walls were built, the towers continued to rise—now to fortify noble families feuding within a town (Montague and Capulet-style).

In the 14th century, San Gimignano's good times turned very bad. In the year 1300, about 13,000 people lived within the walls. Then in 1348, a six-month plague decimated the population, leaving the once-mighty town with barely 4,000 survivors. Once fiercely independent, now crushed and demoralized, San Gimignano came under Florence's control and was forced to tear down most of its towers. (The Banca CR Firenze building occupies the remains of one such toppled tower.) And, to add insult to injury, Florence redirected the vital trade route away from San Gimignano. The town never recovered, and poverty left it in a 14th-century architectural time warp. That well-preserved cityscape, ironically, is responsible for the town's prosperity today.

• *From the well, walk 30 yards uphill to the adjoining square with the cathedral.*

Piazza del Duomo

Stand at the base of the stairs in front of the church. Since before there was gelato, people have lounged on these steps. Take a

360-degree spin clockwise: The cathedral's 12th-century facade is plain-Jane Romanesque—finished even though it doesn't look it. To the right, the two Salvucci Towers (a.k.a. the "Twin Towers") date from the 13th century. Locals like to brag that the architect who designed New York City's Twin Towers was inspired by these. The towers are empty shells, built by the wealthy Salvucci family simply to show off. At that time, no one was allowed a vanity tower higher than the City Hall's 170 feet. So the Salvuccis built two 130-foot towers—totaling 260 feet of stony ego trip.

The stubby tower next to the Salvucci Towers is the Merchant's Tower. Imagine this in use: ground-floor shop, warehouse upstairs (see the functional shipping door), living quarters, and finally the kitchen on the top (for fire-safety reasons). The holes in the walls held beams that supported wooden balconies and exterior staircases. The tower has heavy stone on the first floor, then cheaper and lighter brick for the upper stories.

Opposite the church stands the first City Hall, with its 170-foot tower, nicknamed "the bad news tower." While the church got to ring its bells in good times, these bells were for wars and fires. The tower's arched public space hosted a textile market back when cloth was the foundation of San Gimignano's booming economy.

Next is the super-sized "new" City Hall with its 200-foot tower (the only one in town open to the public; for visiting info, see the Civic Museum and Tower listing, later). The climbing lion is the symbol of the city. The coats of arms of the city's leading families have been ripped down or disfigured. In medieval times locals would have blamed witches or ghosts. For the last two centuries, they've blamed Napoleon instead.

Between the City Hall and the cathedral, a statue of St. Gimignano presides over all the hubbub. The fourth-century bishop protected the village from rampaging barbarians—and is now the city's patron saint. (To enter the cathedral, walk under that statue.)
• *You'll also see the…*

Duomo (Collegiata)

Inside San Gimignano's Romanesque cathedral, Sienese Gothic art (14th century) lines the nave with parallel themes—Old Testament on the left and New Testament on the right. (For example, from back to front: Creation facing the Annunciation, the birth of Adam facing the Nativity, and—farther forward—the suffering of Job opposite the suffering of Jesus.) This is a classic use of art to teach. Study the fine Creation series (along the left side). Many scenes are portrayed with a 14th-century "slice of life" setting to help lay townspeople relate to Jesus—in the same way that many white Christians are more comfortable thinking of Jesus as Caucasian.

To the right of the altar, the St. Fina Chapel honors the devout, 13th-century local girl who brought forth many miracles on her death. Her tomb is beautifully frescoed with scenes from her life by Domenico Ghirlandaio (famed as Michelangelo's teacher). The altar sits atop Fina's skeleton, and its centerpiece is a reliquary that contains her skull (€4, includes dry audioguide; April-Oct Mon-Sat 10:00-19:30, Sun from 12:30; shorter hours off-season; buy ticket and enter from courtyard around left side).
• *From the church, hike uphill (passing the church on your left) following signs to* Rocca e Parco di Montestaffoli. *Keep walking until you enter a peaceful hilltop park and olive grove, set within the shell of a 14th-century fortress the Medici of Florence built to protect this town from Siena.*

Hilltop Views at the Rocca

On the far side, 33 steps take you to the top of a little tower (free) for the best views of San Gimignano's skyline; the far end of town and the Sant'Agostino Church (where this walk ends); and a commanding 360-degree view of the Tuscan countryside. San Gimignano is surrounded by olives, grapes, cypress trees, and—in the Middle Ages—lots of wild dangers. Back then, farmers lived inside the walls and were thankful for the protection.

VOLTERRA & SAN GIMIGNANO

• *Return to the bottom of Piazza del Duomo, turn left, and continue your walk, cutting under the double arch (from the town's first wall). In around 1200, this defined the end of town. The* **Church of San Bartolo** *stood just outside the wall (on the right). The Maltese cross over the door indicates that it likely served as a hostel for pilgrims. As you continue down Via San Matteo, notice that the crowds have dropped by at least half. Enjoy the breathing room as you pass a fascinating array of stone facades from the 13th and 14th centuries—now a happy cancan of wine shops and galleries. Reaching the gateway at the end of town, follow signs to the right to reach...*

Sant'Agostino Church

This tranquil church, at the far end of town (built by the Augustinians who arrived in 1260), has fewer crowds and more soul. Behind the altar, a lovely fresco cycle by Benozzo Gozzoli (who painted the exquisite Chapel of the Magi in the Medici-Riccardi Palace in Florence) tells of the life of St. Augustine, a North African monk who preached simplicity (pay a few coins for light). The kind, English-speaking friars (from Britain and the US) are happy to tell you about their church and way of life. Pace the peaceful cloister before heading back into the tourist mobs (free, April-Oct daily 7:00-12:00 & 15:00-19:00, shorter hours off-season; Sunday Mass in English at 11:00).

Sights in San Gimignano

▲Civic Museum and Tower (Musei Civici and Torre Grossa)

This small, entertaining museum, consisting of three unfurnished rooms, is inside the City Hall (Palazzo Comunale). The main reason to visit is to scale the tower, which offers sweeping views over San Gimignano and the countryside.

Cost and Hours: €7.50 includes museum and tower; daily April-Oct 9:30-19:00, Nov-March 11:00-17:30, audioguide-€2, Piazza del Duomo, tel. 0577-990-312, www.sangimignanomusei. it.

Visiting the Museum: You'll enter the complex through a delightful stony courtyard (to the left as you face the Duomo). Climb up to the loggia to buy your ticket.

The main room (across from the ticket desk), called the **Sala di Consiglio** (a.k.a. Dante Hall, recalling his visit in 1300), is covered in festive frescoes, including the *Maestà* by Lippo Memmi (from 1317). This virtual copy of Simone Martini's *Maestà* in Siena proves that Memmi didn't have quite the same talent as his famous brother-in-law. The art gives you a peek at how people dressed, lived, worked, and warred back in the 14th century.

Upstairs, the **Pinacoteca** displays a classy little painting collection of mostly altarpieces. The highlight is a 1422 altarpiece by Taddeo di Bartolo honoring St. Gimignano (far end of last room). You can see the saint, with the town—bristling with towers—in his hands, surrounded by events from his life.

Before going back downstairs, be sure to stop by the **Mayor's Room** (Camera del Podestà, across the stairwell from the Pinacoteca). Frescoed in 1310, it offers an intimate and candid peek into the 14th century. As you enter, look right up in the corner to find a young man ready to experience the world. He hits his parents up for a bag of money and is on his way. Suddenly (above the window), he's in trouble, entrapped by two prostitutes, who lead him into a tent where he loses his money, is turned out, and is beaten. Above the door, from left to right, you see a parade of better choices: marriage, the cradle of love, the bride led to the groom's house, and newlyweds bathing together and retiring happily to their bed.

The highlight for most visitors is a chance to climb the **Tower** (Torre Grossa, entrance halfway down the stairs from the Pinacoteca). The city's tallest tower, 200 feet and 218 steps up, rewards those who climb it with a commanding view. See if you can count the town's 14 towers. It's a sturdy, modern staircase most of the way, but the last stretch is a steep, ladder-like climb.

San Gimignano 1300

Artists and brothers Michelangelo and Raffaello Rubino share an interesting attraction in their workshop: a painstakingly rendered 1:100 scale clay model of San Gimignano at the turn of the 14th century. Step through a shop selling their art to enjoy the model. You can see the 72 original "tower houses," and marvel at how unchanged the street plan remains today. You'll peek into cross-sections of buildings, view scenes of medieval life both within and outside the city walls, and watch a video about the making of the model.

Cost and Hours: Free, daily April-Oct 10:00-18:00, Nov-March until 17:00, on a quiet street a block over from the main square at Via Costarella 3, mobile 327-439-5165.

Sleeping in San Gimignano

Although the town is a zoo during the daytime, locals outnumber tourists when evening comes, and San Gimignano becomes mellow and enjoyable.

NEAR PORTA SAN MATTEO, AT THE QUIET END OF TOWN

If arriving by bus, save a crosstown walk to these by asking for the Porta San Matteo stop (rather than the main stop near Porta San Giovanni). Drivers can park at the less-crowded Bagnaia lots (P3 and P4), and walk around to Porta San Matteo.

$$$ Hotel l'Antico Pozzo is an elegantly restored, 15th-century townhouse with 18 tranquil, comfortable rooms, a peaceful interior courtyard terrace, and an elite air (Sb-€95, Db-€119-180, air-con, elevator, Via San Matteo 87, tel. 0577-942-014, www. anticopozzo.com, info@anticopozzo.com; Emanuele, Elisabetta, and Mariangela).

$$ Le Undici Lune ("The 11 Moons") is situated in a tight but characteristic circa-1300 townhouse with steep stairs at the tranquil end of town. Its three rooms and one apartment have been tastefully decorated with modern flair by Gabriele. While there's no air-conditioning, the building was designed as a storehouse for food, so it's naturally cool (Db-€85, apartment-€100, book directly for these prices, Via Mainardi 9, mobile 389-236-8174, www. leundicilune.com, leundicilune@gmail.com).

$ Locanda il Pino has just seven rooms and a big living room. It's dank but clean and quiet. Run by English-speaking Elena and her family, it sits above their elegant restaurant at the quiet end of town, just inside Porta San Matteo (Db-€55, Tb-€75, breakfast-€7.50, fans, Via Cellolese 4, tel. 0577-940-415, locanda@ ristoranteilpino.it).

NEAR THE MAIN SQUARE, AT THE BUSY END OF TOWN

$$$ Hotel la Cisterna, right on Piazza della Cisterna, feels old and stately, with 48 aging rooms, some with panoramic view terraces—a scene from the film *Tea with Mussolini* was filmed from one (Sb-€78, Db-€100, Db with view-€125, Db with view terrace—€140, 10 percent direct-booking discount with this book, air-con, elevator, good restaurant with great view, closed Jan-Feb, Piazza della Cisterna 23, tel. 0577-940-328, www.hotelcisterna.it, info@hotelcisterna.it, Alessio).

$$ Palazzo al Torrione, on an untrampled side street just inside Porta San Giovanni, is quiet and handy, and generally better than most local hotels. Their 10 modern rooms are spacious and tastefully appointed (Db-€90, terrace Db-€110, Tb-€100, terrace Tb-€120, Qb-€120-130, 10 percent direct-booking discount with this book, breakfast-€7, parking-€6/day, inside and left of gate at Via Berignano 76; operated from tobacco shop 2 blocks away, on the main drag at Via San Giovanni 59; tel. 0577-940-480, mobile

338-938-1656, www.palazzoaltorrione.com, palazzoaltorrione@
palazzoaltorrione.com, Vanna and Francesco).

$ Le Vecchie Mura Camere offers three good rooms above
their recommended restaurant along a rustic lane, clinging just
below the main square (Db-€65, no breakfast, air-con, Via Piandornella 15, tel. 0577-940-270, www.vecchiemura.it, info@
vecchiemura.it, Bagnai family).

IN THE COUNTRYSIDE, WITH A
VIEW OF SAN GIMIGNANO

$$$ Ponte a Nappo, run by enterprising Carla Rossi and her
English-speaking sons Francesco and Andrea, has six basic rooms
and two apartments in a kid-friendly farmhouse. Located a mile
below town, this place has stunning San Gimignano views. A pic-
nic dinner lounging on their comfy garden furniture next to the big
swimming pool as the sun sets is good Tuscan living (Db-€90-135,
2-to-6 person apartment-€130-250, book direct and mention Rick
Steves—or use promo code "RickSteves" on their website, air-con,
tel. 0577-907-282, mobile 349-882-1565, www.accommodation-
sangimignano.com, info@rossicarla.it). About 100 yards below the
monument square at Porta San Giovanni, find tiny Via Baccanella/
Via Vecchia and drive downhill. They also rent a dozen rooms and
apartments in town (Db-€60-120, each room described on their
website).

Eating in San Gimignano

My first two listings cling to quiet, rustic lanes overlooking the
Tuscan hills (yet just a few steps off the main street); the rest are
buried deep in the old center.

Dulcis in Fundo Ristorante, small and family-run, proudly
serves modest portions of "revisited" Tuscan cuisine (with a mod-
ern twist and gourmet presentation) in a jazzy ambience. This en-
lightened place uses top-quality ingredients, many of which come
from their own farm. They also offer vegetarian and gluten-free op-
tions (€10-12 pastas, €13-17 *secondi,* Thu-Tue 12:30-14:30 & 19:15-
21:45, closed Wed, Vicolo degli Innocenti 21, tel. 0577-941-919,
Roberto and Cristina).

Le Vecchie Mura Ristorante has good service, great prices,
tasty if unexceptional home cooking, and the ultimate view. It's
romantic indoors or out. They have a dressy, modern interior where
you can dine with a view of the busy stainless-steel kitchen under
rustic vaults, but the main reason to come is for the incredible, cliff-
side garden terrace. Cliff-side tables are worth reserving in ad-
vance by calling or dropping by: Ask for "front view" (€9-11 pastas,

€12-15 *secondi,* open only for dinner 18:00-22:00, closed Tue, Via Piandornella 15, tel. 0577-940-270, Bagnai family).

Cum Quibus ("In Company"), tucked away near Porta San Matteo, has a small dining room with soft music, beamed ceilings, modern touches, and a sophisticated vibe; it also offers al fresco tables in its interior patio. Lorenzo and Simona produce tasty and creative Tuscan cuisine (€10 pastas, €19-24 *secondi,* Wed-Mon 12:30-14:30 & 19:00-22:00, closed Tue, reservations advised, Via San Martino 17, tel. 0577-943-199).

Trattoria Chiribiri, just inside Porta San Giovanni on the left, serves homemade pastas and desserts at good prices. While its petite size and tight seating make it hot in the summer, it's a good budget option—and as such, it's in all the guidebooks (€8 pastas, €8-11 *secondi,* daily 11:00-23:00, Piazza della Madonna 1, tel. 0577-941-948, Maria and Maurizio).

Locanda di Sant'Agostino spills out onto the peaceful square, facing Sant'Agostino Church. It's cheap and cheery, serving lunch and dinner daily—big portions of basic food in a restful setting. Dripping with wheat stalks and atmosphere on the inside, it has shady on-the-square seating outside (€8-12 pizzas, pastas, and *bruschette;* €10-15 *secondi,* daily 11:00-23:00, closed Wed off-season, closed Jan-Feb, Piazza Sant'Agostino 15, tel. 0577-943-141, Genziana and sons).

Near Porto San Matteo: Just inside Porta San Matteo are a variety of handy and inviting good-value restaurants, bars, cafés, and *gelaterias.* Eateries need to work harder at the nontouristy end of town.

Picnics: The big, modern **Coop supermarket** sells all you need for a nice spread (Mon-Sat 8:30-20:00, Sun 8:30-12:30 except closed Sun Nov-March, at parking lot below Porta San Giovanni). Or browse the little shops guarded by boar heads within the town walls; they sell pricey boar meat *(cinghiale).* Pick up 100 grams (about a quarter pound) of boar, cheese, bread, and wine and enjoy a picnic in the garden at the Rocca or the park outside Porta San Giovanni.

Gelato: To cap the evening and sweeten your late-night city stroll, stop by **Gelateria Dondoli** on Piazza della Cisterna (at #4). Gelato-maker Sergio was a member of the Italian team that won the official Gelato World Cup—and his gelato really is a cut above (tel. 0577-942-244, Dondoli family).

San Gimignano Connections

Bus tickets are sold at the bar just inside the town gate or at the TI. Many connections require a change at Poggibonsi (poh-jee-BOHN-see), which is also the nearest train station.

From San Gimignano by Bus to: Florence (hourly, less on Sun, 1.5-2 hours, change in Poggibonsi), **Siena** (8/day direct, on Sun must change in Poggibonsi, 1.25 hours), **Volterra** (4/day Mon-Sat; 1/day Sun—in the late afternoon and usually crowded—with no return to San Gimignano; 2 hours, change in Colle di Val d'Elsa, one connection also requires change in Poggibonsi). Note that the bus connection to Volterra is four times as long as the drive; if you're desperate to get there faster, you can pay about €70 for a taxi.

By Car: San Gimignano is an easy 45-minute drive from Florence (take the A-1 exit marked *Firenze Certosa,* then a right past tollbooth following *Siena per 4 corsie* sign; exit the freeway at Poggibonsi). From San Gimignano, it's a scenic and windy half-hour drive to Volterra.

THE HEART OF TUSCANY

*Montepulciano • Pienza • Best of the Heart of Tuscany •
Montalcino*

If your Tuscan dreams feature vibrant neon-green fields rolling to infinity, punctuated by snaking cypress-lined driveways; humble but beautiful (and steep) hill towns; and world-class wines to make a connoisseur weep, set your sights on the heart of this region.

An hour south of Siena, this slice of splendor—which specializes in views and wine—is a highlight, particularly for drivers. With an astonishing diversity of towns, villages, abbeys, wineries, countryside restaurants and accommodations, all set within jaw-dropping scenery, this sub-region of Tuscany is a fine place to abandon your itinerary and just slow down.

Even though the area's towns sometimes seem little more than a rack upon which to hang the vine-draped hills, each one has its own endearing personality. The biggest and most interesting, Montepulciano, boasts a medieval cityscape wearing a Renaissance coat, wine cellars that plunge deep down into the cliffs it sits upon, and a classic town square. Pienza is a sure-of-itself planned Renaissance town that once gave the world a pope. And mellow Montalcino is (even more than most towns around here) all about its wine: the famous Brunello di Montalcino.

PLANNING YOUR TIME

This region richly rewards whatever time you're willing to give it. As this compact region is hemmed in by Italy's two main north-south thoroughfares—the A-1 expressway and SR-2 highway—even those with a few hours to spare can get an enticing taste. But ideally, spend two nights and three full days (see my three-day plan, later). Many travelers enjoy home-basing here for up to a week, appreciating not only the area's many attractions, but also

Heart of Tuscany at a Glance

▲▲▲**Montepulciano** Hill town (with grand vistas, wonderful wine cellars, and a medieval soul) that corrals the essence of Tuscany within its walls. See page 88.

▲▲▲**Heart of Tuscany Driving Tour** An unforgettable day lacing together the views, villages, and disparate rural attractions of the region (including both Montepulciano and Pienza). See page 111.

▲▲**Pienza** Unique, pint-sized planned Renaissance town that's amazingly well-preserved, very touristy, and relatively unhilly. See page 103.

▲▲**Montalcino** Touristy "Brunello-ville" wine capital that still exudes a stony charm; aside from the wine, it feels like a second-rate repeat of Montepulciano. See page 118.

▲▲**Brunello Wineries** My favorite countryside places to sample the famous Brunello di Montalcino, all gorgeously situated among hills and vineyards. **Hours**: Occasionally welcoming to drop-ins, but it's much better to call ahead to schedule a tour and tasting. See page 121.

▲▲**Sleeping at an** *Agriturismo* **or Countryside B&B** The best way to experience rural Tuscany: rustic, rural accommodations, most run by families who are dedicated to making sure their cows and their guests are both well-fed. See page 127.

▲**La Foce Gardens** Delightful, unique gardens with gorgeous plantings, engaging history, and fine panoramas. **Hours**: Visit by 50-minute tour only; April-Oct Wed at 15:00, 16:00, 17:00, and 18:00; Sat-Sun at 11:30 and 15:00; no tours in winter. Reserve in advance. See page 115.

▲**Bagno Vignoni** Quirky little spa town that's simply fun to check out, whether you take a dip or not. See page 116.

HEART OF TUSCANY

its strategic position for day trips to Siena (less than an hour away), or even to Volterra, San Gimignano, Florence, and Orvieto (each about 1.5 hours away).

Choosing a Home Base: Montepulciano is the most all-around engaging town; it's the best choice for those without a car (though connections can still be tricky), and also works well for drivers. With its easy access to the vineyards, Montalcino makes sense for wine pilgrims. And for drivers who'd like to home-base

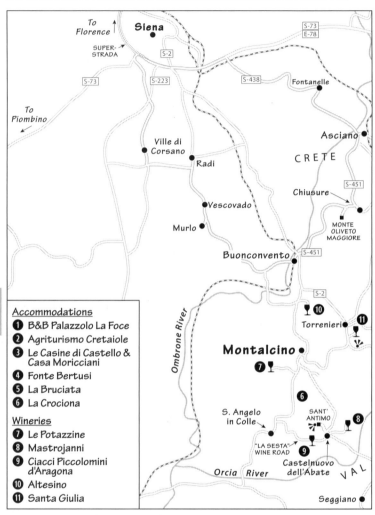

HEART OF TUSCANY

Accommodations
1. B&B Palazzolo La Foce
2. Agriturismo Cretaiole
3. Le Casine di Castello & Casa Moricciani
4. Fonte Bertusi
5. La Bruciata
6. La Crociona

Wineries
7. Le Potazzine
8. Mastrojanni
9. Ciacci Piccolomini d'Aragona
10. Altesino
11. Santa Giulia

in the countryside, I've listed several *agriturismi* and other rural accommodations at the end of this chapter.

The Heart of Tuscany in Three Days

Three days is enough to get a good look at the area's many highlights. Here's a smart plan, assuming you're coming from Siena. (If coming from the south, do it in reverse.)

Day One: On your way south from Siena, visit a winery north of Montalcino before settling into Montepulciano (or your choice of countryside accommodations).

Day Two: Follow my "Heart of Tuscany" drive, including a sight-

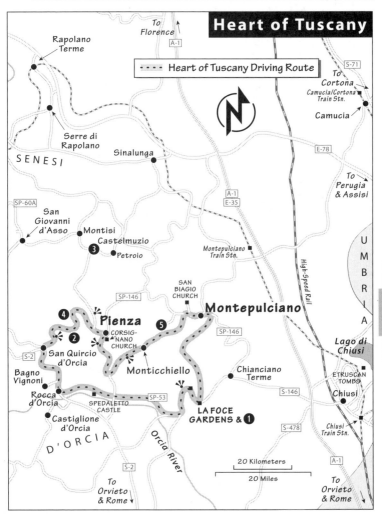

seeing-and-gelato stop in Pienza. Have dinner back in Montepulciano, or in the nearby countryside.

Day Three: Your day is free to enjoy and sightsee Montepulciano or drive to any countryside attractions you've missed so far. You could head to your next destination this afternoon, or spend a third night.

GETTING AROUND THE HEART OF TUSCANY

By Car: This area is ideal by car. Distances are short, and it's easy to mix-and-match sights. Navigate by town names and use a good map or—better yet—a mapping app with GPS to keep you on track (Google Maps works well here). Some of the at-

tractions I've described are on tiny back lanes, marked only with easy-to-miss, low-profile signs from the main roads. I've given distances in kilometers to match up with your rental car's odometer. In small hill towns, make it a habit to park at the lot just outside town and walk in. White lines indicate free parking; blue lines indicate paid parking (pay at the station, then display the ticket on your windshield); and yellow lines are only for locals. Parking machines typically don't accept bills or give change; have plenty of coins on hand.

By Public Transportation: While you can reach many of this chapter's sights by public buses, connections are slow, infrequent, and often require a transfer. Taxis can help connect the dots more efficiently. Montepulciano is the best home base for those without a car (though it's still not entirely convenient).

TOURS IN TUSCANY

A good local guide can help you take full advantage of everything this area has to offer. One with a car can save you lots of time and stress.

Antonella Piredda, who lives in the village of Montisi (just north of Pienza) is smart, well-organized, and enjoyably opinionated (€60/hour, 3-hour minimum, €350/all day, she can join you in your car or hire a driver for extra, mobile 347-456-5150, anto@antonellapiredda.com, www.antonellapiredda.com).

Roberto Bechi runs all-day minibus tours with a passion for local culture, hands-on experiences, and offbeat sights. The price is reasonable, since he assembles groups of up to eight people to share the experience...and the cost (full-day van tours-€90/person, other services and tours explained on his website, www.toursbyroberto.com, toursbyroberto@gmail.com).

Montepulciano

Curving its way along a ridge, Montepulciano (mohn-teh-pull-chee-AH-noh) delights visitors with *vino,* views, and—perhaps more than any other large town in this area—a sense of being a real, bustling community rather than just a tourist depot.

Alternately under Sienese and Florentine rule, the city still retains its medieval *contrade* (districts), each with a mascot and flag. The neighborhoods compete the last Sunday of August in the Bravio delle Botti, where teams of men push large wine casks uphill from Piazza Marzocco to Piazza Grande, all hoping to win a banner and bragging rights. The entire last week of August is a festival: Each *contrada* arranges musical entertainment and serves food at outdoor eateries along with generous tastings of the local *vino.*

The city is a collage of architectural styles, but the elegant San Biagio Church, just outside the city walls at the base of the hill, is its best Renaissance building. Most visitors ignore the architecture and focus more on the city's other creative accomplishment, the tasty Vino Nobile di Montepulciano red wine.

Orientation to Montepulciano

Commercial action in Montepulciano centers in the lower town, mostly along Via di Gracciano nel Corso (nicknamed "Corso"). This stretch begins at the town gate called Porta al Prato (near the TI, bus station, and some parking) and winds slowly up, up, up through town—narrated by my self-guided walk. Strolling here, you'll find eateries, gift shops, and tourist traps. The back streets are worth exploring. The main square, at the top of town (up a steep switchback lane from the Corso), is Piazza Grande. Standing proudly above all the touristy sales energy, the square has a noble, Florentine feel.

TOURIST INFORMATION

The helpful TI is just outside the Porta al Prato city gate, directly underneath the small tree-lined parking lot (Mon-Sat 9:30-12:30 & 15:00-18:00, Sun 9:30-12:30, daily until 20:00 in July-Aug, books rooms for no fee, public computer, Piazza Don Minzoni, tel. 0578-757-341, www.prolocomontepulciano.it).

The office on the main square that looks like a TI is actually a privately run "Strada del Vino" (Wine Road) agency. They don't have city info, but they do provide wine-road maps, wine tours in the city, minibus winery tours farther afield, and cooking classes and other culinary experiences (Mon-Fri 10:00-13:00 & 15:00-18:00, Piazza Grande 7, tel. 0578-717-484, www.stradavinonobile.it).

ARRIVAL IN MONTEPULCIANO

By Car: Well-signed pay-and-display parking lots ring the city center (marked with blue lines). A lot of free spaces are mixed in (marked with white lines)—look around before you park.

To start your visit by following my self-guided walk (up the length of the Corso to the main square), park at the north end of town, near the Porta al Prato gate. Around here, the handiest lots are P1 (in front of the TI, with some free spaces) and the unnumbered lot just above, directly in front of the stone gate. If these are full, try lots P2 or P4. Lot P5 is near the bus station (ride up to the gate on the elevator described under "By Bus," later).

To reach the main square quickly, you can ride the twice-hourly shuttle bus up from near the TI (see "Helpful Hints," later). Or you can drive up to parking lots at the top end of town: Approaching Montepulciano, follow signs for *centro storico, duomo,* and *Piazza Grande,* and use the *Fortezza* or *San Donato* lots (flanking the fortress).

Avoid the "ZTL" no-traffic zone (marked with a red circle). If you're sleeping in town, your hotelier can give you a permit to park within the walls; be sure to get very specific instructions.

By Bus: Buses leave passengers at the bus station on Piazza Nenni, downhill from the Porta al Prato gate. From the station, cross the street and head inside the modern orange-brick structure burrowed into the hillside, where there's an elevator. Ride to level 1, walk straight down the corridor (following signs for *centro storico*), and ride a second elevator (to a different level 1 and the Poggiofanti Gardens); walk to the end of this park and hook left to find the gate. This is the starting point for my self-guided walk up the Corso to the main square. To get to the top of town in a hurry, you can hop on the shuttle bus either at the bus station itself, or near the TI (see "Helpful Hints," next).

HELPFUL HINTS

Market Day: It's on Thursday morning (8:00-13:00), near the bus station.

Services: There's no official **baggage storage** in town, but the TI might let you leave bags with them if they have space. Public **WCs** are located at the TI, to the left of Palazzo Comunale, and at the Sant'Agostino Church.

Shuttle Bus: To avoid the hike up through town to Piazza Grande, you can hop on the orange shuttle bus that departs from near the TI (look for the gray metal canopy over a hotel-booking booth; also stops at the bus station; 2/hour, €1.10, buy tickets at bars or tobacco shops).

Laundry: An elegant self-service launderette is at Via del Paolino

Montepulciano

1. Mueblè il Riccio
2. La Locanda di San Francesco Rooms & E Lucevan le Stelle Wine Bar
3. Albergo Duomo
4. Camere Bellavista
5. Vicolo dell'Oste B&B
6. Ai Quattro Venti
7. Ost. dell'Aquacheta
8. Osteria del Conte
9. Le Pentolaccia
10. Caffè Poliziano
11. Mazzetti Copper Shop
12. Ramaio Cesare Copper Workshop
13. Contucci Cantina
14. De' Ricci Cantine del Redi
15. Cantina della Talosa
16. Launderette

WALK BEGINS

200 Meters

200 Yards

- - - - Self-Guided Walk

HEART OF TUSCANY

2, just around the corner from the recommended Camere Bellavista (daily 8:00-22:00, tel. 0578-717-544).

Taxis: Two taxi drivers operate in Montepulciano. Call 330-732-723 for short trips within town (€10 for rides up or down hill); to reach other towns, call 348-702-4124 (www.strollingintuscany.com).

Montepulciano Walk

This two-part self-guided walk traces the spine of the town, from its main entrance up to its hilltop seat of power. Part 1 begins at the big gate at the bottom of town, Porta al Prato (near the TI and several parking lots); Part 2 focuses on the square at the very top of town, and the nearby streets. Note that Part 1 is steeply uphill; if you'd rather skip straight to the more level part of town (and Part 2), ride the twice-hourly shuttle bus up, or park at one of the lots near the Fortezza. (When you're done, you can still do Part 1—backwards—on the way back down.)

PART 1: UP THE CORSO

This guided stroll takes you up through Montepulciano's commercial (and touristy) gamut, which curls ever so gradually from the bottom of town to the top. While the street is lined mostly with gift shops, you'll pass a few relics of an earlier age.

Begin in front of the imposing Porta al Prato, one of the many stout city gates that once fortified this highly strategic town. Facing the gate, find the sign for the Porta di Bacco *"passaggio segreto"* on the left. While Montepulciano did have secret passages tunneled through the rock beneath it (handy during times of siege), this particular passage—right next to the city's front door—was probably no *segreto*...though it works great for selling salami.

Walk directly through the **Porta al Prato,** looking up to see the slot where the portcullis (heavily fortified gate) could slide down to seal things off. Notice that there are two gates, enabling defenders to trap would-be invaders in a no-man's land where they could be doused with hot tar. Besides having a drop-down portcullis, each gate also had a hinged door—effectively putting four barriers between the town and its enemies.

Pass through the gate and head a block uphill to reach the **Colonna del Marzocco.** This column, topped with a lion holding the Medici shield, is a reminder that Montepulciano existed under the auspices of Florence—but only for part of its history. Originally the column was crowned by a she-wolf suckling human twins, the civic symbol of Siena. At a strategic crossroads of mighty regional powers (Florence, Siena, and the Papal States), Montepulciano often switched allegiances—and this column became a flagpole where the overlords du jour could tout their influence.

The column is also the starting point for Montepulciano's masochistic tradition, the **Bravio delle Botti,** held on the last Sunday of August, in which each local *contrada* (fiercely competitive neighborhood, like Siena's) selects its two stoutest young men to roll a 180-pound barrel up the hill through town. If the vertical climb through town wears you out, be glad you're only toting a camera.

A few steps up, on the right (at #91, with stylized lion heads), is one of the many fine noble palaces that front Montepulciano's main strip. The town is fortunate to be graced with so many bold and noble *palazzos*—Florentine nobility favored Montepulciano as a breezy and relaxed place for a secondary residence. Grand as this palace is, it's small potatoes—the higher you go in Montepulciano, the closer you are to the town center...and the fancier the mansions.

Farther up on the right, at #75 (Palazzo Bucelli), take a moment to examine the **Etruscan and Roman fragments** embedded

in the wall, left here by a 19th-century antiques dealer. You can quickly distinguish which pieces came from the Romans and those belonging to the earlier Etruscans by their alphabets: The "backwards" Etruscan letters (they read from right to left) resemble Greek. Many of the fragments show a circle flanked by a pair of inward-facing semicircular designs. This symbol represents the libation cup used for drinking at an Etruscan banquet.

At the top of the block on the right is the **Church of Sant'Agostino.** Its late-Gothic facade features a terra-cotta sculpture group by the architect Michelozzo, a favorite of the Medicis in Florence. Throughout Montepulciano, Florentine touches like this underline that city's influence.

Hike up a few more steps, then take a breather to look back and see the **clock tower** in the middle of the street. The bell ringer at the top takes the form of the character Pulcinella, one of the wild and carefree revelers familiar from Italy's *commedia dell'arte* theatrical tradition.

Continuing up, at the *alimentari* on the right (at #23), notice the classic old sign advertising milk, butter, margarine, and olive and canola oil. Keep on going (imagine pushing a barrel now), and bear right with the street under another sturdy **gateway**—indicating that this city grew in concentric circles. Passing through the gate and facing the loggia (with the Florentine Medici seal—a shield with balls), turn left and keep on going.

As you huff and puff, notice (on your right, and later on both sides) the steep, narrow, often covered lanes called *vicolo* ("little street"). You're getting a peek at the higgledy-piggledy medieval Montepulciano. Only when the rationality of Renaissance aesthetics took hold was the main street realigned, becoming symmetrical and pretty. Beneath its fancy suit, though, Montepulciano remains a rugged Gothic city.

Again, notice the fine and ever-bulkier palaces. On the left, a tiny courtyard makes it easier to appreciate the grandiosity of the next palace, now home to **Banca Etruria.** "Etruria"—a name you'll see everywhere around here—is a term for the Etruscan territory of today's Tuscany. By the way, the stone scrolls under the window are a design element called a "kneeling window"—created by Michelangelo and a popular decorative element in High Renaissance and Mannerist architecture. You'll see kneeling windows all over town.

Just after is a fine spot for a coffee break (on the left, at #27): **Caffè Poliziano,** the town's most venerable watering hole (from 1868). Step inside to soak in the genteel atmosphere, with a busy espresso machine, loaner newspapers on long sticks, and a little terrace with spectacular views (open long hours daily). It's named for a famous Montepulciano-born 15th-century poet who was a protégé of Lorenzo the Magnificent de Medici and tutored his two sons. So important is he to civic pride that townspeople are nicknamed *poliziani.*

A bit farther up, on the right, notice the precipitous **Vicolo dello Sdrucciolo**—literally "slippery lane." Any *vicolo* on the right can be used as a steep shortcut to the upper part of town, while those on the left generally lead to fine vistas. Many of these side lanes are spanned by brick arches, allowing centuries-old buildings to lean on each other for support rather than toppling over—a fitting metaphor for the tight-knit communities that vitalize Italian small towns.

The next church on the left, the Jesuit **Church of Gesù,** is worth a look. Its interior is elliptical in shape and full of 3-D illusions (don't miss the side chapels and the cupola—all painted on flat surfaces). Soon the street levels out—enjoy this nice, lazy, easy stretch, with interesting shops and artisan workshops (such as the mosaics studio at #14). Across from #64, a lane leads to a charming terrace with a commanding view of the Tuscan countryside.

The **Mazzetti** copper shop (#64) is crammed full of decorative and practical items. Because of copper's unmatched heat conductivity, it's a favored material in premium kitchens. The production of hand-hammered copper vessels like these is a dying art; in this shop, you can see works by Cesare, who makes them in his workshop just up the street. To reach the workshop, go up the tiny covered lane just after the copper shop (Vicolo Benci, on the right). When you emerge, turn right and head uphill steeply; at #4 (on the

HEART OF TUSCANY

left), marked *Ramaio,* is Cesare's workshop and museum. Continuing steeply uphill will take you to the main square. At the bend just before the square, Cesare's buddy Adamo loves to introduce travelers to Montepulciano's fine wines at the Contucci Cantina. Visit Cesare and Adamo now, or head up to the square for Part 2 of this walk.

Either way, Montepulciano's main square is just ahead. You made it!

PART 2: PIAZZA GRANDE AND NEARBY

This pleasant, lively piazza is surrounded by a grab bag of architectural sights. The medieval **Palazzo Comunale,** or town hall, resembles Florence's Palazzo Vecchio—yet another reminder that Florence dominated Montepulciano in the 15th and 16th centuries. The crenellations along the roof were never intended to hide soldiers—they just symbolize power. But the big, square central tower makes it clear that the city is keeping an eye out in all directions. It's made of locally quarried travertine stone, the same material ancient Romans used for their great buildings.

Take a moment to survey the square, where the town's four great powers stare each other down. Face the Palazzo Comunale, and keep turning to the right. You'll see the one-time building of the courts, behind the well (Palazzo del Capitano); the noble Palazzo Tarugi, a Renaissance-arcaded confection (with a public loggia at ground level and a private loggia—now enclosed—directly above); and the aristocratic Palazzo Contucci, with its 16th-century Renaissance facade. (The Contucci family still lives in their palace, producing and selling their own wine.) Continuing your spin, you see the unfinished Duomo looking glumly on, wishing the city hadn't run out of money for its facade.

A cistern system fed by rainwater draining from the roofs of surrounding palaces supplied the fine **well** in the corner. Check out its 19th-century pulleys, the grilles to keep animals from contaminating the water supply, and its decorative top: the Medici coat of arms flanked by lions (representing Florence) dwarfing griffins (representing Montepulciano).

Climbing the town hall's **tower** rewards you with a windblown but commanding panorama from the terrace below the clock. Go into the Palazzo Comunale, head up the stairs to your left, and pay on the second floor. You can pay to go just as far as the terrace, at

HEART OF TUSCANY

the base of the tower (€2.50, 71 stairs, or ride the elevator halfway up); or pay more to go all the way to the top, twisting up extremely narrow brick steps past the antiquated bell-ringing mechanism (€5, 76 additional stairs). If you don't mind the claustrophobic climb, it's worth paying extra to reach the very top, from where you can see all the way to Pienza (look just to the right of San Biagio Church; tower open daily May-Oct 10:00-18:00, closed in winter).

To the Church of San Francesco and Views: From the main square, it's a short, mostly level walk to a fine viewpoint. You could head 200 yards straight down the wide street to the right as you face the tower. But for a more interesting look at Montepulciano behind its pretty Renaissance facades, instead go down the narrow lane between the two palaces in the corner of the square **(Via Talosa).** Pause at the recommended Mueblè il Riccio B&B (with a fine courtyard—peek inside) and look high up across the street to see how centuries of structures have been stitched together, sometimes gracelessly. Across the street is the recommended Cantina della Talosa wine cellar (described later).

Follow this lane as it bends left, and eventually you'll pop out just below the main square, a few doors from the recommended De' Ricci Cantine del Redi wine cellar (described later). Turn right and head down toward the church. Just before #21 (on the left), look for a red-and-gold **shield** over a door with the name *Talosa.* This marks the home of one of Montepulciano's *contrade*, or neighborhoods; birth and death announcements for the *contrada* are posted on the board next to the door.

Across the street and a few steps farther (on the right), you hit a **viewpoint.** From here, it's easy to appreciate Montepulciano's highly strategic position. The ancient town sitting on this high ridge was surrounded by powerful forces—everything you see in this direction was part of the Papal States, ruled from Rome. In the distance is Lake Trasimeno, once a notorious swampland that made it even harder to invade this town.

Continue a few steps downhill, then uphill, into the big parking lot in front of the **Church of San Francesco.** Head out to the overlook for a totally different view: the rolling hills that belonged to Siena. And keep in mind that Montepulciano itself belonged to Florence. For the first half of the 16th century, those three formidable powers—Florence, Siena, and Rome (the papacy)—vied to control this small area. You can also see Montepulciano's most impressive church, San Biagio—well worth a visit for drivers or hikers (described later).

From here, you can head back up to the main square, or drop into one of my recommended cantinas to spelunk their wine cellars.

Sights and Experiences in Montepulciano

For me, Montepulciano's best "experiences" are personal: dropping in on Adamo, the winemaker at Contucci Cantina, and Cesare, the coppersmith at Ramaio Cesare. Both will greet you with a torrent of cheerful Italian; just smile and nod, pick up what you can from gestures, and appreciate this rare opportunity to meet a true local character.

▲▲Contucci Cantina

Montepulciano's most popular attraction isn't made of stone—it's the famous wine, Vino Nobile. This robust red can be tasted in any of the cantinas lining Via Ricci and Via di Gracciano nel Corso, but the cantina in the basement of Palazzo Contucci is both historic and fun. Skip the palace's formal wine-tasting showroom facing the square, and instead head down the lane on the right to the actual cellars, where you'll meet lively Adamo (ah-DAH-moh), who has been making wine here since 1961 and welcomes tourists into his cellar. While at the palace, you may meet Andrea or Ginevra Contucci, whose family has lived here since the 11th century. They love to share their family's products with the public. Adamo and the Contuccis usually have a half-dozen bottles open, and at busy times, other members of their staff are likely to speak English.

HEART OF TUSCANY

After sipping a little wine with Adamo, explore the palace basement, with its 13th-century vaults. Originally part of the town's wall, these chambers have been filled since the 1500s with huge barrels of wine. Doz-

ens of barrels of Croatian and French oak (1,000-2,500 liters each) cradle the wine through a two-year in-the-barrel aging process, while the wine picks up the personality of the wood. After about 35 years, an exhausted barrel has nothing left to offer its wine, so it's retired. Adamo explains that the French oak gives the wine "pure elegance," and the Croatian is more masculine. Each barrel is labeled with the size in liters, the year the wine was barreled, and the percentage of alcohol (determined by how much sun shone in that year). "Nobile"-grade wine needs a minimum of 13 percent alcohol.

Cost and Hours: Free drop-in tasting, daily 9:30-12:30 & 14:30-19:00, Piazza Grande 13, tel. 0578-757-006, www.contucci.it.

▲Ramaio Cesare

Cesare the coppersmith is an institution in Montepulciano, carrying on his father's and grandfather's trade by hammering into existence an immense selection of copper objects in his cavernous workshop. Though his English is limited, Cesare (CHEH-zah-ray) is happy to show you photos of his work—including the copper top of the Duomo in Siena and the piece he designed and personally delivered to Pope Benedict. Peruse his tools: a giant Road Runner-style anvil, wooden hammers, and stencils dating from 1857 that have been passed down from his grandfather and father. Next door, he has assembled a fine museum with items he and his relatives have made, as well as pieces from his personal collection. Cesare is evangelical about copper, and if he's not too busy, he'll create personalized mementoes for visitors—he loves meeting people from around the world who appreciate his handiwork (as his brimming photo album demonstrates). Cesare's justifiable pride in his vocation evokes the hardworking, highly skilled craft guilds that once dominated small-town Italy's commercial and civic life.

Cost and Hours: Demonstration and museum are free, Cesare is generally in his workshop Mon-Sat 8:00-12:30 & 14:30-18:30, closed Sun, 50 yards steeply downhill from the Contucci Cantina at Via del Teatro 4, tel. 0578-758-753, www.rameria.com. Cesare's delightful shop is on the main drag, a block below, at Corso #64—look for *Rameria Mazzetti,* open long hours daily.

Duomo

This church's unfinished facade—rough stonework left waiting for the final marble veneer—is not that unusual. Many Tuscan churches were built just to the point where they had a functional interior, and then, for various practical reasons, the facades were left unfinished. But step inside and you'll be rewarded with some fine art. A beautiful blue-and-white, glazed-terra-cotta *Altar of the Lilies* by Andrea della Robbia is behind the baptismal font (on the left as you enter). The high altar, with a top like a pine forest, features a luminous, late-Gothic Assumption triptych by the Sienese artist Taddeo di Bartolo. Showing Mary in her dreamy eternal sleep as she ascends to be crowned by Jesus, it illustrates how Siena clung to the Gothic aesthetic—elaborate gold leaf and lacy pointed arches—to show heavenly grandeur.

Cost and Hours: Free, daily 9:00-13:00 & 15:00-18:30.

▲De' Ricci Cantine del Redi

The most impressive wine cellars in Montepulciano sit below the Palazzo Ricci, just a few steps off the main square (toward the

Church of San Francesco). Enter through the unassuming door and find your way down a spiral staircase—with rounded steps designed to go easy on fragile noble feet, and lined with rings held in place by tiny, finely crafted wrought-iron goat heads. You'll wind up in the dramatic cellars, with gigantic barrels under even more gigantic vaults—several stories high. As you go deeper and deeper into the cellars, high up, natural stone seems to take over the brick. At the deepest point, you can peer into the atmospheric Etruscan cave, where a warren of corridors spins off from a filled-in well. Finally you wind up in the shop, where you're welcome to taste a few wines (with some local cheese). Don't miss their delightful Vin Santo.

Cost and Hours: While tasting is normally €3, it's free for people with this book; €12-20 bottles, affordable shipping, daily 10:30-19:00; enter next to Palazzo Ricci at Via Callazzi 7, look for signs for *Cantine de' Ricci* (the maker's name) or *Cantine del Redi* (the wine's name); tel. 0578-757-166, www.dericci.it, Enrico.

Cantina della Talosa

This historic cellar, which goes down and down to an Etruscan tomb at the bottom, ages a well-respected wine. With a passion and love of their craft, Cristian Pepi and Andrea give enthusiastic tours and tastings. While you can drop by for a free tasting, I'd call ahead to book a tour—€10 including five wines to taste.

Cost and Hours: Free tasting, daily March-Oct 10:00-19:30, shorter hours off-season, a block off Piazza Grande at Via Talosa 8, tel. 0578-757-929, www.talosa.it.

JUST OUTSIDE MONTEPULCIANO
▲San Biagio Church

The church is at the base of Montepulciano's hill, down a picturesque cypress-lined driveway. Often called the "Temple of San Biagio" because of its Greek-cross style, the church—designed by Antonio da Sangallo the Elder and built of locally quarried travertine—feels like perfection (free, generally daily 8:30-18:30). The soaring interior, with a high dome and lantern, creates a quintessential Renaissance space. Stand on the center stone and do a slow 360-degree spin, enjoying the harmony and mathematical perfection in the design. Consider a picnic or snooze on the grass in back, with fine vistas over the Chiana Valley. The restaurant across the street from the church is a local favorite.

Sleep Code

Abbreviations   **(€1=about $1.10, country code: 39)**
S=Single, D=Double/Twin, T=Triple, Q=Quad, b=bathroom
Price Rankings
  $$$ **Higher Priced**—Most rooms €100 or more
   $$ **Moderately Priced**—Most rooms €70-100
    $ **Lower Priced**—Most rooms €70 or less
Unless otherwise noted, credit cards are accepted, breakfast
is included, free Wi-Fi or a guest computer is generally available, and English is spoken. Many towns in Italy levy a hotel
tax of €1.50-5 per person, per night (often collected in cash;
usually not included in the rates I've quoted). Prices change;
verify current rates online or by email. For the best prices, always book directly with the hotel.

Sleeping in Montepulciano

$$$ Mueblè il Riccio ("The Hedgehog") is medieval-elegant, with 10 modern and spotless rooms, an awesome roof terrace, and friendly owners. Five are new "superior" rooms with grand views across the Tuscan valleys (Sb-€80, Db-€100, view Db-€110, superior Db-€150, superior Db with balcony-€180, Tb-€116, superior Tb-€180, superior Qb-€200, breakfast-€8, air-con, limited free parking—request when you reserve, a block below the main square at Via Talosa 21, tel. 0578-757-713, www.ilriccio.net, info@ilriccio.net, Gió and Ivana speak English). Charming Gió and his son Iacopo give tours of the countryside (€50/hour) in one of their classic Italian cars; for details, see their website. Ivana makes wonderful breakfast tarts.

$$$ La Locanda di San Francesco is pricey but luxurious, with four stylish view rooms over a classy wine bar on a quiet square at Montepulciano's summit (standard Db-€185, superior Db-€205, suite-€225, these are nonrefundable prices—pay €20 more for "flexible" rates, closed Nov-Easter, air-con, free parking nearby, Piazza San Francesco 5, tel. 0578-758-725, www.locandasanfrancesco.it, info@locandasanfrancesco.it, Cinzia and Lucca).

$$ Albergo Duomo is big, modern, and nondescript, with 13 rooms (with small bathrooms) and a comfortable lounge downstairs. With a handy location just a few steps from the main square, it's at the very top of town, with free parking nearby (Sb-€60, small Db-€80, standard Db-€100, Tb-€120, family deals, elevator, air-con in some rooms for €5 extra, loaner laptops, Via di San Donato 14, tel. 0578-757-473, www.albergoduomo.it, albergoduomo@libero.it, Elisa and Saverio).

$$ Camere Bellavista has 10 tidy rooms. True to its name, each room has a fine view—though some are better than others. Room 6 has a view terrace worth reserving (Db-€80, terrace Db-€110, cash only, optional €3-10 breakfast at a bar in the piazza, lots of stairs with no elevator, reception not always staffed—call before arriving or ring bell, Via Ricci 25, mobile 347-823-2314, www. camerebellavista.it, bellavista@bccmp.com, Gabriella speaks just enough English).

$$ Vicolo dell'Oste B&B, just off the main drag halfway up through town, has five family-friendly modern rooms (Db-€95-105, Tb-€130, Qb-€135-150, includes breakfast at nearby café, 5 percent discount when you reserve direct and mention this book, on Via dell'Oste 1—an alley leading right off the main drag just after Caffè Poliziano and opposite the *farmacia* at #47, tel. 0578-758-393, www.vicolodelloste.it, info@vicolodelloste.it, Luisa and Giuseppe).

Eating in Montepulciano

These places are all open for lunch (about 12:30-14:30) and again for dinner (about 19:30-22:00). I've noted closed days.

Ai Quattro Venti is fresh, flavorful, fun, and right on Piazza Grande, with a simple dining room and outdoor tables right on the square. It distinguishes itself by offering reasonable portions of tasty, unfussy Tuscan food in an unpretentious setting. Try their very own organic olive oil and wine (€9 pastas, €9-10 *secondi*, closed Thu, next to City Hall on Piazza Grande, tel. 0578-717-231, Chiara).

Osteria dell'Aquacheta is a carnivore's dream come true, beloved among locals for its beef steaks. Its long, narrow room is jammed with shared tables and tight, family-style seating, with an open fire in back and a big hunk of red beef lying on the counter like a corpse on a gurney. Giulio and his wife, Chiara, run a fun-loving but tight ship—posing with slabs of red meat yet embracing 23 years of trattoria tradition (you'll get one glass to use alternately for wine and water). Steaks are sold by weight (€32/kilo). Typically two people split a 1.6-kilo steak (that's 3.5 pounds; the smallest they'll cook is 1.2 kilos). They also serve hearty €6-8 pastas and salads, other  meaty €10 plates, and a fine house wine (reservations required, seatings at 12:30, 14:30, 19:30, and 21:30 only, closed Tue, Via del Teatro 22, tel. 0578-717-086, www.acquacheta.eu).

Osteria del Conte, an attractive but humble family-run bistro, offers a €30 *menù del Conte*—a four-course dinner of local specialties including wine—as well as à la carte options and cooking like Mom's. While the interior is very simple, they also have outdoor tables on a stony street at the edge of the historic center (€9 pastas, €9-15 *secondi,* closed Wed, Via San Donato 19, tel. 0578-756-062).

Le Pentolaccia is a small, family-run restaurant at the upper, relatively untouristy end of the main drag. With both indoor and outdoor seating, they make tasty traditional Tuscan dishes as well as daily fish specials. Cristiana serves, and husband-and-wife team Jacobo and Alessia stir up a storm in the kitchen (€8-10 pastas, €8-15 *secondi,* closed Thu, Corso 86, tel. 0578-757-582).

Wine Bar/Bistro: **E Lucevan le Stelle** (part of La Locanda di San Francesco), with a terrace on a tranquil square in front of the Church of San Francesco, is a fine place to nurse a glass of local wine (€4-9 glasses; also €7-10 pastas, salads, and soups; daily 12:00-24:00, closed Nov-Easter, Piazza San Francesco 5, tel. 0578-758-725, Lucca).

Near Montepulciano, in Monticchiello: If you'd enjoy getting out of town for dinner—but not *too* far—consider the 15-minute drive to the picturesque hill town of Monticchiello, where you can dine at the excellent **Osteria La Porta** with its fine view terrace, or at the modern-feeling **La Cantina della Porta**. To get there, follow signs to Pienza; then, shortly after passing the road to San Biagio Church (on the right), watch on the left for the Albergo San Biagio. Turn off, take the rough little road that runs up past the left side of this big hotel, and follow it to Monticchiello.

Montepulciano Connections

Get bus schedules at the TI or the bus station on Piazza Pietro Nenni, which seems to double as the town hangout, with a lively bar and locals chatting inside. In fact, there's no real ticket window—buy your tickets at the bar. Check www.sienamobilita.it or www.tiemmespa.it for schedules.

By Bus to: Florence (1-2/day, 2 hours, change in Bettolle, LFI bus, www.lfi.it; or take a bus to Chiusi to catch a train, explained below), **Siena** (6-8/day, none on Sun, 1.5 hours), **Pienza** (8/day, 30 minutes), **Montalcino** (3-4/day, none Sun, change in Torrenieri, 1 hour; or consider a taxi—explained below).

By Train: Trains are impractical here; the Montepulciano train station, five miles from town and connected by an infrequent bus, has only milk-run trains (but could be useful for reaching Siena on a Sunday—get details at the TI). More convenient, consider riding the hourly bus 50 minutes to the town of **Chiusi,** which is on the main Florence-Rome rail line.

Taxi Alternatives: As the **Montalcino** bus connection is infrequent and complicated, consider hiring a taxi (about €70; see contact info under "Helpful Hints," earlier).

Pienza

Set on a crest and surrounded by green, rolling hills, the small town of Pienza packs a lot of Renaissance punch. In the 1400s, locally born Pope Pius II of the  Piccolomini family decided to remodel his birthplace into a city fit for a pope, in the style that was all the rage: Renaissance. Propelled by papal clout, the town of Corsignano was transformed—in only five years' time—into a jewel of Renaissance architecture. It was renamed Pienza, after Pope Pius. The plan was to remodel the entire town, but work ended in 1464 when both the pope and his architect, Bernardo Rossellino, died. Their vision—what you see today—was completed a century later.

Pienza's architectural focal point is its main square, Piazza Pio II, surrounded by the Duomo and the pope's family residence, Palazzo Piccolomini. While Piazza Pio II is Pienza's pride and joy, the entire town—a mix of old stonework, potted plants, and grand views—is fun to explore, especially with a camera or sketchpad in hand. You can walk every lane in the tiny town in a few minutes. Pienza is situated on a relatively flat plateau rather than the steep pinnacle of more dramatic towns like Montepulciano and Montalcino. (This is a plus for visitors with limited mobility, who find basically level Pienza easy to explore.)

Tourists flood Pienza in peak season, and boutiques selling gifty packages of pecorino cheese and local wine greatly outnumber authentic local shops. Restaurants here tend to be more expensive and less reliable than alternatives in the nearby countryside. For these reasons, Pienza is made to order as a stretch-your-legs break to enjoy the townscape and panoramas, but it's not ideal for lingering overnight. For the best experience, visit late in the day, after the day-trippers have dispersed.

Nearly every shop sells the town's specialty: pecorino, a pungent sheep's cheese (you'll smell it before you see it) that's sometimes infused with other ingredients, such as truffles or cayenne

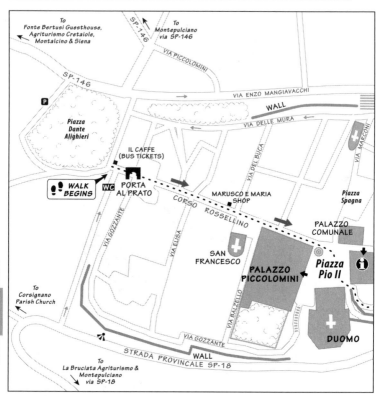

pepper. Look on menus for warm pecorino *(al forno* or *alla griglia),* often topped with honey or pears and served with bread. Along with a glass of local wine, this just might lead you to a new understanding of *la dolce vita.*

Orientation to Pienza

Tourist Information: The TI is 10 yards up the street from Piazza Pio II, inside the skippable Diocesan Museum (Wed-Mon 10:30-13:30 & 14:30-18:00, closed Tue, Sat-Sun only in Nov-March, Corso il Rossellino 30, tel. 0578-749-905). Ignore the *Informaturista* kiosk just outside the gate—it's a private travel agency.

Arrival in Pienza: If **driving,** read signs carefully—some parking spots are reserved for locals, others require the use of a cardboard clock, and others are pay-and-display. Parking is tight, so if you don't see anything quickly, head for the large pay lot at Piazza del Mercato near Largo Roma outside the old town: As you approach town and reach the "ZTL" cul-de-sac (marked with a red circle) in front of the town gate, head up the left side of town and look for the parking turnoff on the left (closed Fri morning during

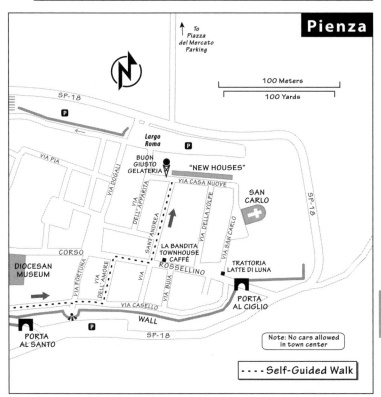

market). **Buses** drop you just a couple of blocks directly in front of the town's main entrance.

Helpful Hints: On Friday mornings, a **market** fills Piazza del Mercato, the main parking lot just outside the town walls. A public **WC,** marked *gabinetti pubblici*, is on the right as you face the town gate from outside, on Piazza Dante Alighieri (down the lane next to the faux TI).

Sights in Pienza

I've connected Pienza's main sights with walking directions, which can serve as a handy little orientation to the town. You could do this stroll in 30 minutes, but entering some of the sights could extend your visit to a few hours.

• *Begin in the little park just in front of the town (near the main round-about and bus stop), called Piazza Dante Alighieri. Facing the town, go through the big, ornamental gateway on the right (which was destroyed in World War II and rebuilt in 1955), and head up the main street...*

Pope Pius II

Pope Pius II (Enea Silvio Bartolomeo Piccolomini, 1405-1464) was born into one of the most powerful families in Siena. He had an illustrious career as a diplomat, traveled far and wide (fathering two illegitimate children, in Switzerland and Scotland), and gained a reputation for his erotic writings *(The Tale of Two Lovers)*. Upon donning the frock, Piccolomini went from ordination to the papacy in just 11 years—a stunning pace spurred, no doubt, by his esteemed lineage. Owing to his educated and worldly upbringing, upon ascending to the papacy Piccolomini chose a name that was not religious, but literary: the ancient poet Virgil first used the term "pious" to describe his hero, Aeneus. One of the most enlightened popes of his time, Pius embraced the burgeoning Renaissance and set out to remake his hometown in pure Renaissance style. Pius was also the first prominent figure known to have suggested the notion of a united Europe, with a common heritage and shared goals (at that time, facing off against the invading Ottomans).

Corso il Rossellino

This main drag—named for Bernardo Rossellino (1409-1464), the Renaissance architect who redesigned Pienza according to Pius' orders—is jammed with touristy boutiques. While you won't find great values, these shops are (like Pienza) cute and convenient.

At the end of the second block on the left, at #21, step into the **Marusco e Maria** cheese-and-salami shop. Take a deep whiff and survey the racks of pecorino cheese, made from sheep's milk. For €3 per couple, Fabio or his staff can give you a quick taste of three types of pecorino: *fresco* (young, soft, and mild), *medio* (medium), and *stagionato* (hard, crumbly, and pungent). Consider stocking up at one of these shops for a pricey but memorable picnic. *Finocchiona* is salami with fennel seeds. This was first popularized by wine traders, because fennel seeds make wine taste better. To this day, Italians use the word *infinocchiare* ("fennel-ize") to mean "to trick."

Farther along, watch for the **Church of San Francesco** on the right. It's the only important building in town that dates from before the Pius II extreme makeover. Its humble facade, simple nave, wood-beamed ceiling, bits of 14th-century frescoes, and tranquil adjacent cloister have a charm that's particularly peaceful in the 21st century. But this gloomy medieval style was exactly what Pius wanted to get away from.

• *Continuing one more block, you'll pop out at Pienza's showcase square...*

▲Piazza Pio II

Pienza's small main piazza gets high marks from architecture highbrows for its elegance and artistic unity. The piazza and surrounding buildings were all designed by Rossellino to form an "outdoor room." Everything is perfectly planned and plotted.

Do a clockwise spin to check out the buildings that face the square, starting with the **Duomo** (which we'll enter soon). High up on the facade is one of many examples you'll spot around town of the Piccolomini family crest: five half-moons, advertising the number of crusades that his family funded. To the right of the Duomo is the **Piccolomini family palace,** now a tourable museum (described later). Notice that the grid lines in the square's pavement continue all the way up the sides of this building, creating a Renaissance cube. Looking farther right, you'll see **City Hall** (Palazzo Comunale), with a Renaissance facade and a fine loggia (to match the square) but a 13th-century bell tower that's shorter than the church's tower. (That's unusual here in civic-minded Tuscany, where municipal towers usually trumpet the importance of town over Church.)

Looking up the lane to the left of City Hall, notice the cantilevered upper floors of the characteristic old houses—a reminder that, while Pienza appears Renaissance on the surface, much of that sheen was added later to fit Pius' vision. Looking farther right, see the **Bishop's Palace,** also called the Borgia Palace (now housing the TI and the skippable Diocesan Museum). Pius invited prominent cardinals to occupy the real estate in his custom-built town. The Borgia clan, who built this palace, produced one of the most controversial popes of that age, Alexander VI, who ascended to the papacy a few decades after Pius II. The Borgia were notorious for their shrewd manipulation of power politics. Our word "nepotism"—which comes from the Italian *nipote* (nephew)—dates from this era, when a pope would pull strings to ensure his relatives would succeed him.

Finally, between the Bishop's Palace and the Duomo, a lane leads to the best **view terrace** in town.

• *Now take the time to tour whichever of the square's sights interest you:*

Duomo

The cathedral's classic, symmetrical Renaissance facade (1462) dominates Piazza Pio II. The interior, bathed in light, is an illuminating encapsulation of Pius II's architectural philosophy (free, generally daily 7:00-13:00 & 14:30-19:00). Pius envisioned this church as an antidote to dark, claustrophobic medieval churches, like the Church of San Francesco we saw earlier. Instead, this was to be a "house of glass," representing the cultural enlightenment that came with the Renaissance. The church decoration is also a bit unusual. Rather than Jesus and Mary, the emphasis is on the pope and his family (like the crescent-moon crest of Pius II on the windows). Instead of the colorful frescoes you'd expect, the church has clean, white walls to reflect the light.

▲Palazzo Piccolomini

The home of Pius II and the Piccolomini family (until 1962) can only be visited on an escorted audioguide tour. While the palace is not quite the interesting slice of 15th-century aristocratic life that it could be (I'd like to know more about the pope's toilet), this is still the best small-town palace experience I've found in Tuscany. (It famously starred as the Capulets' home in Franco Zeffirelli's 1968 Academy Award-winning *Romeo and Juliet*.) You can peek inside the door for free to check out the well-preserved, painted courtyard. In Renaissance times, most buildings were covered with elaborate paintings like these.

Cost and Hours: €7, 30-minute tours depart on the half-hour Tue-Sun 10:30-12:30 & 14:00-18:00, until 16:30 off-season, closed Mon, Piazza Pio II 2, tel. 0578-748-392, www.palazzopiccolominipienza.it.

View Terrace

As you face the church, the upper lane leading left brings you to a panoramic promenade. Views from the terrace include the Tuscan countryside and, in the distance, Monte Amiata, the largest mountain in southern Tuscany. You can exit the viewpoint down the first alley, Via del'Amore—the original Lover's Lane—which leads back to the main drag.

JUST OUTSIDE PIENZA

Corsignano Parish Church (Pieve di Corsignano)

This classic Romanesque parish church *(pieve)*, hugging the slope just below Pienza, is a reminder of a much earlier, rougher, simpler time (before Pope Pius II). This was one of the medieval pilgrimage stops on the Via Francigena. If the church is open, step inside and let your eyes adjust to the very low light. This gloomy, cave-like interior—with just slits for windows—is a far cry from later, brighter architectural styles. Near the entrance on the right, look for the font that was used to baptize the man who would grow up to be Pope Pius II.

Getting There: On foot from Pienza, it's a steep 10-minute downhill walk (as you exit Pienza into the main park, look to your left for *pieve di Corsignano* signs). Similar signs direct drivers to the turnoff just below the old town.

The Via Francigena

Many of the sights in this region—and others in this book (including Siena, Lucca, and San Gimignano)—line up along the route of the Via Francigena (VEE-ah frahn-CHEE-jeh-nah). During the Middle Ages, when devout Christians undertook a once-in-a-lifetime pilgrimage to Rome, this route was heavily trod by the footsore faithful flowing in from northern Europe (hence the name, "Road of the Franks"—referring to the Germanic tribes who lived in present-day Germany and France). While there were many variations and feeder paths, the main Via Francigena followed more or less the route of today's SR-2 highway, from Florence to Siena, then through the Val d'Orcia south to Rome. Without even realizing it, many modern-day tourists follow this millennium-old route as they travel through this part of Italy.

The first documented pilgrimages along here took place around A.D. 725, and the trend continued for many centuries. In 990, Archbishop Sigeric of Canterbury undertook the entire 1,100-mile round-trip from England. Upon his return, he documented tips for fellow pilgrims about where to sleep, where to eat, what to see, and how to pack light in a carry-on-the-plane-size rucksack...arguably the world's first travel guidebook.

The history of Tuscany is inextricably tied to the Via Francigena. During those oh-so-Dark Ages, a long journey was treacherous, rife with opportunity for illness, injury, robbery, and murder. Pilgrim traffic represented an injection of wealth into communities along the Via Francigena, and fortresses popped up—or were repurposed—to keep the route safe. Abbeys and churches were built to cater to the masses. And many shrewd communities leveraged the passing pilgrim trade into enormous prosperity; for example, Siena boomed both as a financial center and a trading outpost for Via Francigena pilgrims.

Like the recently-in-vogue Camino de Santiago in northern Spain, this medieval pilgrim route—forgotten for centuries—has recently enjoyed a renewed interest. Though the numbers are still small—and the path lacks the well-orchestrated conveniences of the Camino de Santiago—a handful of modern-day pilgrims are, once again, walking through Tuscany south to Rome.

Eating in Pienza

La Bandita Townhouse Caffè offers a break from Tuscan rusticity, focusing instead on tempting modern Italian cuisine (such as spring pea soup or peppered Chianina beef carpaccio). Diners watch the chef work in his open kitchen (lunch served Tue-Sun and dinner nightly, indoor/outdoor seating, Corso il Rossellino 111, tel. 0578-749-005).

Trattoria Latte di Luna, with outdoor tables filling a delightful little square, is the more traditional choice (closed Tue, near the end of Corso il Rossellino at Via San Carlo 2, tel. 0578-748-606).

Gelato: **Gelateria Buon Gusto** is run by Nicola, who focuses on quality ingredients and intense flavors (Tue-Sun 11:00-20:00, until 22:00 in summer, closed Mon, Via delle Case Nuove 26, mobile 335-704-9165).

Quick Lunch: For something cheap, characteristic, and fast, just grab a tasty porchetta sandwich (€3.50) at the little shop 30 yards off the main square (at Corso il Rossellino 81) to munch under the loggia or at the viewpoint.

Pienza Connections

Bus tickets are sold at the bar/café (marked *Il Caffè*, closed Tue) just outside Pienza's town gate (or pay a little extra and buy tickets from the driver). Buses leave from a few blocks up the street, directly in front of the town entrance. Montepulciano is the nearest transportation hub.

From Pienza by Bus to: Siena (6/day, none on Sun, 1.5 hours), **Montepulciano** (8/day, 30 minutes), **Montalcino** (3-4/day Mon-Sat, none Sun, change in Torrenieri, 45-60 minutes). **Bus info:** www.tiemmespa.it.

Best of the Heart of Tuscany

If you have just one day to connect the ultimate Tuscan towns and views, this is the loop I'd stitch together with a driving tour. Most of this journey is through velvety, gentle, rolling hillsides generously draped with vivid-green crops in the springtime, and a parched moonscape in the late summer and fall. This almost otherworldly smoothness constitutes many travelers' notions of Tuscan perfection.

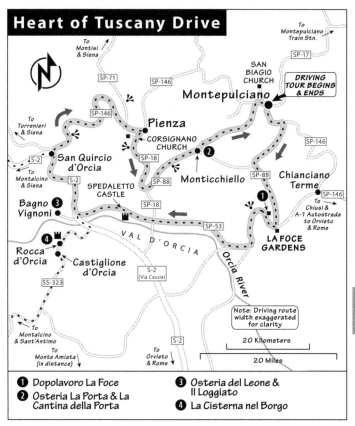

Heart of Tuscany Drive

To Montepulciano Train Stn.

To Montisi & Siena

SP-71

SP-146

SAN BIAGIO CHURCH

DRIVING TOUR BEGINS & ENDS

Montepulciano

SP-146

SP-146

SP-17

To Torrenieri & Siena

Pienza

CORSIGNANO CHURCH

SP-18

❷

SP-88

SP-146

To Montalcino & Siena

S-2

San Quirico d'Orcia

S-2

SPEDALETTO CASTLE

SP-88

Monticchiello

SP-88

Chianciano Terme

SP-146

To Chiusi & A-1 Autostrada to Orvieto & Rome

SP-18

SP-53

❶

Bagno ❸ Vignoni ●

V A L   D ' O R C I A

LA FOCE GARDENS

❹

Rocca d'Orcia

Castiglione d'Orcia

S-2 (Via Cassia)

Orcia River

SS-323

Note: Driving route width exaggerated for clarity

To Montalcino & Sant'Antimo

To Monte Amiata (in distance)

To Orvieto & Rome

S-2

20 Kilometers

20 Miles

❶ Dopolavoro La Foce

❷ Osteria La Porta & La Cantina della Porta

❸ Osteria del Leone & Il Loggiato

❹ La Cisterna nel Borgo

Heart of Tuscany Driving Tour

In addition to larger towns (Montepulciano, Pienza) and smaller ones (Bagno Vignoni, Rocca d'Orcia), this self-guided loop drive, worth ▲▲▲, gives you a good look at the area called the Val d'Orcia (val DOR-chah), boasting some of the best scenery in Italy.

If you're in a rush and don't linger in any of the towns, you could do this drive in a couple of hours. To hit the sights, explore the towns, and linger over a meal or a glass of wine, spread it out over an entire day. (You could even splice in a side-trip to a Brunello winery for a tasting, if you like.) I've started and ended the clockwise loop in Montepulciano, but you could just as easily start and end in Pienza. If gardens are your thing, do this loop when La Foce Gardens are open (Wed, Sat, or Sun afternoons only).

Leg #1: Montepulciano to La Foce to Bagno Vignoni

Before leaving Montepulciano, consider dropping by the showpiece Renaissance **San Biagio Church,** which sits at the base of the town (watch for its long, level, tree-lined driveway exactly where you leave Montepulciano on the road toward Pienza).

To begin our loop, drive south, at first following signs to *Chianciano Terme* and *Chiusi.* Just one kilometer south of Montepulciano, watch on the right for the turnoff to *Castelluccio* and *Monticchiello.* Turn off here and zip along a pastoral back road for five kilometers. Pass the turnoff for Monticchiello on your right, and carry on straight ahead, as the road continues uphill and becomes gravel. Grinding your way up, watch on your right for the jagged Tuscan cliffs called *calanchi.* You'll pop out at the T-intersection in front of the entrance to the **La Foce Gardens** (from this intersection, parking and reception is 50 yards to the left—look for *Loc. La Foce*).

From La Foce, head downhill toward *Siena* and *Roma.* After a few hundred yards, watch on the left for the big gravel parking lot of the recommended **Dopolavoro La Foce** restaurant (across the street). From this lot, you have a fine view of one of *the* iconic cypress-lined driveways of Tuscany.

Continue downhill along this road for about five kilometers, through pristine farm fields, until you reach a major intersection, where you'll turn right toward *Pienza* and *Siena* (on SP-53). Immersed in spectacular scenery, you'll twist between giant cypresses for about 10 kilometers. This road parallels the region's namesake Orcia River ("Val d'Orcia" means "Orcia River Valley"). Take a moment to simply appreciate your surroundings. The famous Chianti region to the north (right) and the Brunello region to the west (straight ahead) are each a short drive away; in those places, the rocky soil is perfect for grapes. But here, instead of rocks, you're surrounded by clay hills—once the floor of a prehistoric sea—that are ideal for cereal crops. Grains alternate every few years with a crop of fava beans, which help reintroduce nitrogen to the soil. It seems that every grassy hilltop is capped with a family farmhouse. Partway along this road, you'll pass a turnoff (on the right) offering a speedy shortcut to Pienza, just 8 stunning kilometers away. But there's so much more to see; I'd rather carry on with our loop.

The tower looming on the hill ahead of you is **Rocca d'Orcia**'s Tentennano Castle. Nearing the end of the road, you'll pass (on the left) the front door of an old farmhouse with oddly formidable, crenellated towers, like a little castle in the field. This is **Spedaletto Castle,** built during the 12th century as a hospice for pilgrims walking the Via Francigena to Rome. Today it serves a similar purpose, as an *agriturismo* called La Grancia ("The Granary"), housing wayfarers like you.

When you reach a T-intersection with the main S-2 highway, turn left (toward *Roma*), then immediately take the exit for **Bagno Vignoni.** To see the empty fortress at **Rocca d'Orcia**, stay on the S-2 highway just one kilometer past Bagno Vignoni, then watch for the next turnoff.

Leg #2: Bagno Vignoni to Pienza (with Possible Detours to Brunello Wineries and Tuscan Views)

From Bagno Vignoni, head north on SR-2 (toward *San Quirico d'Orcia* and *Siena*). After just four kilometers, in San Quirico d'Orcia, turn off onto the SP-146 road to Pienza, also marked for *Chiusi, Chianciano Terme,* and *Montepulciano.*

But before heading down that road, consider a few potential detours: First, if you won't have time to delve deeply into Brunello wine country, but would like just a taste, now is a good time to side-trip to your choice of **Brunello wineries.** Another option is to zip into the town of **Montalcino** itself—an easy and well-signed 15-minute drive from San Quirico—and taste some local vintages at a wine bar there.

Back on the SP-146 road from San Quirico to Pienza, you enjoy one of the region's most postcard-worthy stretches—with grand panoramas in both directions, including two quintessential Tuscan scenes: the **Chapel of Madonna di Vitaleta** (after 2 kilometers, on the right); and a classic **farmhouse-with-trees,** just before Pienza (about 9 kilometers after San Quirico, on the left).

Finally you'll pull into **Pienza,** where you can park and tour the town.

Leg #3: Pienza to Montepulciano (via Monticchiello)

If you're in a hurry or losing sunlight, just hop back on the main SP-146 road for the 12-kilometer straight-shot back to Montepulciano (enjoying some pullouts with fine views of the town on the left). But I prefer this longer, even more dramatic route, via the fortified village of Monticchiello.

From the traffic circle at the entry to Pienza's town center, instead of heading for Montepulciano, follow the road that runs along the left side of town (marked *Amiata* and *Monticchiello*—as you face Pienza, you'll continue straight when the main road bends left). This road loops around behind and below the far end of the village, where you can consider a brief detour to see Pienza's oldest church: Turn off on the right at the brown sign for *Pieve di Corsigiano* and drive a few hundred yards to **Corsignano Parish Church.**

The Beauty of Tuscany's Geology (and Vice Versa)

While tourists have romanticized notions of the "Tuscan" landscape, there's a surprisingly wide variety of land forms in the region. Never having been crushed by a glacier, Tuscany is anything but flat. Its hills and mountains are made up of different substances, each suited to very different types of cultivation.

The Chianti region (between Florence and Siena) is rough and rocky, with an inhospitable soil that challenges grape vines to survive while coaxing them to produce excellent wine grapes.

Farther south, the soil switches from rock to clay, silt, and sand. The region called the Crete Senesi is the perfectly described "Sienese Clay Hills." Seen from a breezy viewpoint, you can easily visualize how these clay hills were once at the bottom of the sea floor. The soil here is perfect for truffles and for vast fields of wheat, sun-yellow rapeseed (for canola oil), and periodically fava beans (to add nitrogen to the soil). In the spring and summer, the Crete Senesi is blanketed with brightly colorful crops and flowers. But by the fall, after the harvest, it's brown, dusty, and desolate—still picturesque, but in a surface-of-the-moon way. Within the Crete Senesi, you can distinguish two types of hills shaped by erosion: smooth, rounded *biancane* and pointy, jagged *calanchi*.

The area around Montepulciano and Montalcino is more varied, with rocky protuberances that break up the undulating clay hills and provide a suitable home for wine grapes. Even farther south is the Val d'Orcia. This valley of the Orcia River is similar to the Crete Senesi, but has fewer rocks and jagged *calanchi*. Montepulciano sits in a unique position between the Val d'Orcia and a much flatter valley, the Val di Chiana, through which Italy's main north-south expressway runs.

You'll see many hot springs in this part of Tuscany, as well as town names with the word Terme (for "spa" or "hot spring") or Bagno ("bath"). These generally occur where clay meets rock: Water moving through the clay encounters a barrier and gets trapped. A byproduct of these mineral springs is the limestone called travertine, explaining the quarries you may see around spa towns.

Continuing on the main road past that turnoff, you'll drop steeply down into the valley, feeling as if you're sinking into a lavish painting. Dead ahead is **Monte Amiata,** the tallest mountain in Tuscany. This looming behemoth blocks bad weather, creating a mild microclimate that makes the Val d'Orcia a particularly pleasant place to farm...or to vacation. Meanwhile, don't forget to savor the similarly stellar views of Pienza in your rearview mirror. After five kilometers, watch on the left for the turnoff to *Monticchiello* (brown sign). From here, carry on for four kilometers—watching on the left for fine vistas of Pienza, and for another classic "twisty cypress-lined road")—to the pleasant town of **Monticchiello.** This town, with an excellent recommended restaurant (Osteria La Porta) and a compact, fortified townscape worth exploring, is a good place to stretch your legs.

From Monticchiello, there are two routes back to Montepulciano: For the shorter route (6 kilometers), partly on gravel roads, drive all the way to the base of the Monticchiello old town, then turn right. For the longer route (10 kilometers), which stays on paved roads but circles back the way our loop started, turn off for *Montepulciano* at the main intersection, in the flat part of town that's lower down.

Sights in the Heart of Tuscany

Below are the main sights you'll pass on my Heart of Tuscany driving route. Remember that two of the main stops—the towns of **Montepulciano** and **Pienza**—are covered earlier in this chapter.

▲La Foce Gardens

One of the finest gardens in Tuscany, La Foce (lah FOH-cheh) caps a hill with geometrical Italian gardens and rugged English gardens that flow seamlessly into the Tuscan countryside. An English-born, Italian-bred aristocrat—Iris Origo—left her mark on this area, and wrote evocatively about her time here. The gardens—which are worth a pilgrimage for garden lovers—can be visited only  with a guided tour, and only three days each week (Wed, Sat, Sun).

Cost and Hours: €10; 50-minute tours offered April-Oct Wed at 15:00, 16:00, 17:00, and 18:00, Sat-Sun at 11:30 and 15:00; no tours in winter, confirm tour time and reserve in advance, tel. 0578-69101, www.lafoce.com.

Getting There: La Foce sits in the hills above the busy town of Chianciano Terme. To avoid driving through Chianciano (heavy traffic, poor signage), consider a more scenic route through the countryside from Montalcino.

Eating and Sleeping near La Foce: Near the gardens, the Origo family runs a remote, restful B&B and a memorably charming roadside restaurant, **Dopolavoro La Foce** ("After Work"). Once the quitting-time hangout for local farmers, today its interior is country-chic, but with a respect for local tradition. The garden terrace out back is a chirpy delight, and the parking lot across the busy road offers one of the best vantage points on that perfect Tuscan road (Tue-Sun 8:00-23:00, closed Mon, Strada della Vittoria 90, tel. 0578-754-025).

▲Bagno Vignoni

Thanks to the unique geology of this part of Tuscany, several natural hot springs bubble up between the wineries and hill towns. And the town of Bagno Vignoni (BAHN-yoh veen-YOH-nee)—with a quirky history, a pleasant-to-stroll street plan punctuated  with steamy canals, and various places to take a dip—is the most accessible and enjoyable to explore. If you'd like to recuperate from your sightseeing and wine tasting by soaking in the thermal baths, bring your swimsuit.

Getting There: Bagno Vignoni is well-signed, just off the main SR-2 highway linking Siena to Rome (3 miles south of San Quirico d'Orcia). Park in the pay lot by the big roundabout and walk into town, taking the left fork (in front of Hotel Le Terme).

Bagno Vignoni Town Walk: Emerging into the main square, walk under the covered loggia and look out over the aptly named Piazza delle Sorgenti ("Square of the Sources"), filled with a vast pool. Natural spring water bubbles up at the far end at temperatures around 125 degrees Fahrenheit. Known since Roman times, these hot springs were harnessed for their medicinal properties in the Middle Ages. You're not allowed to wade or swim in this main pool today, but an easy stroll through town shows you other facets of these healing waters. Facing the pool, turn left, walk to the end of the loggia, then turn left again down Via delle Sorgenti. Listen for the water that gushes under your feet, as it leaves the pool and heads for its big plunge over the cliff. You'll emerge at an open zone with the cliff-capping ruins of medieval mills and cisterns that once made full use of Bagno Vignoni's main resource. Here you have a chance to dip your toes or fingers into streams of now-tepid water. At the canals' end, the water plunges down into the gorge carved by the Orcia River.

Taking the Waters: The modern **Piscina Val di Sole** bath complex, inside Hotel Posta Marcucci, is simple but sophisticated—a serene spot to soak (€15, €5 towel rental with €10 deposit, April-Sept Fri-Wed 9:30-18:00, shorter hours off-season, closed Thu year-round, tel. 0577-887-112, www.piscinavaldisole.it).

Eating in Bagno Vignoni: **Osteria del Leone,** on the cheery little *piazzetta* just behind the loggia, is the town's class act, with charming tables out on the square (closed Mon, Via dei Mulini 3, tel. 0577-887-300, www.osteriadelleone.it). For something a bit more affordable and casual, drop by the nearby **Il Loggiato** (closed Thu, Via delle Sorgenti 36, tel. 0577-888-973).

Rocca d'Orcia

The looming fortress overlooking Rocca d'Orcia (ROH-kah DOR-chah) perches high above the main SR-2 highway from Siena to Rome. Likely inhabited and fortified since Etruscan times, this strategic hilltop was a seat of great regional power in the 12th century. During this time, Rocca d'Orcia was one of a chain of forts that watched over pilgrims walking the Via Francigena to Rome. Today the **Rocca di Tentennano** fortress—an empty shell of a castle with modern steel stairs and a grand 360-degree panorama at its top—looks stark and abandoned. It seems to dare you to pay €3 to take the very steep hike up from the parking lots below (June-Sept daily 10:00-13:00 & 16:00-19:00; Fri-Sun only in May; shorter hours off-season, mobile 333-986-0788, www.parcodellavaldorcia. com).

Eating in Rocca d'Orcia: **La Cisterna nel Borgo** sits on Rocca's main square, facing the town's namesake cistern. Marta and Fede serve up deliciously executed dishes in a classic setting (cash only, closed Mon, Borgo Mestro 37, tel. 0577-887-280).

▲Monticchiello

This 200-person fortified village clings to the high ground in the countryside just south of Pienza and Montepulciano. While not quite "undiscovered," Monticchiello is relatively untrampled, and feels like a real place where you can get in touch with authentic Tuscan village life.

Eating in Monticchiello: **Osteria La Porta** is just inside the town's gate, where warm and classy Daria pleases diners either indoors or out with traditional Tuscan dishes presented with flair. As this is a destination restaurant, reservations are a must (€23 lunch *menu*, dinner à la carte, seatings at 12:30, 14:00, 19:30, and 21:30—but they'll seat you at other times if they have room, closed Thu, Via del Piano 1, tel. 0578-755-163, www.osterialaporta.it).

La Cantina della Porta, 50 yards up the hill and to the right, is run by the same family (closed Wed, Via San Luigi 3, tel. 0578-755-170).

Montalcino

On a hill overlooking vineyards and valleys, Montalcino is famous for its delicious and pricey Brunello di Montalcino red wines. It's a pleasant, low-impact town crawling with wine-loving tourists, a smattering of classy shops, but little sightseeing. Everyone touring this area seems to be relaxed and in an easy groove...as if enjoying a little wine buzz.

In the Middle Ages, Montalcino (mohn-tahl-CHEE-noh) was considered Siena's biggest ally. Originally aligned with Florence, the town switched sides after the Sienese beat up Florence in the Battle of Montaperti in 1260. The Sienese persuaded the Montalcinesi to join their side by forcing them to collect corpses and sleep one night in the bloody, Florentine-strewn battlefield. Later, the Montalcinesi took in Sienese refugees. To this day, in gratitude for their support, the Sienese invite the Montalcinesi to lead the parade that kicks off Siena's Palio celebrations.

Montalcino prospered under Siena, but like its ally, it waned after the Medici family took control of the region. The village became a humble place. Then, in the late 19th century, the Biondi Santi family created a fine, dark red wine, calling it "the brunette" (Brunello). Today's affluence is due to the town's much-sought-after wine. If you're not a wine lover, you may find Montalcino (a.k.a. Brunello-ville) to be too touristy.

Montalcino provides a handy springboard for exploring the surrounding wine region. "Montalcino" literally means "Mountain of Oaks"—and sure enough, its surrounding hills are generously forested.

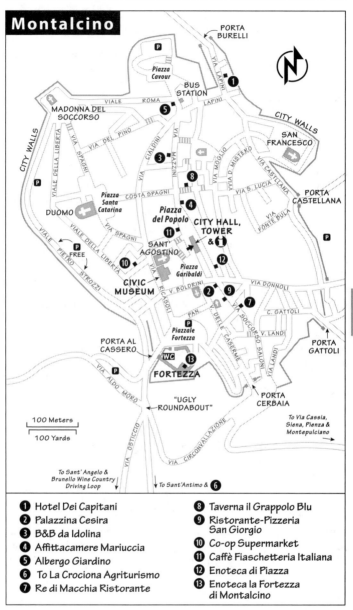

Montalcino

PORTA BURELLI

Piazza Cavour

BUS STATION

VIA LAPINI

LAPINI

CITY WALLS

VIALE ROMA

MADONNA DEL SOCCORSO

VIA DEL PINO

VIA CIALDINI

VIA MAZZINI

VIA D. MISTERO

SAN FRANCESCO

CITY WALLS

VIALE DELLA LIBERTA

VIA SPAGNI

VIA MOGLIO

VIA CASTELLANA

VIA S. LUCIA

PORTA CASTELLANA

COSTA SPAGNI

Piazza Santa Catarina

DUOMO

VIA SPAGNI

Piazza del Popolo

CITY HALL, TOWER & ①

VIA FONTE BULA

VIALE PIETRO STROZZI

VIALE DELLA LIBERTA

FREE

SANT' AGOSTINO

CIVIC MUSEUM

Piazza Garibaldi

VIA RICASOLI

V. BOLDRINI

PAN.

VIA DONNOLI

C. GATTOLI

V. LANDI

PORTA GATTOLI

Piazzale Fortezza

V. DELLE CASERME

VIA SOCCORSO SALONI

VIA LANDI

PORTA AL CASSERO

VIA ALDO MORO

WC ⑬

FORTEZZA

PORTA CERBAIA

"UGLY ROUNDABOUT"

VIA OSTICCIO

VIA CIRCONVALLAZIONE

To Via Cassia, Siena, Pienza & Montepulciano

100 Meters

100 Yards

To Sant' Angelo & Brunello Wine Country Driving Loop

To Sant'Antimo & ⑥

❶ Hotel Dei Capitani
❷ Palazzina Cesira
❸ B&B da Idolina
❹ Affittacamere Mariuccia
❺ Albergo Giardino
❻ To La Crociona Agriturismo
❼ Re di Macchia Ristorante
❽ Taverna il Grappolo Blu
❾ Ristorante-Pizzeria San Giorgio
❿ Co-op Supermarket
⓫ Caffè Fiaschetteria Italiana
⓬ Enoteca di Piazza
⓭ Enoteca la Fortezza di Montalcino

Orientation to Montalcino

Sitting atop a hill amidst a sea of vineyards, Montalcino is surrounded by walls and dominated by the Fortezza (a.k.a. "La Rocca"). From here, roads lead down into the two main squares: Piazza Garibaldi and Piazza del Popolo.

Tourist Information: The helpful TI, just off Piazza Garibaldi in City Hall, sells bus tickets; can call ahead to book a visit at a countryside winery (€1/person fee); and has information on taxis to nearby towns, abbeys, and monasteries (daily 10:00-13:00 & 14:00-17:50, tel. 0577-849-331, www.prolocomontalcino.com).

Arrival in Montalcino: Drivers coming in for a short visit should head to the pay lot in Piazzale Fortezza: Skirt around the fortress, take the first right (just past a little park), and follow signs to *parking* and *Fortezza* (€1.50/hour, free 20:00-8:00). Or, if you don't mind a short climb, park for free below the fortress: At the roundabout with the ugly statue, take the small downhill lane into the big lower parking lot (blue lines mean that you have to pay, but the lower-level unmarked spots are always free). If these lots are full, follow the town's western wall toward the Madonna del Soccorso church and a long pay lot.

The **bus** station is on Piazza Cavour, about 300 yards from the town center. From here, simply follow Via Mazzini straight up into town. While Montalcino has no official baggage storage, a few shops are willing to hold onto one or two bags on a short-term basis; ask at the TI.

Helpful Hints: Market day is Friday (7:00-13:00) on Viale della Libertà, near the Fortezza.

Sights in Montalcino

Fortezza

This 14th-century fort, built under Sienese rule, is now little more than an empty shell. You're welcome to enter the big, open courtyard (with WCs out the far end), or just enjoy a picnic in the park surrounding the fort; but if you want to climb the ramparts for a panoramic view, you'll have to pay (€4, enter through wine bar, daily 9:00-20:00, shorter hours off-season). Most people visit the fortress for its wine bar.

Piazza del Popolo

All roads in tiny Montalcino lead to the main square, Piazza del Popolo ("People's Square"). Since 1888, the **Caffè Fiaschetteria Italiana** has been *the* elegant place to enjoy a drink. Its founder, inspired by Caffè Florian in Venice, brought fine coffee to this humble town of woodcutters. **City Hall** was the fortified seat of government. It's decorated by the coats of arms of judges who, in the interest of fairness, were from outside of town. Like Siena, Montalcino was a republic in the Middle Ages. When Florentines took Siena in 1555, Siena's ruling class retreated here and held out for four more years. The Medici coat of arms (with the six balls, or pills) dominates the others. This, and the much-reviled statue of Cosimo de' Medici in the loggia, are reminders that Florence finally took Montalcino in 1559. The one-handed **clock** was the norm until 200 years ago. For five centuries, the arcaded **loggia** hosted the town market. And, of course, it's fun to simply observe the *passeggiata*—these days mostly a parade of tourists here for the wine.

For some wine-centric whimsy, go around the right side of the City Hall and find a series of plaques (each designed by a different artist), which show off the annual rating of the Brunello harvest from two to five stars—important, as wine is the lifeblood of the local economy.

Montalcino Museums (Musei di Montalcino)

While technically three museums in one (archaeology, medieval art, and modern art), and surprisingly big and modern for this little town, Montalcino's lone museum ranks only as a decent bad-weather activity. The cellar is filled with interesting artifacts dating back as far as—gulp—200,000 B.C. The ground, first, and second floors hold the medieval and modern art collections, with an emphasis on Gothic sacred art (with works from Montalcino's heyday, the 13th to 16th centuries). The ground floor is best, with a large collection of crucifixes and the museum's highlights, a glazed-terra-cotta altarpiece and statue of St. Sebastian, both by Andrea della Robbia.

Cost and Hours: €4.50, Tue-Sun 10:00-13:00 & 14:00-17:50, closed Mon, Via Ricasoli 31, to the right of Sant'Agostino Church, tel. 0577-846-014.

Wineries near Montalcino

The countryside around Montalcino is littered with wineries, some of which offer tastings. As Brunello is the poshest of Italian wines, these wineries feel a bit upscale. While most will accommodate those just dropping by in the afternoon for a quick taste, it's highly recommended and in your interest to reserve ahead. It's a simple process (just call and arrange a time), and they'll delight in showing you around. Tours generally last 45-60 minutes, cost €10-15 per person, and conclude with a tasting of three or four wines. The Montalcino TI can give you a list of more than 150 regional wineries and will call ahead for you. Or check with the vintners' consortium (tel. 0577-848-246, www.consorziobrunellodimontalcino.it).

If you lack a car (or don't want to drive), you can take a tour on the **Brunello Wine Bus,** which laces together a variety of wineries (€25, mid-June-Oct Tue, Thu, and Sat, departs at 9:00, returns at 20:00, tel. 0577-846-021, www.lecameredibacco.com).

If you're paying for a wine tasting, you aren't obligated to buy. But if a winery is doing a small tasting just for you, they're hoping you'll buy a bottle or two.

SOUTH OF MONTALCINO
Le Potazzine
This endearingly small (38,000 bottles per year), friendly, family-run winery, about a five-minute drive south of Montalcino, is operated by gregarious Gigliola and her assistant, Michele. The name is a type of small bird that also means "Little Girls," in honor of Gigliola's daughters. Call or email ahead to schedule a one-hour tour and tasting (€10-36 bottles, Loc. Le Prata 262, tel. 0577-846-168, www.lepotazzine.it, tenuta@lepotazzine.it). From SP-14 south of Montalcino, take the turnoff on the right for *Camigliano* and *Tavernelle* onto SP-103; after a minute, follow the *Castiglion del Bosco* sign; and in another minute, when the road becomes gravel, you'll hit the driveway into Le Potazzine (on the left).

Mastrojanni
Perched high above the Romanesque Sant'Antimo Abbey, overlooking sprawling vineyards, this winery (owned by the Illy coffee company) is big and glitzy—yet doesn't feel as corporate or soulless as some of the bigger players (€17-36 bottles, Podere Loreto e San Pio, tel. 0577-835-681, www.mastrojanni.com, Andrea). To reach it, head up into the town of Castelnuovo dell'Abate (just above Sant'Antimo Abbey), bear left at the Bassomondo restaurant, and continue up along the gravel road (enjoying vineyard and abbey views) to the end.

Ciacci Piccolomini d'Aragona
This well-respected, family-run vineyard has a classy tasting room/ *enoteca* and an outdoor view terrace. If you're just dropping in, belly up to the wine bar for two or three free tastes. Or reserve ahead for a more formal tasting of top-quality wines for €10-25, which includes a tour of the cellar (open Mon-Fri 9:00-19:00, Sat 10:30-18:30, head toward Castelnuovo dell'Abate but go right before entering that town, following signs toward Sant'Angelo in Colle, tel. 0577-835-616, www.ciaccipiccolomini.com, visite@ ciaccipiccolomini.com).

NORTH OF MONTALCINO
Altesino
Elegant and stately, Altesino owns perhaps the most stunning location of all, just off the back road connecting Montalcino north to

Buonconvento. You'll twist up on cypress-lined gravel lanes to this perch, which looks out over an expanse of vineyards with Montalcino hovering on the horizon (€12.50 for tour and basic tasting, daily, may close for midafternoon break, Loc. Altesino 54, tel. 0577-806-208, www.altesino.it, info@altesino.it). You'll find the turnoff for Altesino along the back road (SP-45) between Montalcino and Buonconvento (not the main SR-2 highway).

Santa Giulia

On the outskirts of Torrenieri, this may be the quintessential family-run winery, with an emphasis on quality over quantity (only 10,000 bottles a year). They also produce excellent olive oil, prosciutto, and salami. Flatter, a bit less picturesque, and much more rustic (with a working-farm feel rather than a swanky tasting room) than the others listed here, a tour here is a Back Door experience. The son, Gianluca, and his wife, Kae, enjoy showing off the entire farm—ham hocks, cheese, and winery—before giving you a chance to taste their produce. Call to find a time that fits their schedule; around lunchtime, you can arrange a "Zero Kilometer" meal, with everything farm-made (€15 for tasting and tour, 2-person minimum, €12-27 bottles, Loc. San Giulia 48, tel. 0577-834-270, www.santagiulia montalcino.it, info@santagiuliamontalcino.it). From Torrenieri's main intersection, follow the brown *Via Francigena* signs. After crossing the train tracks and a bridge, watch on the left to follow signs for *Sasso di Sole*, then *Sta. Giulia*; you'll take gravel roads through farm fields to the winery.

Sleeping in Montalcino

$$$ **Hotel Dei Capitani,** at the end of town near the bus station, has plush public spaces, an inviting pool, and a cliffside terrace offering plenty of reasons for lounging. About half of the 29 rooms come with vast Tuscan views for the same price (request a view room when you reserve), the nonview rooms are bigger, and everyone has access to the terrace (Db-€138 in 2016 when you book directly with the hotel and mention this book, extra bed-€40, air-con, elevator, limited free parking—first come, first served, Via Lapini 6, tel. 0577-847-227, www.deicapitani.it, info@deicapitani. it).

$$ **Palazzina Cesira,** right in the heart of the old town, is a gem renting five spacious and tastefully decorated rooms in a fine 13th-century residence with a palatial lounge and a pleasant garden. You'll enjoy a refined and tranquil ambience, a nice breakfast (with eggs), and the chance to get to know Lucilla and her American husband Roberto, who are generous with local advice (Db-€105, superior Db-€115, suites-€125, 2-night minimum, 3-night

Wines in the Region

This region has two well-respected red wines, each centered on a specific town: Montepulciano is known for its Vino Nobile, while Montalcino is famous for its Brunello. In each wine, the predominant grape is a clone of sangiovese (Tuscany's main red wine grape).

Vino Nobile di Montepulciano ("noble wine of Montepulciano") is a high-quality, dry ruby red, made mostly with the Prugnolo Gentile variety of sangiovese (70 percent), plus other varieties including Mammolo (30 percent). Aged two years (or three for a *riserva*)—one year of which must be in oak casks—it's more full-bodied than a typical Chianti and less tannic than a Brunello. It pairs well with meat, especially roasted  lamb with rosemary, rabbit or boar ragu over pasta, grilled portobello mushrooms, and local cheeses like pecorino. Several large wineries produce and age their Vino Nobile in the sprawling cellars beneath the town of Montepulciano. Two of these—Contucci Cantina and De' Ricci Cantine del Redi—are fun and easy to tour (see "Sights and Experiences in Montepulciano" on page 97). The oldest red wine in Tuscany, Vino Nobile has been produced since the late 1500s. (Don't mistake this wine for lesser quality wines from the Le Marche or Abruzzo regions that use a grape confusingly named Montepulciano.)

Brunello di Montalcino ("the little brown one of Montalcino"—named for the color of the grapes before harvest) is even more highly regarded and ranks among Italy's finest and most expensive wines. Made from 100 percent Sangiovese Grosso (a.k.a. Brunello) grapes, it's smooth, dry, and aged for a minimum of two years in wood casks, plus an additional four months in the bottle. *Riserva* wines are aged an additional year. Brunello is designed to cellar for 10 years or longer—but who can wait? It pairs well with the local cuisine, but the perfect match is the fine Chianina beef.

First created by the Biondi Santi clan in the late 19th century,

minimum on holiday weekends, air-con, free off-street parking, Via Soccorso Saloni 2, tel. 0577-846-055, www.montalcinoitaly.com, info@montalcinoitaly.com).

$$ B&B da Idolina has four good, midrange rooms above a wine shop on the main street (Sb-€60, Db-€85, Tb-€100, includes basic breakfast in shared kitchen, check-in 14:00-20:00—call if arriving later, Via Mazzini 65, tel. 0577-849-212, mobile 333-771-2102, www.poggiorubino.it, camereidolina@poggiorubino.it, Alessandro).

this wine quickly achieved a sterling reputation. Today, there are around 240 mostly small producers of Brunello in the Montalcino region; I've recommended just a few, which I find fun and accessible (see listings on page 121). A simpler option is to sample a few different wines at one of the good wine bars in Montalcino (see page 126).

You'll also see Rosso di Montalcino (a younger version of Brunello), which is aged for one year. This "poor man's Brunello" is very good, at half the price. Note that in lesser-quality years, only Rosso di Montalcino is produced.

Touring a winery, you'll see that many winemakers age Brunello in giant oak casks. You'll also notice glass jars (an invention of Leonardo da Vinci) poking up from the tops of those casks, which allow expansion of the liquid during fermentation, and—by providing a small overflow reservoir—ensure that the wine reaches the very top of the cask. Before placing the wine in casks, modern wineries ferment it in temperature-controlled cement or stainless steel tanks, which are easier to maintain than wood and preserve a more fruity bouquet.

Strolling through vineyards, you may notice "sentinel" roses at the ends of some of the rows of vines. These aren't just decorative; because disease affects roses before grapes, historically the flowers acted as a canary in a coal mine, giving vintners advance notice if a phylloxera epidemic was imminent. Today the roses can warn of mildew.

But disease isn't the only pest: Locals say that wild boars make the best winemakers—they wait to raid the vineyards until the grapes are perfectly sweet. At that magic moment, it becomes a race between the boars and the human harvesters. But humans have the last laugh (or bite)—boar is found on many Tuscan menus and is considered the perfect accompaniment to the local wines.

HEART OF TUSCANY

$ Affittacamere Mariuccia has three small, colorful, good-value, Ikea-chic rooms on the main drag over a heaven-scented bakery (Sb-€40, Db-€60, air-con, check in across the street at Enoteca Pierangioli before 20:00 or let them know arrival time, Piazza del Popolo 16, rooms at #28, tel. 0577-849-113, mobile 347-365-5364, www.affittacameremariuccia.it, enotecapierangioli@hotmail.com, Alessandro and Stefania).

$ Albergo Giardino, old and basic, has nine big simple rooms, no public spaces, and a convenient location near the bus station (Db-€60, 10 percent discount with this book outside May and Sept, no breakfast, Piazza Cavour 4, tel. 0577-848-257, mobile 338-684-3163, www.albergoilgiardino.it, info@albergoilgiardino.it, Roberto and dad Mario).

Eating in Montalcino

RESTAURANTS

Re di Macchia is an invitingly intimate restaurant where Antonio serves up the Tuscan fare Roberta cooks. Look for their seasonal menu and a fine Montalcino wine list. Consider the €25 fixed-price meal. For €17 more, it's paired with local wines carefully selected to accompany each dish (€10 pastas, €16 *secondi*, Fri-Wed 12:00-14:00 & 19:00-21:00, closed Thu, reservations strongly recommended, Via Soccorso Saloni 21, tel. 0577-846-116).

Taverna del Grappolo Blu is unpretentious, friendly, and serious about its wine, game, homemade pasta, and vegetarian options (€9 pastas, €9-14 *secondi*, Sat-Thu 12:00-15:00 & 19:00-22:00, closed Fri, reservations smart, a few steps off Via Mazzini at Scale di Via Moglio 1, tel. 0577-847-150, Luciano, www.grappoloblu.it).

Ristorante-Pizzeria San Giorgio is a homey trattoria/pizzeria with traditional decor and reasonable prices. It's great for families and a reliable choice for a simple meal (€5-6 pizzas, €8 pastas, €8-13 *secondi*, daily 12:00-15:30 & 19:00-23:00, closed Tue off-season, Via Soccorso Saloni 10, tel. 0577-848-507, Mara).

Picnic: Gather ingredients at the **Co-op supermarket** on Via Sant'Agostino (Mon-Sat 8:30-13:00 & 16:00-20:00, closed Sun, just off Via Ricasoli in front of Sant'Agostino Church), then enjoy your feast up at the Madonna del Soccorso Church, with vast territorial views.

Wine Bars: The places listed next also serve light food.

WINE BARS *(ENOTECHE)*

Caffè Fiaschetteria Italiana, a classic café/wine bar, was founded by Ferruccio Biondi Santi, the creator of the famous Brunello wine. The wine library in the back of the café boasts many local choices. A meeting place since 1888, this grand café also serves light lunches and espresso to tourists and locals alike (€6-13 Brunellos by the glass, €3-5 light snacks, €8-12 plates; same prices inside, outside, or in back room; daily 7:30-23:00, Piazza del Popolo 6, tel. 0577-849-043). And if it's coffee you need, this place—with its classic 1961 espresso machine—is considered the best in town.

Enoteca di Piazza is one of a chain of wine shops with a system of mechanical dispensers. A "drink card" (like a debit card) keeps track of the samples you take, for which you'll pay from €1 to €9 for each 60-milliliter taste of 100 different wines, including some whites—rare in this town. They hope you'll buy a bottle of the samples you like, and are happy to educate you in English. (Rule of thumb: A bottle costs about 10 times the price of the sample. If you buy a bottle, the sample of that wine is free.) While the place feels a little formulaic, it can be fun—the wine is great, and the staff is casual and helpful. Their small restaurant lets you enjoy your drink card with local dishes (daily 9:00-20:00, near Piazza del Popolo at Via Matteotti 43, tel. 0577-848-104, www.enotecadipiazza.com).

Enoteca la Fortezza di Montalcino offers a chance to taste top-end wines by the glass, each with an English explanation. While the prices are a bit higher than other *enoteche* in town, the medieval setting inside Montalcino's fort is a hit for most visitors. Spoil yourself with Brunello in the cozy *enoteca* or at an outdoor table (tastings start at €13 for 3 wines and go up from there; sampler plates of cheeses, *salumi*, honeys, and olive oil; daily 9:00-20:00, closes at 18:00 Nov-March, inside the Fortezza, tel. 0577-849-211, Luciano).

Montalcino Connections

Montalcino is well-connected to Siena; other bus connections are inconvenient but generally workable. Montalcino's bus station is on Piazza Cavour, within the town walls. Bus tickets are sold at the bar on Piazza Cavour, at the TI, and at some tobacco shops, but not on board. Check schedules at the TI, at the bus station, or online (at www.sienamobilita.it or www.tiemmespa.it). The nearest train station is a 20-minute bus ride away, in Buonconvento (bus runs nearly hourly).

From Montalcino by Bus: The handiest direct bus is to **Siena** (6/day Mon-Sat, 4/day Sun, 1.25 hours). To reach **Pienza** or **Montepulciano,** ride the bus to Torrenieri (3-4/day Mon-Sat, none on Sun, 20 minutes), where you'll switch to line #112 for the rest of the way (from Torrenieri: 25 minutes to Pienza, 45 minutes to Montepulciano). Anyone going to **Florence** by bus changes in Siena; since the bus arrives at Siena's train station, it's handier to go the rest of the way to Florence by train.

Countryside Accommodations

While I've listed fine accommodations in Siena, Montepulciano, and Montalcino, a beautiful way to more fully experience the Heart of Tuscany is to sleep in a farmhouse B&B. Some of these are working farms (a prerequisite to be officially called an *agriturismo*) and give a great sense of living with a family on a farm. Others are just lovely homes in the countryside. The beautiful common denominator about these listings is the wonderful people you'll meet as your hosts.

IN THE VAL D'ORCIA, NEAR PIENZA

$$$ Agriturismo Cretaiole, ideally situated in pristine farmland just outside Pienza, is perfect for those who want to settle in and fully experience Tuscany. One of my favorite *agriturismo* experiences in Italy, this family-friendly farm welcomes visitors for weeklong stays (Sat-Sat) in six comfortable apartments. Carlo and his father, Luciano, tend to the farm, while Isabella and her helper Carlotta assist guests in finding the Tuscan experience they're

dreaming of (each for a reasonable extra charge): pasta-making and olive-oil tasting classes, family-style Tuscan dinners, winery tours, truffle hunts and grape and olive harvesting (in season), artisan studio visits, Siena side-trips, watercolor classes, and more (Db-€890/week, small Db apartment-€1,120/week, large Db apartment-€1,390/week, same apartment for a family with up to two kids on sofa bed-€1,650/week, larger apartments available, these prices promised with this book in 2016; weeklong stays preferred but shorter stays possible when it's slow—Db-€130/night, 3-night minimum, you can only book one month ahead; fewer activities and lower prices mid-Nov-mid-March, no air-con or swimming pool, loaner bikes, loaner mobile phones, Isabella's mobile 338-740-9245, Carlotta's mobile 338-835-1614, tel. 0578-748-083, www.cretaiole.it, info@cretaiole.it). The same family runs two properties in the atmospheric medieval village of Castelmuzio, five miles north of Pienza (**Le Casine di Castello** and **Casa Moricciani;** for details see www.buongiornotoscana.com).

$$$ Fonte Bertusi, a classy and artistic guesthouse between Pienza and Cretaiole, is well-run by young couple Manuela and Andrea, Andrea's father Edoardo, and their attention-starved cats. They have a cozy library/lounge/art gallery that hosts installations and occasional music events, and they've scattered vivid, whimsical bits and pieces of artwork around the complex. The eight apartments mix rustic decor with avant-garde creations; it's a bit pricey, but the setting is sublime (nightly rate: 1-bedroom apartment-€130, 2-bedroom apartment-€260, includes breakfast; weekly rate: €600-1,150, €50 extra per person for breakfast all week; laundry service, swimming pool, grand sunset-view terrace, communal BBQ and outdoor kitchen, just outside Pienza toward San Quirico d'Orcia on the right—just after the turnoff for "Il Fonte," tel. 0578-748-

077, Manuela's mobile 339-655-5648, www.fontebertusi.it, info@ fontebertusi.it).

$$$ La Bruciata is a family-friendly *agriturismo* charmingly tucked in remote-feeling countryside a five-minute drive outside Montepulciano (on the way to Pienza). Can-do Laura and her family produce wine and olive oil, and rent seven tasteful, modern rooms split among four apartments (for 2-6 people each) that share a peaceful yard with swimming pool. In the summer (June-Aug), they prefer one-week stays, but shorter visits are possible at other times (Db-€100-120 depending on size, air-con for extra charge, farm-fresh meals and cooking classes, Via del Termine 9, tel. 0578-757-704, mobile 339-781-5106, www.agriturismolabruciata. it, info@agriturismolabruciata.it). Leaving Montepulciano toward Pienza, turn off on the left for *Poggiano,* then carefully track red *La Bruciata* signs (using gravel roads).

NEAR MONTALCINO

$$ La Crociona, an *agriturismo* farm and working vineyard, rents seven fully equipped apartments with dated furnishings. Fiorella Vannoni and Roberto and Barbara Nannetti offer cooking classes and tastes of the Brunello wine grown and bottled on the premises (Db-€95, or €65 in Oct-mid-May; Qb-€140, or €95 in Oct-mid-May; lower weekly rates, reception open 9:00-13:00 & 14:30-19:30, laundry service-€8/load, covered pool, hot tub, fitness room, La Croce 15, tel. 0577-847-133, www.lacrociona.com, info@ lacrociona.com). The farm is two miles south of Montalcino; don't turn off at the first entrance to the village of La Croce—wait for the second one, following signs to *Tenuta Crocedimezzo e Crociona.* A good restaurant is next door.

AT LA FOCE GARDENS, NEAR MONTEPULCIANO

$$$ B&B Palazzolo La Foce lets you sleep aristocratically in a small villa just below the La Foce Gardens. Its four colorful rooms share a welcoming kitchen/lounge with a giant fireplace, and an outdoor swimming pool with glorious Tuscan views. All of the rooms bask in fine panoramas, and two rooms share a bathroom (D-€120, Db-€140, no air-con but breezy, Strada della Vittoria 61—but check in at gardens' main entrance to get specific directions to your room, more expensive villas available, tel. 0578-69101, www.lafoce.com, info@lafoce.com).

ASSISI

Assisi is famous for its hometown boy, St. Francis, who made very, very good. While Francis the saint is interesting, Francesco Bernardone the man is even more so, and mementos of his days in Assisi are everywhere—where he was baptized, a shirt he wore, a hill he prayed on, and a church where a vision changed his life.

About the year 1200, this simple friar from Assisi countered the decadence of Church government and society in general with a powerful message of non-materialism and a "slow down and smell God's roses" lifestyle. Like Jesus, Francis taught by example, living without worldly goods and aiming to love all creation. A huge monastic order grew out of his teachings, which were gradually embraced (some would say coopted) by the Church. Christianity's most popular saint and its purest example of simplicity is now glorified in beautiful churches, along with his female counterpart, St. Clare. In 1939, Italy made Francis one of its patron saints; in 2013, the newly elected pope took his name.

Francis' message of love, simplicity, and sensitivity to the environment has a broad and timeless appeal. But every pilgrimage site inevitably gets commercialized, and Francis' legacy is now Assisi's basic industry. In summer, this Umbrian town bursts with flash-in-the-pan Francis fans and Franciscan knickknacks. Those able to see past the glow-in-the-dark rosaries and bobblehead friars can actually have a "travel on purpose" experience. Even a block or two off the congested main drag, you'll find pockets of serenity that, it's easy to imagine, must have made Francis feel at peace.

PLANNING YOUR TIME

Assisi is worth a day and a night. Its old town has a half-day of sightseeing and another half-day of wonder. The essential sight is the Basilica of St. Francis. For a good visit, take my self-guided Assisi Walk, going from the top of town to the basilica at the bottom, and my Basilica of St. Francis Tour. With more time, be sure to wander the back streets and linger on the main square, Piazza del Comune.

Most visitors are day-trippers. While the town's a zoo by day, it's a delight at night. Assisi after dark is closer to a place Francis could call home.

Orientation to Assisi

Crowned by a ruined castle, Assisi spills downhill to its famous Basilica of St. Francis. The town is beautifully preserved and rich in history. A 5.5-magnitude earthquake in 1997 did more damage to the tourist industry than to the town's buildings. Fortunately, tourists—whether art lovers, pilgrims, or both—have returned, drawn by Assisi's special allure.

The city stretches across a ridge that rises from a flat plain. The Basilica of St. Francis sits at the low end of town; Piazza Mat-

teotti (bus stop and parking lot) is at the high end; and the main square, Piazza del Comune, lies in between. The main drag (called Via San Francesco for most of its course) runs from Piazza del Comune to the basilica. Capping the hill above the town is the ruined castle, called the Rocca Maggiore, and rising above that is Mount Subasio. The town is smaller than its fame might lead you to think: Walking uphill from the basilica to Piazza Matteotti takes 30 minutes, while the downhill journey takes about 15 minutes. Some Francis sights lie outside the city walls, in the valley beneath the ridge (the modern part of town, called Santa Maria degli Angeli) and in the hills above.

TOURIST INFORMATION

The **TI** is in the center of the old town on Piazza del Comune (Mon-Fri 8:00-14:00 & 15:00-18:00, Sat-Sun 9:30-17:00—until 18:00 in April-Oct, tel. 075-813-8680). From April to October, there's also a branch down in the valley in Santa Maria degli Angeli, across the street from the big piazza in front of the Basilica of St. Mary of the Angels.

Discovery Station Assisi, located in the train station in Santa Maria degli Angeli, is a volunteer-run children's science and tech

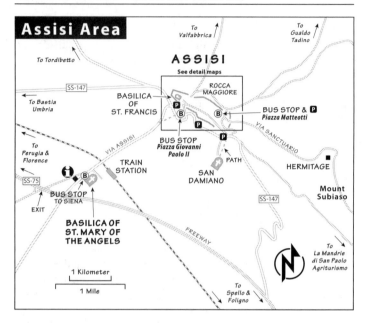

center that also serves as an unofficial TI. Here you can store luggage (€3, confirm closing time), access Wi-Fi (€2 donation, unlimited use), buy bus tickets, and get maps and advice for the entire region (open daily, irregular hours, exit station and go left 20 yards, donations appreciated, tel. 075-804-4507).

ARRIVAL IN ASSISI

By Train: The train station is about two miles below Assisi, in Santa Maria degli Angeli. You can check bags in the station at the newsstand (daily 6:45-12:30 & 13:00-19:30) or at Discovery Station Assisi (listed earlier), but not in the old town.

Orange city **buses** connect the station with the old town on the hilltop. Buses (line #C) usually leave at :16 and :46 past the hour from the bus stop immediately to your left as you exit the station (daily 5:30-23:00, 15 minutes; buy tickets at the newsstand inside the train station for €1.30, or on board the bus for €2—exact change only, validate in yellow box as you board, valid 1.5 hours after being stamped, good for any bus within the old town). The bus may actually be awaiting the arrival of your train. If so, don't dawdle or you may just miss it.

While these big train-station-to-Assisi buses don't go into town, they stop at three convenient places just outside the wall: at the bottom (Piazza Giovanni Paolo II, near Basilica of St. Francis), the middle (Largo Properzio, just outside the Porta Nuova city gate), and at the top (Piazza Matteotti).

Going from the old town to the train station, the orange buses reverse the route, starting at the top (Piazza Matteotti, usually at :10 and :40 past the hour), stopping in the middle next (outside Porta Nuova at Largo Properzio), and then at the bottom (Piazza Giovanni Paolo II), before zipping down to the station.

All buses are marked either *SM degli Angeli/Stazione* or *Matteotti/S. Francesco*. While you may find yourself looping into the hinterland, most of these buses also go to the Basilica of St. Mary of the Angels (Santa Maria degli Angel, one stop beyond the station, confirm with the driver). The middle Assisi stop (Porta Nuova) is best for hotels in the center, leaving you a long but level walk to the main square.

Taxis from the train station to the old town cost about €15. You can be charged extra for luggage, night service, additional people (four is customary)...and sometimes just for being a tourist. When departing the old town, you'll find taxi stands at Piazza Giovanni Paolo II, the Basilica of St. Francis, the Basilica of St. Clare, and Piazza del Comune (or have your hotel call for you, tel. 075-813-100). Expect to pay a minimum of €10 for any ride.

By Bus: Buses from Siena may arrive at the stop next to the Basilica of St. Mary of the Angels (Santa Maria degli Angel), near the train station (see above for directions from the station into town). Most other intercity buses arrive at the base of the old town.

By Car: Drivers coming in for the day can follow the signs to several handy parking lots *(parcheggi)*. Piazza Matteotti's wonderful underground parking garage is at the top of the town and comes with bits of ancient Rome in the walls. Another big lot, Parcheggio Giovanni Paolo II, is at the bottom end of town, 200 yards below the Basilica of St. Francis. At Parcheggio Porta Nuova, an escalator delivers you to Porta Nuova near St. Clare's. The lots vary in price (€1.30-1.60/hour, most €12/day). For day-trippers, the best plan is to park at Piazza Matteotti, follow my self-guided town walk, tour the basilica, and then either catch a bus back to Piazza Matteotti or simply wander back up through town to your car.

HELPFUL HINTS

Best Shopping: Tacky knickknacks line the streets leading to the Basilica of St. Francis. For better shops (with local handicrafts), head to Via San Rufino and Corso Mazzini (both just off Piazza del Comune, shops described later in the Assisi self-guided walk). A Saturday-morning market fills Via Borgo San Pietro (along the bottom edge of town).

Festivals: Assisi annually hosts several interesting festivals commemorating St. Francis and life in the Middle Ages. **Festa di Calendimaggio** is a springtime medieval festival featuring costume parades, concerts, and competitions among Assisi's

St. Francis of Assisi (1181-1226)

In 1202, young Francesco Bernardone donned armor and rode out to battle the Perugians (residents of Umbria's capital city). The battle went badly, and Francis was captured and imprisoned for a year. He returned a changed man. He avoided friends and his father's lucrative business and spent more and more time outside the city walls fasting, praying, and searching for something.

In 1206, a vision changed his life, culminating in a dramatic confrontation. He stripped naked before the town leaders, threw his clothes at his father—turning his back on the comfortable material life—and declared his loyalty to God alone.

Idealistic young men flocked to Francis, and they wandered Italy like troubadours, spreading the joy of the Gospel to rich and poor. Francis became a cult figure, attracting huge crowds. They'd never seen anything like it—sermons preached outdoors, in the local language (not Church Latin), making God accessible to all. Francis' new order of monks was also extremely unmaterialistic, extolling poverty and simplicity. Despite their radicalism, the order eventually gained the pope's approval and spread through the world. Francis, who died in Assisi at the age of 45, left a legacy of humanism, equality, and love of nature that would eventually flower in the Renaissance.

In Francis' Sandal Steps

1. Baptized in Assisi's **Cathedral of San Rufino** (then called St. George's).
2. Raised in the family home just off Piazza del Comune (now the **Chiesa Nuova**).
3. Heard call to "rebuild church" in **San Damiano.** (The crucifix of the church is now in the **Basilica of St. Clare.**)
4. Settled and established his order of monks at the **Porziuncola Chapel** (inside today's St. Mary of the Angels Basilica).
5. Met Clare. (Her tomb and possessions are at the **Basilica of St. Clare.**)
6. Received the pope's blessing for his order (1223 document in the reliquary chapel at the **Basilica of St. Francis**).
7. Had many visions and was associated with miracles during his life (depicted in **Giotto's frescoes** in the Basilica of St. Francis' upper level).
8. Died at the **Porziuncola,** his body later interred beneath the **Basilica of St. Francis.**

ASSISI

rival neighborhoods (www.calendimaggiodiassisi.it). Rustic medieval "taverns" pop up around the center offering *porchetta* (roasted pig) and *vino* (starts the first Wed in May and lasts four days; if one of these days is already a public holiday, it's held the following week). The **Settimana Francescana** commemorates the beginning of the end of Francis' life, when he made his way for the last time to the Porziuncola Chapel (Sept 28). This week-long celebration culminates in the **Festa di San Francesco,** which marks his death with religious processions, special services, and an arts, crafts, and folklore fair. The TI has a monthly *Assisi Informa* leaflet with details on upcoming festivals and celebrations; see also the event listings at www. assisi.regioneumbria.eu.

Internet Access: Many cafés in town have free Wi-Fi for customers. Wi-Fi is also available at the train station in the Discovery Center Assisi (see "Tourist Information," earlier).

Laundry: 3 elleblu' Lavanderia can do a load of laundry for you at a reasonable price on the same day, if they're not too busy (Mon-Fri 9:00-18:00, Sat 9:00-13:00, closed Sun, Via Borgo Aretino 6a, tel. 075-816-084).

Travel Agencies: You can purchase train, bus, and plane tickets at **Agenzia Viaggi Stoppini,** centrally located between Piazza del Comune and the Basilica of St. Clare. Manager Fabrizio is patient with tourists' needs (Mon-Fri 9:00-12:30 & 15:30-19:00, Sat 9:00-12:30, closed Sun, also offers day trips to nearby towns, Corso Mazzini 31, tel. 075-812-597, www. viaggistoppiniassisi.it).

Local Guides: Giuseppe Karabotis is a good licensed guide (€130/3 hours, €260/6 hours, mobile 328-867-0567, iokarabot@libero. it). **Daniela Moretti** is a hardworking young guide from Perugia who knows both Assisi and all of Umbria (€120/half-day, €240/day, mobile 335-829-9984, www.danyguide.com, danyguide@hotmail.com). If they're busy, they can recommend other guides.

GETTING AROUND ASSISI

Most visitors need only their feet to get everywhere in Assisi, except to the train station and nearby Basilica of St. Mary of the Angels (via bus #C—see directions in "Arrival in Assisi").

Within the old town, pale yellow minibuses #A and #B run every 20-40 minutes, linking the lower end (near the Basilica of St. Francis) with the middle (Piazza del Comune) and the top (Piazza Matteotti). While it's only a 15-minute stroll from the upper end to the lower, the climb back up can have you looking for a lift. Hop on a bus marked *Piazza Matteotti* if you're exhausted after your basilica visit and need a sweat-free five-minute return to the top of the old town (near many of my recommended hotels). Before boarding, confirm the destination (catch the bus below the Basilica of St. Francis, just outside the Porta San Francisco).

You can buy a bus ticket (good on any city bus) at a newsstand or kiosk for €1.30, or get a ticket from the driver for €2 (exact change only). After you've stamped your ticket on board the bus, it's valid for 90 minutes.

Assisi Walk

There's much more to Assisi than just St. Francis and what the blitz tour groups see. This self-guided walk, worth ▲▲, covers the town from top to bottom. To get to Piazza Matteotti, ride the bus from the train station (or from Piazza Giovanni Paolo II) to the last stop; drive up (and park in the underground lot); or hike five minutes uphill from Piazza del Comune.

∩ Download my free Assisi Town Walk audio tour.

• *Start 50 yards beyond Piazza Matteotti (down the small lane between two stone houses, away from city center—see map).*

❶ The Roman Amphitheater (Anfiteatro Romano)

A lane named Via Anfiteatro Romano skirts the cozy neighborhood built around a Roman amphitheater—a reminder that Assisi was once an important Roman town. Circle the amphitheater counterclockwise. Imagine how colorful the town laundry basin (on the right) must have been in previous generations, when the women of Assisi gathered here to do their wash. Just beyond the basin is a small rectangular pool; above it are the coats of arms of Assisi's leading families. A few steps farther, leave the amphitheater, hiking up the stairs on the right to the top of the hill, for an aerial view of the ancient oval. The Roman stones have long been absorbed into the medieval architecture. It was Roman tradition to locate the amphitheater outside of town, which this used to be. While the amphitheater dates from the first century A.D., the buildings filling it today were built in the 13th and 14th centuries. Notice how carefully maintained the town's complexion is and how when redoing a roof, locals will mix old and new tiles.

• *Continue on, enjoying the grand view of the fortress in the distance. The lane leads down to a city gate and an...*

❷ Umbrian View

Step outside of Assisi at the Porta Perlici for a commanding view. Umbria, called the "green heart of Italy," is the country's geographical center and only landlocked region. Enjoy the various shades of green: silver green on the valley floor (olives), emerald green (grapevines), and deep green on the hillsides (evergreen oak trees).

The valleys are dotted by small family farms, many of which rent rooms as *agriturismos.* Also notice Rocca Maggiore ("big fortress"), which provided townsfolk a refuge in times of attack, and, behind you atop the nearer hill, Rocca Minore ("little fortress"), which gives the town's young lovers a little privacy. The quarry (under the Rocca Maggiore) was a handy source for Assisi's characteristic pink limestone.

• *Go back through the gate and follow Via Porta Perlici—it's immediately on your right—downhill into town (toward Hotel La Rocca).*

Enjoy the higgledy-piggledy architecture (this neighborhood has some of the most photogenic back lanes in town). Fifty yards down, to the left of the arched gate, find the wall containing an aqueduct that dates back to Roman times. It still brings water from a mountain spring into the city (push the brass tap for a taste). After another 50 yards, turn left through a medieval town gate (with Hotel La Rocca on your right). Just after the hotel, you'll pass a second gate dating from Roman times. Follow Via Porta Perlici downhill until you hit a fine square facing a big church.

❸ Cathedral of San Rufino (Cattedrale San Rufino)

Trick question: Who's Assisi's patron saint? While Francis is one of Italy's patron saints, Rufino (the town's first bishop, martyred and

buried here in the third century) is Assisi's. This cathedral (seat of the local bishop) is 11th-century Romanesque with a Neoclassical interior, and dedicated to Rufino. Although it has what is considered to be one of the best and purest Romanesque facades in all of Umbria, the big triangular top (just a decorative wall) was added in Gothic times.

Cost and Hours: Cathedral-free, daily 7:30-19:00, Nov-mid-March closed Mon-Fri 12:30-14:30, tel. 075-812-283, www.assisimuseodiocesano.com.

Visiting the Church: Before going in, study the facade—a jungle of beasts emphasizing how the church was a refuge and sanc-

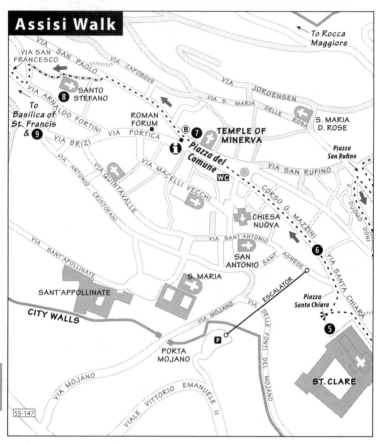

Assisi Walk

tuary in a scary world. Notice the lions at the base of the facade, flanking each door. One is eating a Christian martyr, reminding worshippers of the courage of early Christians.

Enter the church. While the front of the church is an unremarkable mix of 17th- and 18th-century Baroque and Neoclassical, the rear (near where you enter) has several points of interest. Notice first the two fine statues: *St. Francis* and *St. Clare* (by Giovanni Dupré, 1888). To your right is an old baptismal font (in the corner with the semicircular black iron grate). In about 1181, a baby boy was baptized in this font. His parents were upwardly mobile Francophiles who called him Francesco ("Frenchy"). In 1194, a nobleman baptized his daughter Clare here. Eighteen years later, their paths crossed in this same church, when Clare attended a class and became mesmerized by the teacher—Francis. Traditionally, the children of Assisi are still baptized here.

The striking glass panels in the floor reveal foundations preserved from the ninth-century church that once stood here. You're

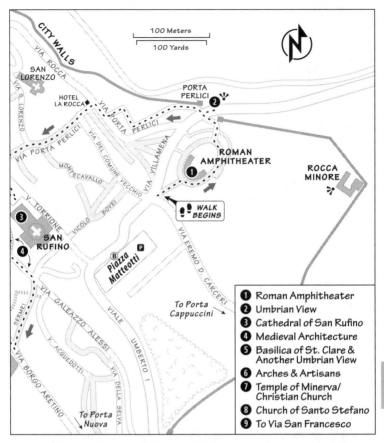

1 Roman Amphitheater
2 Umbrian View
3 Cathedral of San Rufino
4 Medieval Architecture
5 Basilica of St. Clare & Another Umbrian View
6 Arches & Artisans
7 Temple of Minerva/ Christian Church
8 Church of Santo Stefano
9 To Via San Francesco

walking on history. After the 1997 earthquake, structural inspectors checked the church from ceiling to floor. When they looked under the paving stones, they discovered graves (until Napoleon decreed otherwise, it was common practice to bury people in churches). Underneath that level, they found Roman foundations and some animal bones (suggesting the possibility of animal sacrifice). There might have been a Roman temple here; churches were often built upon temple ruins. Stand at the back of the church facing the altar, and look left to the Roman cistern that collected rain water (just beyond the great stone archway, next to where you entered). Take the three steps down (to trigger the light) and marvel at the fine stonework and Roman engineering. In the Middle Ages, this was the town's emergency water source when under attack.

Diocesan Museum: Underneath the church, incorporated into the Roman ruins and columns, are the foundations of an earlier Church of San Rufino, now the crypt and the fine little Diocesan museum. When it's open, you can go below to see the saint's sarcophagus (third century) and the small museum featuring the cathedral's art from centuries past (€3.50, down the stairs, near the baptismal font, well-described in English).

• *Leaving the church, take a sharp left (at the pizza-by-the-slice joint, on Via Dono Doni). After 20 yards, take a right and go all the way down the stairway to see some...*

❹ Medieval Architecture

At the bottom of the stairs, notice the pink limestone pavement, part of the surviving medieval town. The arches built over doorways indicate that the buildings date from the 12th through the 14th century, when Assisi was booming. Italian cities such as Assisi—thriving on the north-south trade between northern Europe and Rome—were in the process of inventing free-market capitalism, dabbling in democratic self-rule, and creating the modern urban lifestyle. The vaults you see that turn lanes into tunnels are reminders of medieval urban expansion—creating more living space (mostly 15th century). While the population grew, people wanted to live within the town's protective walls. Medieval Assisi had several times the population density of modern Assisi.

Notice the blooming balconies; Assisi holds a flower competition each June.

• *From the bottom of the stairs, head to the left and continue downhill. When you arrive at a street, turn left, going slightly uphill for a long block, then take the low road (right) at the Y, and head down Via Sermei. Continue down to the big church. Walk right, under the three massive buttresses, to Piazza Santa Chiara and the front of the church.*

❺ Basilica of St. Clare (Basilica di Santa Chiara)

Dedicated to the founder of the Order of the Poor Clares, this Umbrian Gothic church is simple, in keeping with the nuns' dedication

to a life of contemplation. In Clare's lifetime, the order was located in the humble Church of San Damiano, in the valley below, but after Clare's death, they needed a bigger and more glorious building. The church was built in 1265, and the huge buttresses were added in the next century.

Cost and Hours: Free, daily 6:30-12:00 & 14:00-19:00, until 18:00 in winter.

Visiting the Basilica: The interior's fine frescoes were whitewashed in Baroque times. The battered remains of one on the left show how the fresco surface was hacked up so whitewash would

St. Clare (1194-1253)

The 18-year-old rich girl of Assisi fell in love with Francis' message, and made secret arrangements to meet him. The night

of Palm Sunday, 1212, she slipped out of her father's mansion in town and escaped to the valley below. A procession of friars with torches met her and took her to (what is today) St. Mary of the Angels Basilica. There, Francis cut her hair, clothed her in a simple brown tunic, and welcomed her into a life of voluntary poverty. Clare's father begged, ordered, and physically threatened her to return, but she would not budge.

Clare was joined by other women who banded together as the Poor Clares. She spent the next 40 years of her life within the confines of the convent of San Damiano: barefoot, vegetarian, and largely silent. Her regimen of prayer, meditation, and simple manual labor—especially knitting—impressed commoners and popes, leading to her canonization almost immediately after her death. St. Clare is often depicted carrying a monstrance (a little temple holding the Eucharist wafer).

stick. Imagine all the pristine frescoes hiding behind the whitewash (here and all over Europe).

The Chapel of the Crucifix of San Damiano, on the right, has the wooden crucifix that changed Francis' life. In 1206, an emaciated, soul-searching, stark-raving Francis knelt before this crucifix of a living Christ (then located in the Church of San Damiano) and asked for guidance. According to legend, the crucifix spoke: "Go and rebuild my Church, which you can see has fallen into ruin." Francis followed the call.

Stairs lead from the nave down to the tomb of St. Clare. Her tomb—discovered in about 1850—is at the far right end of the richly ornamented neo-Gothic crypt (the image is fiberglass; her actual bones lie underneath). As you circulate with the crowd of pilgrims, notice the paintings on the walls depicting spiritual lessons from Clare's life and death. At the opposite end of the crypt (back between the stairs, in a large glassed-in area, well-described on the wall) are important relics: the saint's robes, hair (in a silver box), and an enormous tunic she made—along with relics of St. Francis (including a blood-stained stocking he wore after receiving the stigmata). The attached cloistered community of the Poor Clares has flourished for 700 years.

• *Leave the church and belly up to the viewpoint at the edge of the square for...*

Another Umbrian View: On the left is the convent of St. Clare (global headquarters of all the Poor Clares). Below you lies the olive grove of the Poor Clares, which has been there since the 13th century. In the distance is a grand Umbrian view. Assisi overlooks the richest and biggest valley in otherwise hilly and mountainous Umbria. Across the valley (and over the Tiber River), the rival town Perugia, where Francis was imprisoned, sits on its own hill. The municipality of Assisi has a population of 25,000, but only 3,500 people live in the old town. The lower town, called Santa Maria degli Angeli, grew up with the coming of the railway in the 19th century. In the haze, the church with the greyish-blue dome is St. Mary of the Angels (described later), the cradle of the Franciscan order. A popular pilgrimage site today, it marks the place where St. Francis lived, worked, and died.

Spanish-speaking Franciscans settled in California. Three of their missions grew into major cities: Los Angeles (named after this church), San Francisco (named after St. Francis), and Santa Clara (named after St. Clare).

• *From the church square, step out into Via Santa Chiara.*

❻ Arches and Artisans

Notice the three medieval town gates (two behind the church, and one uphill toward the town center). The gate over the road behind the church dates from 1265. (Farther on, you can just see the crenellations of the 1316 Porta Nuova, which marks the final medieval expansion of Assisi.) Toward the city center (on Via Santa Chiara, the high road), an arch marks the site of the Roman wall. These three gates represent the town's three walls, illustrating how much the city has grown since ancient times.

Walk uphill along Via Santa Chiara (which becomes Corso Mazzini) to the city's main square. As you pass under the arch you enter what was Roman Assisi. The street is lined with interesting shops selling traditional embroidery, religious souvenirs, and gifty local edibles. The shops on Corso Mazzini, on the stretch between the gate and the Piazza del Comune, show off many local crafts. As you browse, watch for the following shops: Galleria d'Arte Perna (on the left, #20b) sells the medieval fantasy townscapes of Paolo Grimaldi, a local painter who runs this shop with his brother, Alessandro. A helpful travel agency is across the street and a few steps up (at #31, Agenzia Viaggi Stoppini; see "Helpful Hints," earlier).

Next, the aptly named Assisi Olive Wood (on the left at #14E) sells olive-wood carvings, as does d'Olivo, across the street at #23. It's said that St. Francis made the first Nativity scene to help humanize and, therefore, teach the Christmas message. That's why you'll see so many crèches in Assisi. (Even today, nearby villages are enthusiastic about their "living" manger scenes, and Italians everywhere enjoy setting up elaborate crèches in churches for Christmas.) Further along at #14A is a bakery, Bar Sensi, selling the traditional raisin-and-apple strudel called *rocciata* (roh-CHAH-tah, splittable and served warm). Farther along on the left (on the corner at #2b) is Il Duomo, selling religious art, manger scenes, and crucifixion figurines. Across the street, on the right, is Centro Ricami, selling finely embroidered linens and baby clothes. And on the square (at #34, opposite the flags), the recommended La Bottega dei Sapori is worth a visit for edible and drinkable souvenirs.

You've walked up what was, in ancient times, the main drag into town. Ahead of you, the six fluted Corinthian columns of the Temple of Minerva marked the forum (today's Piazza del Comune). Sit at the fountain on the piazza for a few minutes of people-watching—don't you just love Italy? Within a few hundred yards of this square, on either side, were the medieval walls. Imagine the commotion of 5,000 people confined within these walls. No wonder St. Francis needed an escape for some peace and quiet.

• *Now, head over to the temple on the square.*

❼ Temple of Minerva/Christian Church

Assisi has always been a spiritual center. The Romans went to great lengths to make this first-century B.C. Temple of Minerva a cen-

terpiece of their city. Notice the columns that cut into the stairway. It was a tight fit here on the hilltop. In ancient times, the stairs went down—about twice as far as they do now—to the main drag, which has gradually been filled in over time. The Church of Santa Maria sopra ("over") Minerva was added in the 9th century. The bell tower is from the 13th century.

Pop inside the temple/church. Today's interior is 17th-century Baroque. Walk to the front. Flanking the altar are the original Roman temple floor stones. You can even see the drains for the bloody sacrifices that took place here. Behind the statues of Peter and Paul, the original Roman embankment peeks through.

Cost and Hours: Free, daily 7:15-19:30, in winter closes at sunset and midday.

• *Across the square at #11, step into the 16th-century frescoed vaults of the...*

Loggia of the Palazzo del Comune: Notice the Italian flair for design. Even this little loggia was once finely decorated. The art style is called "Grotesque," named for the Renaissance-era discovery of Roman paintings, featuring bizarre creatures, on the walls of Nero's Golden House in Rome (the lower levels, still largely unexcavated, appeared cave-like: grotto-esque). This scene was indisputably painted after 1492. How do they know? Because it features turkeys—first seen in Europe after Columbus returned from the Americas with his ship full of exotic souvenirs. The turkeys painted here may have been that bird's European debut.

• *From the main square, hike past the temple up the high road, Via San Paolo. After 200 yards (across from #24), a sign directs you down a stepped lane to the...*

❽ Church of Santo Stefano (Chiesa di Santo Stefano)

Surrounded by cypress, fig, and walnut trees, Santo Stefano—which used to be outside the town walls in the days of St. Francis—is a delightful bit of offbeat Assisi. Legend has it that Santo Stefano's bells miraculously rang on October 3, 1226, the day St. Francis died. Step inside. This is the typical rural Italian Romanesque church—no architect, just built by simple stonemasons who put together the most basic design. Hundreds of years later, it still stands.

Cost and Hours: Free, daily 8:30-20:00, shorter hours off-season.

• *The lane zigzags down to Via San Francesco. Turn right and walk under the arch toward the Basilica of St. Francis.*

❾ Via San Francesco

This main drag leads from the town to the basilica holding the body of St. Francis. Francis was a big deal even in his own day. He was made a saint in 1228—the same year that the basilica's foundations were laid—and his body was moved here by 1230. Assisi was a big-time pilgrimage center, and this street was its booming hub. The arch marks the end of what was Assisi in St. Francis' day. Notice the fine medieval balcony immediately past the arch (on the left). About 30 yards farther down (on the left), cool yourself at the fountain, as medieval pilgrims might have. The hospice next door was built in 1237 to house pilgrims. Notice the three surviving faces of its fresco: Jesus, Francis, and Clare. Farther down, across from #12A (on the left), is the Oratorio dei Pellegrini, dating from the 1450s. A brotherhood ran a hostel here for travelers passing through to pay homage to St. Francis. The chapel offers a richly frescoed 14th-century space designed to inspire pilgrims—perfect for any traveler to pause and contemplate the saint's message.

• *Continuing on, you'll eventually reach Assisi's main sight, the Basilica of St. Francis. For the start of my self-guided tour, walk downhill to the basilica's lower courtyard.*

Basilica of St. Francis Tour

The Basilica of St. Francis (Basilica di San Francesco), worth ▲▲▲, is one of the artistic and religious highlights of Europe. It

rises where, in 1226, St. Francis was buried (with the outcasts he had stood by) outside of his town on the "Hill of the Damned"— now called the "Hill of Paradise." The basilica is frescoed from top to bottom with scenes by the leading artists of the day: Cimabue, Giotto, Simone Martini, and Pietro Lorenzetti. A 13th-century historian wrote, "No more exquisite monument to the Lord has been built."

From a distance, you see the huge arcades "supporting" the basilica. These were 15th-century quarters for the monks. The arcades that line the square and lead to the church housed medieval pilgrims.

ORIENTATION

Cost and Hours: Free entry; lower basilica—daily 6:00-18:45, until 17:45 in Nov-March; reliquary chapel in lower basilica— generally open Mon-Fri 9:00-18:00, often closed Sat-Sun and occasionally at other times for religious services; upper basilica—daily 8:30-18:45, until 17:45 in Nov-March. Modest dress is required to enter the church—no above-the-knee skirts or shorts and no sleeveless tops for men, women, or children.

Information: The church courtyard at the entrance of the lower basilica has an info office, often staffed by native English-speaking friars (April-Oct Mon-Sat 9:15-17:30, Nov-March Mon-Sat 9:15-12:00 & 14:15-17:30, closed Sun year-round, tel. 075-819-0084, www.sanfrancescoassisi.org). Call or check the website to find out about upcoming concerts at the basilica.

Tours: Audioguides (boring and old-school) are available at the kiosk located outside the entrance of the lower basilica (€7 donation requested for 1 or 2 persons, 45 minutes). Hour-long **guided tours** in English are available daily except Sunday (€10 donation requested, must call or email to reserve, tel. 075-819-0084, www.sanfrancescoassisi.org, assisisanfrancesco@libero.it).

🎧 Download my free Basilica of St. Francis **audio tour.**

ASSISI

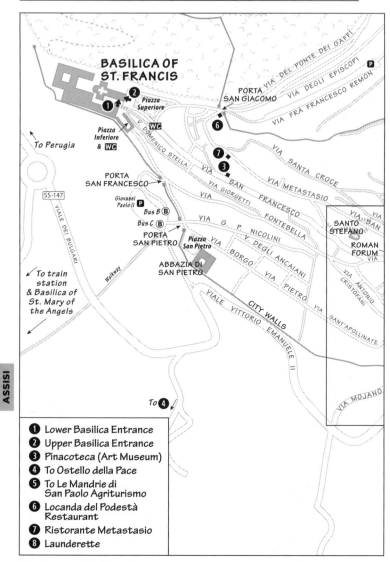

Bookstore: The church bookshop is in the inner courtyard behind the upper and lower basilica. It sells an excellent guidebook, *The Basilica of Saint Francis: A Spiritual Pilgrimage* (€3, by Goulet, McInally, and Wood; I used this book, and a tour with Brother Michael, as sources for this self-guided tour).

Services: Go before you enter, as there aren't any WCs inside. There are two different pay WCs within a half-block of the lower entrance—up the road in a squat building, and halfway down the big piazza on the left.

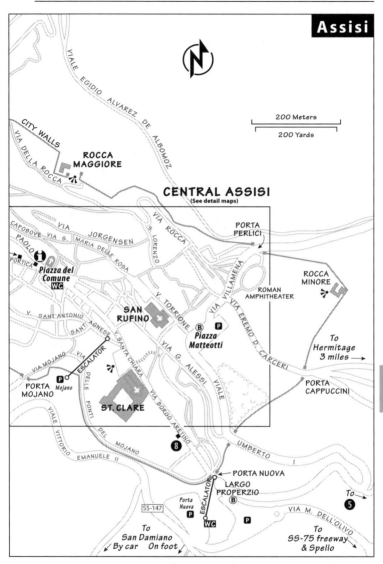

Attending Mass: To worship in the basilica, consider joining the Franciscan brothers for Mass in *Italiano* (Sun at 7:30, 9:00, 10:30, 12:00, 17:00, and 18:30; Nov-March at 7:15, 11:00, and 17:00), or experience a Mass sung by the basilica choir many Sundays at 10:30. On Sundays in summer (Easter-Oct), there's an English Mass in the lower basilica at 9:00. Additional English and sung Masses don't follow a set schedule. Call the basilica to find out when English-speaking pilgrimage groups or choirs have reserved Masses, and attend with

The Franciscan Message

Francis' message caused a stir. Not only did he follow Christ's teachings, he followed Christ's lifestyle, living as a poor, wandering preacher. He traded a life of power and riches for one of obedience, poverty, and chastity. He was never ordained as a priest, but his influence on Christianity was monumental.

The Franciscan realm (Brother Sun, Sister Moon, and so on) is a space where God, man, and the natural world frolic harmoniously. Francis treated every creature—animal, peasant, pope—with equal respect. He and his "brothers" (*fratelli*, or friars) slept in fields, begged for food, and exuded the joy of non-materialism. Franciscan friars were known as the "Jugglers of God," modeling themselves on French troubadours (*jongleurs*, or jugglers) who roved the countryside singing, telling stories, and cracking jokes.

In an Italy torn by conflict between towns and families, Francis promoted peace and the restoration of order. (He set an example by reconstructing the crumbled San Damiano chapel.) While the Church was waging bloody Crusades, Francis pushed ecumenism and understanding. And the Franciscan message had an impact. In 1288, just 62 years after Francis died, a Franciscan became pope (Nicholas IV). Francis' message also led to Church

them—although groups change their plans fairly often (tel. 075-819-0084).

OVERVIEW

The Basilica of St. Francis, a theological work of genius, can be difficult for the 21st-century tourist/pilgrim to appreciate.

Since the basilica is the reason that most people visit Assisi, and the message of St. Francis has even the least devout sightseers blessing the town Vespas, I've designed this self-guided tour with an emphasis on the place's theology (rather than art history).

A disclaimer before we start: Just as Francis used many biblical legends to help teach the Christian message, legends from the life of Francis were told in later ages to teach the same message. Are they true? In general, probably not. Are they in keeping with Francis' message? Yes. Do I share legends here as if they are historic? Sure.

The church has three parts: the upper basilica, the lower basilica, and the saint's tomb (below the lower basilica). To get oriented, stand at the lower entrance in the courtyard. While empty today, reforms that many believe delayed the Protestant Reformation by a century.

This richly decorated basilica seems to contradict the teachings of the poor monk it honors, but it was built as an act of religious and civic pride to remember the hometown saint. It was also designed—and still functions—as a pilgrimage center and a splendid classroom. Though monks in robes may not give off an "easy-to-approach" vibe, the Franciscans of today are still God's jugglers (and many of them speak English).

Here is Francis' message, in his own words:

The Canticle of the Sun

Good Lord, all your creations bring praise to you!
Praise for Brother Sun, who brings the day. His radiance reminds us of you!
Praise for Sister Moon and the stars, precious and beautiful.
Praise for Brother Wind, and for clouds and storms and rain that sustain us.
Praise for Sister Water. She is useful and humble, precious and pure.
Praise for Brother Fire who cheers us at night.
Praise for our sister, Mother Earth, who feeds us and rules us.
Praise for all those who forgive because you have forgiven them.
Praise for our sister, Bodily Death, from whose embrace none can escape.
Praise and bless the Lord, and give thanks, and, with humility, serve him.

ASSISI

centuries ago this main plaza was cluttered with pilgrim services and the medieval equivalent of souvenir shops. Opposite the entry to the lower basilica is the information center.

SELF-GUIDED TOUR

Enter through the grand doorway of the lower basilica. Just inside, decorating the top of the first arch, look up and see St. Francis, who greets you with a Latin inscription. Sounding a bit like John Wayne,

he says the equivalent of, "Slow down and be joyful, pilgrim. You've reached the Hill of Paradise. And, if you're observant and thoughtful, this church will knock your spiritual socks off."

• *Start with the tomb. To get there, turn left into the nave. Midway down, follow the signs and go right, to the tomb downstairs.*

The Tomb

The saint's remains are above the altar in

the stone box with the iron ties. In medieval times, pilgrims came to Assisi because St. Francis was buried here. Holy relics were the "ruby slippers" of medieval Europe. Relics gave you power—they answered your prayers and won your wars—and ultimately helped you get back to your eternal Kansas. Assisi made no bones about promoting the saint's relics, but hid his tomb for obvious reasons of security. His body was buried secretly while the basilica was under construction, and over the next 600 years, the exact location was forgotten. When the tomb was to be opened to the public in 1818, it took more than a month to find his actual remains.

Francis' four closest friends and first followers are memorialized in the corners of the room. Opposite the altar, up four steps between the entrance and exit, notice the small copper box behind the metal grill. This contains the remains of Francis' rich Roman patron, Jacopa dei Settesoli. She traveled to see him on his deathbed but was turned away because she was female. Francis waived the rule and welcomed "Brother Jacopa" to his side. These five tombs—in the Franciscan spirit of being with your friends—were added in the 19th century.

The candles you see are the only real candles in the church (others are electric). Pilgrims pay a coin, pick up a candle, and place it in the small box on the side. Franciscans will light it later.

• *Climb back up to the lower nave.*

Lower Basilica

Appropriately Franciscan—subdued and Romanesque—this nave is frescoed with parallel scenes from the lives of Christ (right) and Francis (left), connected by a ceiling of stars. The Passion of Christ and the Compassion of Francis lead to the altar built over Francis' tomb. After the church was built and decorated, side chapels were erected to provide mausoleums for the rich families that patronized the work of the order. Unfortunately, in the process, huge arches were cut out of some frescoed scenes, but others survive. In the fresco directly above the entry to the tomb, Christ is being taken down from the cross (just the bottom half of his body can be seen, on the left), and it looks like the story is over. Defeat. But in the opposite fresco (above the tomb's exit), we see Francis preaching to the birds, reminding the faithful that the message of the Gospel survives.

These stories directed the attention of the medieval pilgrim to the altar, where he could meet God through the sacraments. The church was thought of as a community of believers sailing toward God. The prayers coming out of the nave (*navis*, or ship) fill the triangular sections of the ceiling—called *vele*, or sails—with spiritual wind. With a priest for a navigator and the altar for a helm, faith propels the ship.

Basilica of St. Francis—Lower Level

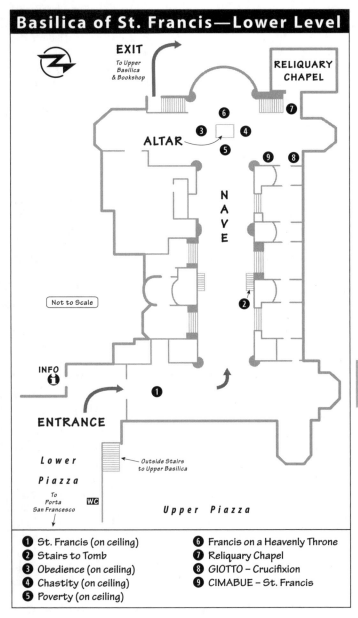

EXIT
To Upper
Basilica
& Bookshop

RELIQUARY CHAPEL

ALTAR

NAVE

Not to Scale

INFO

ENTRANCE

Lower

Piazza

To
Porta
San Francesco

Outside Stairs
to Upper Basilica

WC

Upper Piazza

ASSISI

❶ St. Francis (on ceiling)
❷ Stairs to Tomb
❸ Obedience (on ceiling)
❹ Chastity (on ceiling)
❺ Poverty (on ceiling)
❻ Francis on a Heavenly Throne
❼ Reliquary Chapel
❽ GIOTTO – Crucifixion
❾ CIMABUE – St. Francis

Stand behind the altar (toes to the bottom step, facing the entrance) and look up. The three scenes above you represent the creed of the Franciscans: Directly above the tomb of St. Francis, to the right, **Obedience** (Francis appears twice, wearing a rope harness and kneeling in front of Lady Obedience); to the left, **Chastity** (in her tower of purity held up by two angels); and straight ahead, **Poverty.** Here Jesus blesses the marriage as Francis slips a ring on Lady Poverty. In the foreground, two "self-sufficient" yet pint-size merchants (the new rich of a thriving northern Italy) are throwing sticks and stones at the bride. But Poverty, in her patched wedding dress, is fertile and strong, and even bare brambles blossom into a rosebush crown.

The three knots in the rope that ties the Franciscan robe symbolize the monks' vows of obedience, chastity, and poverty. St. Francis called money the "devil's dung." The jeweled belt of a rich person was all about material wealth. A bag of coins hung from it, as did a weapon to protect that person's wealth. Franciscans instead bound their tunics with a simple rope, its three knots a constant reminder of their vows.

Now put your heels to the altar and—bending back like a drum major—look up for a peek at the reward for a life of obedience, chastity, and poverty: **Francis on a heavenly throne** in a rich, golden robe. He traded a life of earthly simplicity for glory in heaven.

• *Turn to the right and march to the corner, where steps lead down into the...*

ASSISI

Reliquary Chapel

This chapel is filled with fascinating relics (which a €0.50 flier explains in detailed English; often closed Sat-Sun). Step in and circle the room clockwise. You'll see the silver chalice and plate that Francis used for the bread and wine of the Eucharist (in a small, dark, windowed case set into the wall, marked *Calice e Patena*). Francis believed that his personal possessions should be simple, but the items used for worship should be made of the finest materials. Next, the Veli di Lino is a cloth Jacopa wiped her friend's brow with on his deathbed. In the corner display case is a small section of the itchy haircloth *(cilizio)*—not sheep's wool, but cloth made from scratchy horse or goat hair—worn by Francis as penance (the cloth he chose was the opposite of the fine fabric his father sold). In the next corner are the tunic and slippers that Francis donned during his last days. Next, find a prayer (in a fancy silver stand) that St. Francis wrote for Brother Leo and signed with a T-shaped character—his tau cross. The last letter in the Hebrew alphabet, tav ("tau" in Greek) is symbolic of faithfulness to the end, and Francis adopted it for his signature. Next is a papal document (1223) legitimizing the Franciscan order and assuring his followers that they were not risking a (deadly) heresy charge. Finally, just past the altar, see the tunic that was lovingly patched and stitched by followers of the five-foot, four-inch-tall St. Francis.

Before leaving the chapel, notice the modern paintings done recently by local artists. Over the entrance, Francis is shown being born in a stable like Jesus (by Capitini). Scenes from the life of Clare and Padre Pio (a Capuchin priest, very popular in Italy, who was sainted in 2002) were painted by Stefanelli and Antonio.

• *Return up the stairs, stepping into the...*

Lower Basilica's Transept

The decoration of this church brought together the greatest Sienese (Lorenzetti and Simone Martini) and Florentine (Cimabue and Giotto) artists of the day. Look around at the painted scenes. In 1300, this was radical art—believable homespun scenes, landscapes, trees, real people. Directly opposite the reliquary chapel, study **Giotto's painting of the Crucifixion,** with the eight sparrow-like angels. For the first time, holy people are expressing emotion: One angel turns her head sadly at the sight of Jesus, and another scratches her hands down her cheeks, drawing blood. Mary (lower left), previously in control, has fainted in despair. The Franciscans, with their goal of bringing God to the people, found a natural partner in Europe's first naturalist (and therefore modern) painter, Giotto.

To grasp Giotto's artistic leap, compare his work with the painting to the right, by Cimabue. It's Gothic, without the 3-D architecture, natural backdrop, and slice-of-life reality of Giotto's work. **Cimabue's St. Francis** (far right) shows the saint with the stigmata—Christ's marks of the Crucifixion. Contemporaries described Francis as being short, with a graceful build, dark hair, and sparse beard. (This is considered the

most accurate portrait of Francis—done according to the description of one who knew him.) The sunroof haircut (tonsure) was standard for monks of the day. According to legend, the brown robe and rope belt were inventions of necessity. When Francis stripped naked and ran away from Assisi, he grabbed the first clothes he could, a rough wool peasant's tunic and a piece of rope, which became the uniform of the Franciscan order. To the left, at eye level under the sparrow-like angels, are paintings of saints and their exquisite halos (by Simone Martini or his school). To the right of the door at the same level, see five of Francis' closest followers—clearly just simple folk.

Francis' friend, "Sister Bodily Death," was really not all that terrible. In fact, Francis would like to introduce you to her now (above and to the right of the door leading into the reliquary chapel). Go ahead, block the light from the door with this book and meet her. Before his death, Francis added a line to *The Canticle of the Sun:* "Praise for our sister, Bodily Death, from whose embrace none can escape."

• *Now cross the transept to the other side of the altar (enjoying some of the oldest surviving bits of the inlaid local-limestone flooring—c. 13th century), and find the staircase going up. Immediately above the stairs is Pietro Lorenzetti's* Francis Receiving the Stigmata. *(Francis is considered the first person ever to earn the marks of the cross through his great faith and love of the Church.) Make your way up the stairs to the...*

Courtyard

The courtyard overlooks the 15th-century cloister, the heart of this monastic complex. Pope Sixtus IV (of Sistine Chapel fame) had it built as a secure retreat for himself. Balanced and peaceful by design, the courtyard also functioned as a cistern to collect rainwater, supplying enough for 200 monks (today, there are about 40). The Franciscan order emphasizes teaching. This place functioned as a kind of theological center of higher learning, which rotated monks in for a six-month stint, then sent them back home more prepared and better inspired to preach effectively. That explains the complex narrative of the frescoes wallpapering the walls and halls here.

The **treasury** *(Museo del Tesoro)* to the left of the bookstore features ornately decorated chalices, reliquaries, vestments, and altarpieces (free but donation requested, April-Oct daily 10:00-17:30, closed Nov-March).

• *From the courtyard, climb the stairs (next to the bookshop) to the...*

Upper Basilica

Built later than its counterpart below, the brighter upper basilica is considered the first Gothic church in Italy (started in 1228). You've followed the intended pilgrims' route, entering the lower church and finishing here. Notice how the pulpit (embedded in the corner pillar) can be seen and heard from every spot in the packed church. The spirit of the order was to fill the church and preach. See also the design in the round window in the west end (high above the entry). The tiny centerpiece reads "IHS" (the first three letters of Jesus' name in Greek). And, as you can see, this trippy kaleidoscope seems to declare that all light radiates from Jesus.

The windows here are treasures from the 13th and 14th centuries. Those behind the apse are among the oldest and most pre-

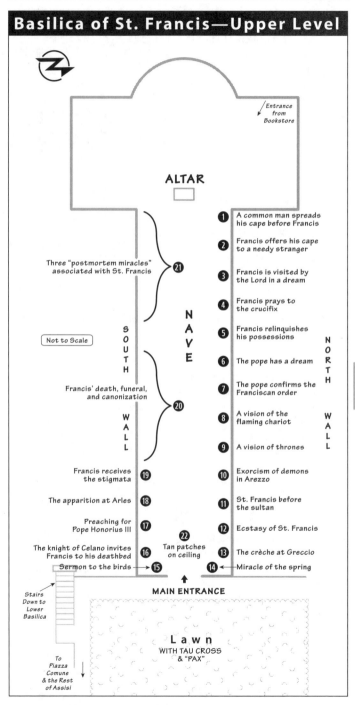

Basilica of St. Francis—Upper Level

ALTAR

Entrance from Bookstore

N A V E

S O U T H   W A L L

N O R T H   W A L L

Not to Scale

ASSISI

Three "postmortem miracles" associated with St. Francis — **21**

Francis' death, funeral, and canonization — **20**

Francis receives the stigmata — **19**

The apparition at Arles — **18**

Preaching for Pope Honorius III — **17**

The knight of Celano invites Francis to his deathbed — **16**

Sermon to the birds → **15**

1 A common man spreads his cape before Francis

2 Francis offers his cape to a needy stranger

3 Francis is visited by the Lord in a dream

4 Francis prays to the crucifix

5 Francis relinquishes his possessions

6 The pope has a dream

7 The pope confirms the Franciscan order

8 A vision of the flaming chariot

9 A vision of thrones

10 Exorcism of demons in Arezzo

11 St. Francis before the sultan

12 Ecstasy of St. Francis

13 The crèche at Greccio

14 ← Miracle of the spring

22 Tan patches on ceiling

MAIN ENTRANCE

Stairs Down to Lower Basilica

To Piazza Comune & the Rest of Assisi

L a w n
WITH TAU CROSS & "PAX"

cious in Italy. Imagine illiterate medieval peasants entranced by these windows, so full of meaning that they were nicknamed "Bibles of the Poor." But for art lovers, the basilica's draw is that Giotto and his assistants practically wallpapered it circa 1297-1300. Or perhaps the job was subcontracted to other artists—scholars debate it. Whatever the case, the anatomy, architectural depth, and drama of these frescoes helped to kick off the Renaissance. The gallery of frescoes shows 28 scenes from the life of St. Francis. The events are a mix of documented history and folk legend.

• *Working clockwise, start on the north wall (to the left, if you just climbed the stairs from the bookstore) and follow along with the help of the numbered map key. The subtitles in the faded black strip below the frescoes describe each scene in clear Latin—and affirm my interpretation.*

❶ **A common man spreads his cape before Francis** in front of the Temple of Minerva on Piazza del Comune. Before his conversion, young Francis was the model of Assisian manhood—handsome, intelligent, and well-dressed, befitting the son of a wealthy cloth dealer. Above all, he was liked by everyone, a natural charmer who led his fellow teens in nights of wine, women, and song. Medieval pilgrims understood the deeper meaning of this scene: The "eye" of God (symbolized by the rose window in the Temple of Minerva) looks over the young Francis, a dandy "imprisoned" in his own selfishness (the Temple—with barred windows—was once a prison).

❷ **Francis offers his cape to a needy stranger.** Francis was always generous of spirit. He became more so after being captured in battle and held for a year as a prisoner of war, then suffering from illness. Charity was a Franciscan forte.

❸ **Francis is visited by the Lord in a dream.** Still unsure of his calling, Francis rode off to the Crusades. One night, he dreams of a palace filled with armor marked with crosses. Christ tells him to leave the army—to become what you might consider the first "conscientious objector"—and go home to wait for a nonmilitary assignment in a new kind of knighthood. He returned to Assisi and, though reviled as a coward, would end up fighting for spiritual wealth, not earthly power and riches.

❹ **Francis prays to the crucifix** in the Church of San Damiano. After months of living in a cave, fasting, and meditating, Francis kneels in the run-down church and prays. The crucifix speaks, telling him: "Go and rebuild my Church, which you can see has fallen into ruin." Francis hurried home and sold his father's cloth to pay for God's work. His furious father dragged him before the bishop.

❺ **Francis relinquishes his possessions.** In front of the bishop and the whole town, Francis strips naked and gives his dad his clothes, credit cards, and time-share on Capri. Francis raises his hand and says, "Until now, I called you father. From now on, my only father is my Father in Heaven." Notice God's hand blessing the action from above. Francis then ran off into the hills, naked and singing. In this version, Francis is covered by the bishop, symbolizing his transition from a man of the world to a man of the Church. Notice the disbelief and concern on the bishop's advisors' faces; subtle expressions like these wouldn't have made it into other medieval frescoes of the day.

❻ **The pope has a dream.** Francis headed to Rome, seeking the pope's blessing on his fledgling movement. Initially rebuffing Francis, the pope then dreams of a simple, barefooted man propping up his teetering Church, and then...

❼ **The pope confirms the Franciscan order,** handing Francis and his gang the document now displayed in the reliquary chapel.

Francis' life was peppered with visions and miracles, shown in three panels in a row: ❽ **vision of the flaming chariot,** ❾ **vision of thrones,** and ❿ **exorcism of demons in Arezzo.**
• *Next see...*

⓫ **St. Francis before the sultan.** Francis' wandering ministry took him to Egypt during the Crusades (1219). He walked unarmed into the Muslim army camp. They captured him, but the sultan was impressed with Francis' manner and let him go, reportedly whispering, "I'd convert to your faith, but they'd kill us both." Here the sultan gestures from his throne.

⓬ **Ecstasy of St. Francis.** This oft-painted scene shows the mystic communing with Christ.

⓭ **The crèche at Greccio.** A creative teacher, Francis invents the tradition of manger scenes.
• *Around the corner, see the...*

⓮ **Miracle of the spring.** Shown here getting water out of a rock to quench a stranger's thirst, Francis felt closest to God when in the hills around Assisi, seeing the Creator in the creation.
• *Cross over to the far side of the entrance door.*

⓯ **Sermon to the birds.** In his best-known miracle, Francis is surrounded by birds as they listen to him teach. Francis embraces all levels of creation. One interpretation of this scene is that the birds, which are of different species, represent the diverse flock of humanity and nature, all created and beloved by God and worthy of one another's love.

ASSISI

This image of well-fed birds is an appropriate one to take with you. It's designed to remind pilgrims that, like the birds, God gave us life, plenty of food, feathers, wings, and a world to fly around in. Francis, patron saint of the environment and animals, taught his followers to count their blessings. A monk here reminded me that even a student backpacker today eats as well as the wealthiest nobleman in the days of Francis.

• *Continue to the south wall for the rest of the panels.*

Despite the hierarchical society of his day, Francis was welcomed by all classes, shown in these three panels: ❻ **the knight of Celano invites Francis to his deathbed;** ❼ **preaching for Pope Honorius III,** who listens intently; and ❽ **the apparition at Arles,** which illustrates how Francis could be in two places at once (something only Jesus and saints can pull off). The proponents of Francis, who believed he was destined for sainthood, show him performing the necessary miracles.

❾ **Francis receives the stigmata.** It's September 17, 1224, and Francis is fasting and praying on nearby Mount Alverna when a six-winged angel (called a seraph) appears with holy laser-like powers to burn in the marks of the Crucifixion, the stigmata. For the strength of his faith, Francis is given the marks of his master, the "battle scars of love." These five wounds suffered by Christ (nails in palms and feet, lance in side) marked Francis' body for the rest of his life.

The next panels deal with ❷⓪ **Francis' death, funeral, and canonization.** The last panels show ❷❶ **miracles** associated with the saint after his death, proving that he's in heaven and bolstering his eligibility for sainthood.

Francis died thanking God and singing his *Canticle of the Sun.* Just as he referred to the sun as his brother and the moon as his sister, Francis called his body "brother." On his deathbed he conceded, "Maybe I was a bit tough on brother ass." Ravaged by an asceticism extreme enough to earn him both the stigmata and tuberculosis, Francis died in 1226.

Before leaving through the front entrance, look up at the ceiling and the walls near the rose window to see ❷❷ **large tan patches.** In 1997, when a 5.5-magnitude quake hit Assisi, it shattered the upper basilica's frescoes into 300,000 fragments. Shortly after the quake, an aftershock shook the ceiling frescoes down, killing two monks and two art scholars standing here. Later, the fragments were meticulously picked up and pieced back together.

Outside, on the lawn, the Latin word *pax* (peace) and the Franciscan tau cross are sculpted from shrubbery. For a drink or snack, the Bar San Francesco (facing the upper basilica) is handy. For *pax,* take the high lane back to town, up to the castle, or into the countryside.

More Sights in Assisi

▲▲Basilica of St. Mary of the Angels
(Basilica di Santa Maria degli Angeli)

This huge basilica, towering above the buildings of Santa Maria degli Angeli—the modern part of Assisi in the flat valley below the hill town—marks the spot where Francis lived, worked, and died. It's a grandiose church built around a humble chapel—reflecting the monumental impact of this simple saint on his town and the world.

Cost and Hours: Free, Mon-Sat 6:15-12:50 & 14:30-19:30, Sun 6:45-12:50 & 14:30-19:30, tel. 075-805-11. A little TI kiosk is across the street from the souvenir stands (generally daily 10:00-13:00 & 15:30-18:30 but hours a bit erratic, tel. 075-804-4554). As you face the church, the best WC is on your right.

Getting There: Whether you're traveling by car or by train, it's practical to visit this sight on the way into or out of town. From Assisi's train station—which has baggage storage—it's a five-minute walk to the basilica (exit station left, after 50 yards take the underground pedestrian walkway—*sottopassaggio*—on your left, then walk straight ahead, passing several handy eateries). There's ample well-marked parking nearby.

If you're coming from the old town, you can reach the basilica on the same orange bus (line #C) that runs down to the train station (stay on one more stop to reach the basilica). In the opposite direction, buses from the basilica up to the old town run twice hourly, usually at :14 and :44 after the hour. Leaving the church, the stop is on your right, by the side of the building. For information on tickets, see "Getting Around Assisi," earlier.

Visiting the Basilica: This grand church was built in the 16th century around the tiny but historic **Porziuncola Chapel** (now directly under the dome) after the chapel became too small to accommodate the many pilgrims wanting to pay homage to St. Francis. Some local monks had given Francis this *porziuncola*, or "small portion," after his conversion—a little land with a fixer-upper chapel. Francis lived here after he founded the Franciscan Order,

ASSISI

and this was where he consecrated St. Clare as a Bride of Christ. What would humble Francis think of the huge church—Christianity's 10th largest—built over his tiny chapel?

Behind the Porziuncola Chapel on the right, find the **Cappella del Transito,** which marks the site of Francis' death on October 3, 1226. Francis died as he'd lived—simply, in a small hut located here. On his last night on earth, he invited some friars to join him in a Last Supper-style breaking of bread. Then he undressed, lay down on the bare ground, and began to recite Psalm 141: "Lord, I cry unto thee." He spoke the last line, "Let the wicked fall into their own traps, while I escape"...and he passed on.

From the right transept, follow *Roseto* signs to the rose garden. You'll walk down a passage with gardens on either side (viewable through the windows)—on the left, a tranquil park with a statue of Francis petting a sheep, and on the right, the **rose garden.** Francis, fighting a temptation that he never named, once threw himself onto the roses. As the story goes, the thorns immediately dropped off. Thornless roses have grown here ever since.

Exiting the passage, turn right to find the **Rose Chapel** (Cappella delle Rose), built over the place where Francis lived.

In the autumn, a room in the next **hallway** displays a giant animated Nativity scene (a reminder to pilgrims that Francis first established the tradition of manger scenes as a teaching aid). You'll pass a room with a free 10-minute video about the church (ask for English, daily 10:00-12:30 & 16:00-18:00). The bookshop has some works in English and an "old pharmacy" selling herbal cures.

Continuing on, you'll pass the **Porziuncola Museum,** featuring early depictions of St. Francis by 13th-century artists, a model of Assisi during Francis' lifetime, and religious art and objects from the basilica. On the museum's upper floor are some monks' cells, which provide intriguing insight into the spartan lifestyles of the pious and tonsured (€4 to see both floors, ask for English brochure, museum open April-Oct Tue-Sun 9:30-12:30 & 15:30-19:00, Nov-March until 18:00, closed Mon, tel. 075-805-1419, www.porziuncola.org).

▲Roman Forum (Foro Romano)

For a look at Assisi's Roman roots, tour the Roman Forum, which is underneath Piazza del Comune. The floor plan is clearly explained in English, as are the surviving odd bits and obscure pieces. During your visit, you'll walk on an ancient Roman road.

Cost and Hours: €4, included in €8 combo-ticket that also covers next two sights, daily June-Aug 10:00-13:00 & 14:30-19:00, shorter hours off-season; from Piazza del Comune, go a half-block to Via Portica 2—it's on your right; tel. 075-815-5077.

Pinacoteca

This small, unexciting museum attractively displays its 13th- to 17th-century art (mainly frescoes), with general English information in nearly every room. There's a damaged Giotto Madonna and a rare secular fresco (to the right of the Giotto art), but it's mainly a peaceful walk through a pastel world—best for art lovers.

Cost and Hours: €3, included in €8 combo-ticket, same hours as Roman Forum, on main drag between Piazza del Comune and Basilica of St. Francis at Via San Francesco 12—look for banner above entryway, tel. 075-815-5234.

▲Rocca Maggiore

The "big castle" offers a few restored medieval rooms, a good look at a 14th-century fortification, and a fine view of Assisi and the Umbrian countryside. If you're pinching your euros, skip it—the view is just as good from outside the castle.

Cost and Hours: €5.50, included in €8 combo-ticket, daily from 10:00 until an hour before sunset—about 19:15 in summer, Via della Rocca, tel. 075-815-5077.

Church of San Damiano (Chiesa di San Damiano)

Located on the slope steeply below the Basilica of St. Clare, this church and convent was where Francis received his call and where Clare spent her days as mother superior of the Poor Clares. Today, there's not much to see, but it's a relatively peaceful escape from touristy Assisi. Drivers can zip right there (watch for the turnoff on the road up to Piazza Matteotti), while walkers descend pleasantly from Assisi for 15 minutes through an olive grove.

In 1206, Francis was inside the church when he heard the wooden crucifix order him to rebuild the church. (The crucifix in San Damiano is a copy; the original is now displayed in the Basilica of St. Clare.) Francis initially interpreted these miraculous words as a call to rebuild crumbling San Damiano. He sold his father's cloth for money to fix the church. (The church we see today, however, was rebuilt later by others.) Eventually, Francis realized his charge was to revitalize the Christian Church at large.

As he approached the end of his life, Francis came to San Damiano to visit his old friend Clare. She set him up in a simple reed hut in the olive grove, where he was inspired to write his poem *The Canticle of the Sun*.

Cost and Hours: Free, daily, convent open 10:00-12:00 & 14:00-18:00, closes at 17:00 in winter, church opens at 6:15, start

ASSISI

walking from the Porta Nuova parking lot at the south end of Assisi and follow the signs, tel. 075-812-273, www.assisiofm.it.

Commune with Nature

For a picnic with the same birdsong and views that inspired St. Francis, leave the tourists behind and hike to the Rocca Minore (small private castle, not tourable) above Piazza Matteotti.

Near Assisi

Hermitage (Eremo delle Carceri)

If you want to follow further in St. Francis' footsteps, take a trip up the rugged slopes of nearby Mount Subasio to the humble, peaceful hermitage where Francis and his followers retreated for solitude. Today the spot is marked by a 14th-century friary that's still occupied by Franciscan monks. A self-guided tour twists you through the head-thumping doorframes and steep stairways of the medieval structure, the highlight of which is the tiny, dank cave where Francis would retire for private prayer. Outside, you'll see the ancient tree (held together with braces) that's said to be where Francis preached to the birds. Rustic paths lead to open-air "chapels" in the surrounding forest.

Cost and Hours: Free, daily 8:30-18:30, until 17:30 in winter, tel. 075-812-301.

Getting There: There is no public transportation; either drive, take a taxi, or hike. Drivers can park on the switchback just above the entrance, along the left side of the road. For hikers starting from Assisi's Porta Cappuccino gate, it's a stiff 3-mile, 1.5-hour hike with an elevation gain of about 1,000 feet. You'll walk along a narrow, switchbacked, paved road (with no shoulders) enjoying brisk air and sporadic views. A souvenir kiosk at the entrance sells drinks and sandwiches.

Sleeping in Assisi

Assisi accommodates large numbers of pilgrims on religious holidays. Finding a room at any other time should be easy. I've listed prices for spring (April-mid-June) and fall (mid-Aug-Oct). At most places, expect slightly lower rates in midsummer and winter.

Few hotels are air-conditioned. Locals suggest that you keep your windows closed through the middle of the day so that your room will be as cool as possible in the evening.

HOTELS AND ROOMS

$$$ Hotel Umbra, a quiet villa in the middle of town, has 24 spacious but overpriced rooms with great views, thinning carpets, and older decor (Sb-€85, standard Db-€110, bigger "superior" Db with better views-€130, Tb-€165, 10 percent direct-booking discount

Sleep Code

Abbreviations   **(€1=about $1.10, country code: 39)**
S=Single, **D**=Double/Twin, **T**=Triple, **Q**=Quad, **b**=bathroom.
Price Rankings
  $$$ **Higher Priced**—Most rooms €100 or more
    $$ **Moderately Priced**—Most rooms €55-100
      $ **Lower Priced**—Most rooms €55 or less
Unless otherwise noted, credit cards are accepted, English is spoken, breakfast is included, and free Wi-Fi and/or a guest computer is generally available. Many towns in Italy levy a hotel tax of €1.50-5 per person, per night (often collected in cash; usually not included in the rates I've quoted). Prices can change; verify current rates online or by email. For the best prices, always book directly with the hotel.

with this book and cash if staying 2 or more nights, air-con, elevator, peaceful garden, and view sun terrace, most rooms have views, closed Dec-March, just off Piazza del Comune under the arch at Via degli Archi 6, tel. 075-812-240, www.hotelumbra.it, info@hotelumbra.it, family Laudenzi).

$$$ Hotel Ideale, on a ridge overlooking the valley, offers 13 airy remodeled rooms with new furnishings (most with views and balconies), a tranquil garden setting, and free parking (view Db-€100, Tb-€130, Qb-€140, two apartments with fully equipped kitchens available, prices good with this book through 2016, 10 percent discount for stays of 3 or more nights, air-con, Piazza Matteotti 1, tel. 075-813-570, www.hotelideale.it, info@hotelideale.it, friendly sisters Lara and Ilaria and their monolingual family). The hotel is across the street from the parking lot at Piazza Matteotti, at the top end of town.

$$ Hotel Belvedere, a great value, is a modern building with 12 spacious, classic-feeling rooms; eight come with sweeping views (Sb-€50, Db-€70, Tb-€90, Qb-€100, breakfast-€5, elevator, large communal view terrace, 2 blocks past Basilica of St. Clare at Via Borgo Aretino 13, tel. 075-812-460, www.assisihotelbelvedere.com, hotelbelvedereassisi@yahoo.it, thoughtful Enrico speaks fluent New Jerseyan). Coming by bus from the train station, get off at Porta Nuova; the hotel is steps away.

$$ Hotel Pallotta offers seven fresh, bright, small rooms and a shared top-floor lounge with view. Friendly and helpful, the owners provide guests with loads of extra niceties including a loaner Assisi guidebook, free use of washer and drying rack, and free hot drinks and cake at teatime (Sb-€45, Db-€79, Tb-€90, 10 percent direct-booking discount with this book; a block off Piazza del Co-

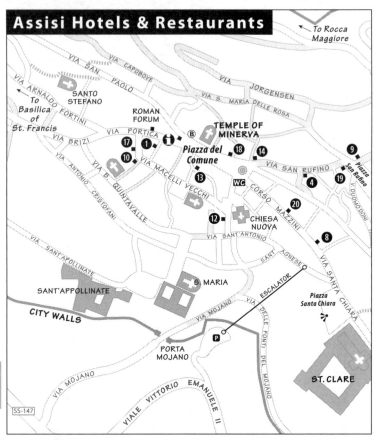

Assisi Hotels & Restaurants

mune at Via San Rufino 6; tel. 075-812-307, www.pallottaassisi.it, pallotta@pallottaassisi.it; Stefano, Serena, and family).

$$ Hotel San Rufino offers a great locale, solid stone quality, and 11 comfortable rooms (Sb-€48, Db-€61, Tb-€85, Qb-€100, breakfast-€5, elevator; from Cathedral of San Rufino, follow sign to Via Porta Perlici 7; tel. 075-812-803, www.hotelsanrufino.it, info@hotelsanrufino.it).

$$ Albergo Il Duomo, Hotel San Rufino's nine-room annex a block away, is tidy and *tranquillo*. Located on a stair-stepped lane, it's more atmospheric and has nicer bathrooms than its parent hotel, but more steps and no elevator (Sb-€46, Db-€60, Tb-€76, breakfast-€5, Wi-Fi in lobby only, Vicolo San Lorenzo 2 but check in at Hotel San Rufino—see earlier, tel. 075-812-742, www.hotelsanrufino.it, info@hotelsanrufino.it).

$$ Hotel La Rocca, on the peaceful top end of town, has 32 solid and modern rooms in a medieval shell (Sb-€49, Db-€62, Tb-€83, breakfast-€5, air-con, elevator, parking-€7, sunny rooftop ter-

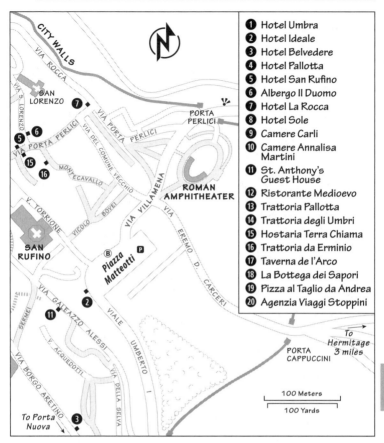

1 Hotel Umbra
2 Hotel Ideale
3 Hotel Belvedere
4 Hotel Pallotta
5 Hotel San Rufino
6 Albergo Il Duomo
7 Hotel La Rocca
8 Hotel Sole
9 Camere Carli
10 Camere Annalisa Martini
11 St. Anthony's Guest House
12 Ristorante Medioevo
13 Trattoria Pallotta
14 Trattoria degli Umbri
15 Hostaria Terra Chiama
16 Trattoria da Erminio
17 Taverna de l'Arco
18 La Bottega dei Sapori
19 Pizza al Taglio da Andrea
20 Agenzia Viaggi Stoppini

race, decent restaurant upstairs, 3-minute walk from Piazza Matteotti at Via Porta Perlici 27, tel. 075-812-284, www.hotelarocca. it, info@hotelarocca.it, Carlo).

$$ Hotel Sole, renting 38 rooms in a 15th-century building, is well-worn and forgettable, but the location is central. Half of its rooms are in a newer annex across the street (Sb-€45, Db-€70, Tb-€85, ask for a discount, breakfast-€5, air-con, elevator in annex only, public parking nearby, 100 yards before Basilica of St. Clare at Corso Mazzini 35, tel. 075-812-373, www.assisihotelsole.com, info@assisihotelsole.com).

$ Camere Carli has six shiny, spacious, new rooms in a solid, minimalist place above an art gallery (Sb-€35, Db-€48, Tb-€60, Qb-€70, no breakfast, show this book to get these prices in 2016, family lofts, lots of stairs and no elevator, free parking 150 yards away, just off Piazza San Rufino at Via Porta Perlici 1, tel. 075-812-490, mobile 339-531-1366, www.camerecarli.it, carliarte@live.it, pleasant Franco speaks limited English).

$ Camere Annalisa Martini is a cheery home amid vines and roses in the town's medieval core. This is a good budget choice—Annalisa enthusiastically accommodates her guests with a picnic garden, washing machine (€7/small load), communal refrigerator, and six homey rooms (S-€25, Sb-€27, D-€40, Db-€45, Tb-€58, Qb-€68, rates soft for last-minute bookings, cash only, 3 rooms share 2 bathrooms, no breakfast; one block from Piazza del Comune—go downhill toward basilica, turn left on Via San Gregorio to #6; tel. 075-813-536, www.cameremartiniassisi. it, cameremartini@libero.it, Mamma Rosignoli doesn't speak English, but Annalisa does).

Hostel: Francis probably would have bunked with the peasants in Assisi's 65-bed **$ Ostello della Pace** (€18 bunk in dorm rooms, €21-26/person in private 2- to 4-person rooms with bath, dinner-€10.50, laundry service-€4, free parking, lockout 10:00-16:00, midnight curfew, closed Nov-Feb; take orange shuttle bus from station to Piazza Giovanni Paolo II, then walk 15 minutes downhill on Via Marconi, then left at bend on Via di Valecchie to #4; tel. 075-816-767, www.assisihostel.com, info@assisihostel.com).

SWEET DREAMS IN A CONVENT

Assisi is filled with convents, most of which rent rooms to pilgrims and travelers. While you don't need to be a pilgrim or even a Christian to be welcome, it's just common sense to stay in a convent *only* if you're approaching Assisi with a contemplative mindset. Convents feel institutional, house many groups, and are not particularly cheap—but they come with all the facilities you might need to enjoy a spirit-filled visit to Assisi.

$$ St. Anthony's Guest House is where the Franciscan Sisters of the Atonement offer a very warm and tranquil welcome. Their oasis of peace is just above the Basilica of St. Clare. With only 35 beds in 19 rooms (some with great views—request when you reserve) at a reasonable price, they book up literally months in advance (Sb-€45, Db-€65, Tb-€85, family rooms available, 2-night minimum, cash only for short stays, no problem if couples want to share a bed, elevator, no air-con but fans, 23:00 curfew, closed mid-Nov-Feb, library, views, picnic garden, parking-€3 donation; from the parking cashier in Piazza Matteotti, take the stairs down to the *"tunnel romano,"* then continue down on the elevator—it's just to the left at Via Galeazzo Alessi 10; tel. 075-812-542, atoneassisi@ tiscali.it).

AGRITURISMO NEAR ASSISI

$$ Le Mandrie di San Paolo ("The Herd of St. Paul") is a meticulously restored 1,000-year-old stone house renting 13 rustic but comfortable rooms. Soulful Alex and the Damiani family are justifiably proud of their fine craftsmanship, passion for hospitality, and connection to the land. They have an olive grove, lots of animals, a beautiful swimming pool, sauna, fine restaurant, and spectacular views over Assisi and the valleys of Umbria (Db-€90; 2-bedroom apartments: Db-€105, Qb-€140, family deals, 3-night minimum in June-mid-Sept, mobile 349-821-7867, tel. 075-806-4070, www. agriturismomandriesanpaolo.it, mandrie10@gmail.com). Their restaurant is a great choice, and worth considering for nonguests who just want to get out of town—they produce their own olive oil and flour, and fire their bread ovens with their own wood (€25-30 for four-course meal, daily 19:30-22:00, in winter on request, reservations preferred). It's about a 10-minute drive from Assisi, on the hill high above the village of Viole (a.k.a. San Vitale). Just head southeast of Assisi following signs for *Viole;* when you enter town, before you reach the arch, turn left and follow signs up the hill.

Eating in Assisi

I've listed decent, central, good-value restaurants. Assisi's food is heavy and rustic. Locals brag about their sausage and love to grate truffles on pasta.

To bump up any meal, consider a glass or bottle of the favorite homegrown red wine, Sagrantino de Montefalco. Sagrantino is Umbria's answer to Brunello (although many wine lovers around here would say that it's vice versa). Before or after dinner, enjoy a drink on the main square facing the Roman temple...or hang out with the local teens with a takeaway beer under the temple's columns.

ASSISI

FINE DINING

Ristorante Medioevo is my vote for your best splurge. With heavy but spacious cellar vaults, William Ventura's restaurant is an elegant, accessible playground of gastronomy. He features traditional cuisine with a modern twist, dictated by what's in season. While his first passion is cooking, his second is music—mellow jazz and bossa nova give a twinkle to the medieval atmosphere. Dishes are well-presented; beef and game dishes are the specialties, and the wonderful Sagrantino wine is served by the glass. To better understand the Italian fascination with "a good marriage" between food and wine, readers of this book will get a small slice of strong pecorino cheese to go with any glass of Sagrantino ordered—just request it (€16 fixed-price lunch, €9-13 pastas, €12-16 *secondi,* €40 tasting menu with matching wines, Tue-Sun 12:15-15:00 & 19:00-22:45, closed Mon, in winter open weekends only; from the fountain on Piazza del Comune, hike downhill two blocks to Via Arco dei Priori 4; tel. 075-813-068).

Trattoria Pallotta is a local favorite with white tablecloths and a living-room ambience. It's run by a friendly and hardworking family—with Margarita in charge of the kitchen—and offers delicious, well-presented regional specialties, such as *piccione* (squab, a.k.a. pigeon) and *coniglio* (rabbit). And they enjoy serving split courses *(bis)* featuring the two local pastas. Reservations are smart (€10 pastas, €8-16 *secondi,* always a vegetarian menu, €18 fixed-price meal includes a simple dessert, wine, and water, better €28 fixed-price meal showcases local specialties; Wed-Mon 12:15-14:30 & 19:15-23:00, last orders at 21:30, closed Tue, a few steps off Piazza del Comune across from temple/church at Vicolo della Volta Pinta 2, tel. 075-812-649, www.pallottaassisi.it).

CASUAL EATERIES

Trattoria degli Umbri is your best bet for a meal overlooking Assisi's main square, with a few nice tables just above the fountain. They serve delightful Umbrian dishes and top-notch wines by the glass (closed Thu, Piazza del Comune 40, tel. 075-812-455).

Hostaria Terra Chiama is a modern little eight-table place run by Diego and his family, who serve traditional Umbrian dishes with seasonal specials (€8-12 plates, daily, lunch from 12:30, dinner from 19:00, Via San Rufino 16, tel. 075-819-9051).

At **Locanda del Podestà,** chef Stelvio cooks up tasty grilled Umbrian sausages, *gnocchi alla locanda,* and all manner of truffles, while Romina graciously serves happy diners who know a good value. Try the tasty *scottadito* ("scorch your fingers") lamb chops (€5-9 pastas, €7-16 *secondi,* €18 fixed-price meal includes coffee, Thu-Tue 12:00-14:45 & 19:00-21:30, closed Wed and Feb, 5-minute walk uphill along Via Cardinale Merry del Val from basilica, Via San Giacomo 6C, tel. 075-816-553).

Ristorante Metastasio, just up the street from Podestà, offers seasonal specials, a traditional menu, and Assisi's best view terrace for dining (€10-13 pastas, €10-18 *secondi,* Thu-Tue 12:00-14:30 & 19:00-21:30, closed Wed, terrace closed in bad weather, Via Metastasio 9, tel. 075-816-525).

Trattoria da Erminio has peaceful tables on a tiny square, and indoor seating under a big, medieval (but air-conditioned) brick vault. Run by Federico and his family for three generations, it specializes in local meat cooked on an open-fire grill. They have good Umbrian wines—before you order, ask Federico or Giuliana for a taste of the Petranera wine (€6-12 pastas, €8-14 grilled meats, Fri-Wed 12:00-14:30 & 19:00-21:00, closed Thu; from Piazza San Rufino, go a block up Via Porta Perlici and turn right to Via Montacavallo 19; tel. 075-812-506).

Taverna de l'Arco is one of the oldest restaurants in Assisi, but its new young owners are bringing a fresh energy to the place.

The spacious vaulted dining room, reasonably priced menu, and homemade pastas and gnocchi make it worth considering (€7-10 pastas, €8-13 *secondi,* Thu-Tue 12:00-14:30 & 19:00-22:00, closed Wed, one block from Piazza del Comune at Via San Gregorio 8, tel. 075-816-680).

PICNIC ON THE MAIN SQUARE

There are many little grocery stores *(alimentari)* near Piazza del Comune (one is a block uphill from the main square, at Via San Rufino 19), plus bakeries selling pizza by the slice.

La Bottega dei Sapori is handy for assembling a picnic of Umbrian treats: good *porchetta* sandwiches and specialty items, including truffle paste and olive oil. Sandwich chefs Sara and Katia make a nice *taglieri misti* (meat and cheese plate) for €7. It can get pricey here (especially if you eat in), so be sure you understand the cost before ordering anything (€4 sandwiches, local wines to go, daily 9:30-21:00, Piazza del Comune 34, tel. 075-812-294, Fabrizio). You can eat your sandwich at a table at the neighboring café if you order a drink there.

Pizza by the Slice: **Pizza al Taglio da Andrea,** facing the Church of San Rufino on Piazza San Rufino, has perhaps the best pizza by the slice in town. Locals also like their *torta al testo*, the Umbrian flatbread sandwich (daily, Via San Rufino 26, tel. 075-815-325).

A Countryside Farm-to-Table Dinner: **Le Mandrie di San Paolo,** in a 1,000-year-old farmhouse (described earlier), makes many of their own ingredients and serves an exquisite dinner to guests and nonguests alike (€25-30 for four-course meal, daily 19:30-22:00, in winter on request, reservations preferred, a 10-minute drive from Assisi—see "Sleeping in Assisi" for details).

Assisi Connections

The train station's ticket office is often open only Mon-Fri 12:30-20:00, closed Sat-Sun; when the office is closed, use the ticket machine (newsstand sells only regional tickets). Up in Assisi's old town, you can get train information and tickets from Agenzia Viaggi Stoppini.

From Assisi by Train to: Rome (nearly hourly, 2-3.5 hours, 5 direct, most others change in Foligno), **Florence** (8/day direct, 2-3 hours), **Orvieto** (roughly hourly, 2-3 hours, with transfer in Terontola or Orte), **Siena** (10/day, about 4 hours, most involve 2 changes; bus is faster). Italian train timetables change frequently—double-check details at www.trenitalia.com.

By Bus: Service to **Rome** is operated by the Sulga bus company (2/day, 3 hours, pay driver, departs from Piazza San Pietro, arrives at Rome's Tiburtina station, where you can connect with the regional train to Fiumicino airport, tel. 800-099-661, www. sulga.it). A bus for **Siena** (daily at 10:20, 2 hours, www.baltour.it, search on "Santa Maria degli Angeli" for timetable) departs from the stop next to the Basilica of St. Mary of the Angels, near the train station; you usually can't buy Siena tickets from the driver— buy them at Assisi's Agenzia Viaggi Stoppini. Don't take the bus to **Florence;** the train is better.

By Plane: Perugia/Assisi Airport, about 10 miles from Assisi, has daily connections to London, Brussels, Barcelona, and a few Mediterranean destinations (airport code: PEG, tel. 075-592-141, www.airport.umbria.it). Bus service between Assisi and the airport is so sporadic (just a few times a day—see www.umbriamobilita.it) that you should plan on taking a taxi (about €30).

ASSISI

ORVIETO AND CIVITA

While Tuscany is justifiably famous for its many fine hill towns, Umbria, just to the south, has some stellar offerings of its own. Assisi is a must for nature lovers and Franciscan pilgrims. But if you're after views, wine, and charming villages, you'll find Umbria's best in Orvieto and in Civita di Bagnoregio (which is technically just across the border in Lazio, the same region as Rome). About a 30-minute drive apart, these hill towns—one big, one small—perch high above scenic plains. Pleasant Orvieto is best known for its colorful-inside-and-out cathedral and its fine Orvieto Classico wine. Tiny Civita di Bagnoregio, my favorite hill town, is an improbable pinnacle of traditional Italian village culture, just accessible enough that modern tourists are keeping it going. Taken together, Orvieto and Civita make a perfect duet for experiencing what all the hill-town fuss is about.

PLANNING YOUR TIME

The town of Orvieto and the village of Civita deserve at least an overnight, although even a few hours in each is enough to sample what they have to offer. Both are also great places to slow down and relax. Stay in one and side-trip to the other (Orvieto has more restaurants and other amenities and is easier to reach, while Civita really lets you get away from it all). The two towns are connected by a 30-minute drive or a 45-minute bus ride, and Orvieto is conveniently close to Rome (about an hour away by train or expressway).

Orvieto

Just off the freeway and the main train line, Umbria's grand hill town entices those heading to and from Rome. While no secret, it's well worth a visit. The town sits majestically on its *tufo* throne a thousand feet above the valley floor. Orvieto became a regional power in the Middle Ages, and even earlier, a few centuries before Christ, it was one of a dozen major Etruscan cities. Some historians believe Orvieto may have been a religious center—a kind of Etruscan Mecca (locals are looking for archaeological proof—the town and surrounding countryside are dotted with Etruscan ruins).

Orvieto has three popular claims to fame: cathedral, Classico wine, and ceramics. Drinking a shot of the local white wine in a ceramic cup as you gaze up at the cathedral lets you experience Orvieto's three C's all at once. (Is the cathedral best in the afternoon, when the facade basks in golden light, or early in the morning, when it rises above the hilltop mist? You decide.) Though loaded with tourists by day, Orvieto is quiet by night, and a visit here comes with a wonderful bonus: close proximity to the unforgettable Civita di Bagnoregio (covered later in this chapter).

Orientation to Orvieto

Orvieto has two distinct parts: the old-town hilltop and the dreary new town below (called Orvieto Scalo). Whether coming by train or car, you first arrive in the nondescript, modern lower part of town. From there you can drive or take the funicular, elevator, or escalator up to the medieval upper town, an atmospheric labyrinth of streets and squares where all the sightseeing action is.

TOURIST INFORMATION

The TI is on the cathedral square at Piazza del Duomo 24 (Mon-Fri 8:15-13:50 & 16:00-19:00, Sat-Sun 10:00-13:00 & 15:00-18:00, tel. 0763-341-772). The ticket office next to the main TI sells combo-tickets and books reservations for Underground Orvieto Tours (tel. 0763-340-688). Depending on funding, the town may also have a branch TI at Piazza Cahen (at the top of the funicular) during summer.

Combo-Ticket: The €20 **Carta Unica** combo-ticket covers Orvieto's top sights (virtually every sight recommended here, including the underground tours) and includes one round-trip on the bus and/or funicular. To cover your funicular ride, you can buy the combo-ticket on your arrival in the lower town—either at the bar or newsstand at the train station (if they haven't run out), or at a seasonal ticket office in the parking lot (below the station, Easter-Sept daily 9:00-16:00, closed Oct-Easter, tel. 0763-302-378). The combo-ticket is also available at the ticket office next to the TI on Piazza del Duomo, as well as at most of the sights it covers.

ARRIVAL IN ORVIETO

By Train: The train station is at the foot of the hill the old town sits on. There's no baggage storage at the train station, but Hotel Picchio, 300 yards from the station at Via G. Salvatori 17, stores day-trippers' luggage for a few euros (leaving the station, go left, then right up Via G. Salvatori, tel. 0763-301-144). Check at the station for the train schedule to your next destination (schedule is also available at the TI or online at www.trenitalia.com).

The easiest way to the top of town (including the cathedral and my recommended hotels) is by **funicular:** Buy your ticket at the entrance to the *funiculare;* look for the *biglietteria* sign (€1.30, good for 1.5 hours, includes minibus from Piazza Cahen to Piazza del Duomo, Mon-Sat 7:15-20:30, Sun 8:00-20:30, about every 10 minutes). Or buy a Carta Unica combo-ticket (described earlier) to cover your funicular ride.

As you exit the funicular at the top, you're in Piazza Cahen, located at the east end of the upper town. To your left is a ruined fortress with a garden and a commanding view. To your right, down a steep path, is St. Patrick's Well. Farther to the right is a park with Etruscan ruins and another sweeping view.

Just in front of you is the small **shuttle bus** (usually white or orange), waiting to take you to Piazza del Duomo at no extra charge (included in your funicular ticket; 3-6/hour). The bus fills up fast, but the views from the ruined fortress are worth pausing for—if you miss the bus, you can wait for the next one, or just walk to the cathedral (head uphill on Corso Cavour; after about 10 minutes, take a left onto Via del Duomo). The bus drops you in Piazza del Duomo, just steps from the main TI and within easy walking distance of most of my recommended sights and hotels.

If you arrive outside the funicular's operating hours, you can reach the upper part of town by **taxi** (see later) or **bus** to Piazza della Repubblica (buses run roughly 2/hour until midnight, buy €1.30 ticket at bar inside station).

By Car: For free parking, use the huge lot below the train station (5 minutes off the autostrada; turn right immediately after the autostrada underpass and follow the *P camping* and *P funiculare* signs). Walk through the station and ride the funicular up the hill (see "By Train," above).

It's also possible to park in the old town. While little free parking is available, there are several pay options: the small lot

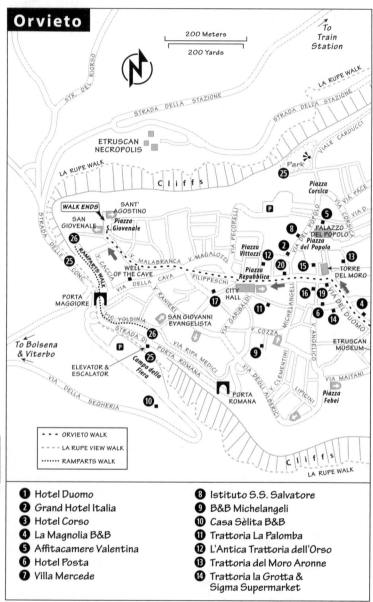

Orvieto

200 Meters
200 Yards

To Train Station

STR. DEL RIORSO

STRADA DELLA STAZIONE

LA RUPE WALK

STRADA DELLA STAZIONE

VIALE CARDUCCI

ETRUSCAN NECROPOLIS

LA RUPE WALK

Cliffs

Park

㉕

Piazza Corsica

VIA PACE

VIA D.

WALK ENDS

SANT' AGOSTINO

SAN GIOVENALE

Piazza S. Giovenale

㉖

VIA CACCIA

RAMPARTS WALK

STRADA DELLE CONC.

㉕

VIA DELLA CAVA

V. MALABRANCA

V. MAGALOTTI

WELL OF THE CAVE

FILIPPESCHI

VIA PECORELLI

Piazza Vittozzi

⑫

Piazza Repubblica

㉒

⑮

VIA CORSICA

VIA DEL POPOLO

⑧

②

PALAZZO DEL POPOLO

Piazza del Popolo

⑤

⑬

TORRE DEL MORO

PORTA MAGGIORE

V. RANIERI

VIC. VOLSINIA

SAN GIOVANNI EVANGELISTA

⑰

CITY HALL

VIA GARIBALDI

⑪

VIA MICHELANGELI

⑯ ⑲

⑥ ⑭

VIA DEL DUOMO

④

To Bolsena & Viterbo

STRADA DI PORTA ROMANA

VIA RIPA MEDICI

㉖

V. COZZA

⑨

VIA DEGLI ALBERICI

VIA S. CLEMENTINI

V. ANGELICO

ETRUSCAN MUSEUM

ELEVATOR & ESCALATOR

㉕

Campo della Fiera

㉕

⑩

PORTA ROMANA

LIPICINI

VIA MAITANI

Piazza Febei

VIA DELLA SEGHERIA

Cliffs

LA RUPE WALK

- - - ORVIETO WALK
- - - LA RUPE VIEW WALK
······ RAMPARTS WALK

❶ Hotel Duomo
❷ Grand Hotel Italia
❸ Hotel Corso
❹ La Magnolia B&B
❺ Affitacamere Valentina
❻ Hotel Posta
❼ Villa Mercede
❽ Istituto S.S. Salvatore
❾ B&B Michelangeli
❿ Casa Sèlita B&B
⓫ Trattoria La Palomba
⓬ L'Antica Trattoria dell'Orso
⓭ Trattoria del Moro Aronne
⓮ Trattoria la Grotta & Sigma Supermarket

ORVIETO & CIVITA

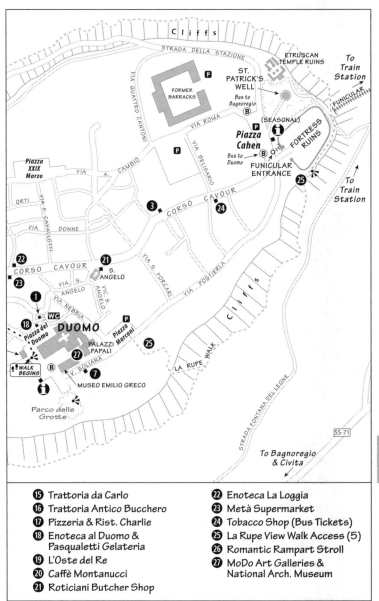

15 Trattoria da Carlo
16 Trattoria Antico Bucchero
17 Pizzeria & Rist. Charlie
18 Enoteca al Duomo & Pasqualetti Gelateria
19 L'Oste del Re
20 Caffè Montanucci
21 Roticiani Butcher Shop

22 Enoteca La Loggia
23 Metà Supermarket
24 Tobacco Shop (Bus Tickets)
25 La Rupe View Walk Access (5)
26 Romantic Rampart Stroll
27 MoDo Art Galleries & National Arch. Museum

ORVIETO & CIVITA

in Piazza Marconi, near Orvieto's cathedral (€1.50 for first hour, €1/hour thereafter); the south half (blue lines) of Piazza Cahen (€1.20/hour); northwest of Piazza Cahen at the lot on Via Roma (€1/hour), and the Campo della Fiera lot just below the west end of town (€1/hour; from top level of lot, walk up into town or take escalator—7:00-21:00—or elevator—7:00-24:00; both free). While white lines generally indicate free parking, much of it is marked for residents only. Blue lines require you to buy a "pay and display" slip from a nearby machine.

While you can drive up Via Postierla and Via Roma to get to central parking lots, Corso Cavour and other streets in the old center are closed to traffic and monitored by cameras (look for red lights, and avoid streets marked by a red circle).

By Taxi: Taxis line up in front of the train station and charge about €15 for a ride to the cathedral (a ridiculous price considering the ease and pleasure of the €1.30 funicular/shuttle-bus ride to the cathedral square; mobile 360-433-057).

HELPFUL HINTS

Market Days and Festivals: On Thursday and Saturday mornings, Piazza del Popolo becomes a busy farmers' market. The same square hosts an arts-and-crafts market some Sundays. Orvieto is also busy during the Umbria Jazz festival that takes place for a few days before New Year's (www.umbriajazz.com).

Internet Access: Many of Orvieto's cafés have Wi-Fi for their customers, including all the popular spots along the Corso.

Bookstore: Libreria dei Sette has a small selection of English-language books (daily 9:00-13:00 & 16:00-20:00, next to Torre del Moro at Corso Cavour 85, tel. 0763-344-436).

Laundry: There's a coin launderette in the lower town, a 10-minute walk from the train station. It's a bit of a haul from central hotels, and instructions are in Italian only, but it's workable if you're desperate (daily 7:00-22:00, Piazza del Comercio, off via Monte Nibbio, mobile 393-758-6120).

Car/Minibus Service: Giuliotaxi is run by charming, English-speaking Giulio and his sister, Maria Serena. They have a car (for up to 4) and a minibus (for up to 8). Giulio offers two special Civita excursions from Orvieto for Rick Steves readers: He'll drive you to and from Civita with a one-hour wait there (€90/car, €120/minibus), or for a longer trip, book a two-hour visit to Civita, then explore around Lake Bolsena for a couple more hours (5 hours total, €160/car, €200/minibus). They can take you to other destinations, as well (mobile 349-690-6547, giuliotaxi@libero.it).

Car Rental: Hertz has an office facing the funicular station, 100 yards to the left at Via Sette Martiri 32f, tel. 0763-301-303.

Local Guide: Manuela del Turco is good (€120/2.5-hour tour, mobile 333-221-9879, manueladel@virgilio.it). **David Tordi,** who also guides for me, leads walking tours of Orvieto and the Duomo (€10/1-1.5-hour tours, Fri-Sun, tel. 0763-340-688, www.orvietoviva.com).

After Dark: In the evening, there's little going on other than strolling and eating. The big *passeggiata* scene is down Via del Duomo and Corso Cavour.

Orvieto Walk

This quickie L-shaped self-guided walk takes you from the Duomo through Orvieto's historic center. Each evening, this route is the scene of the local *passeggiata*.

Facing the cathedral, head left. Stroll past the clock tower (first put here in 1347 for the workers building the cathedral), which marks the start of Via del Duomo, lined with shops selling ceramics. **Via dei Magoni** (second left) has several artisan shops and the crazy little Il Mago di Oz ("Wizard of Oz") shop, a wondrous toyland created by eccentric Giuseppe Rosella (Via dei Magoni 3, tel. 0763-342-063). Have Giuseppe push a few buttons, and you're far from Kansas (no photos allowed).

Via del Duomo continues to Orvieto's main intersection, where it meets Corso Cavour and a tall, stark tower—the **Torre**

del Moro. The tower marks the center of town, serves as a handy orientation tool, and is decorated by the coats of arms of past governors. The elevator leaves you with 173 steps still to go to earn a commanding view (€3, daily March-Oct 10:00-19:00, May-Aug until 20:00, shorter hours off-season).

This crossroads divides the town into **four quarters** (notice the *Quartiere* signs on the corners). In the past, residents of these four districts competed in a lively equestrian competition on Piazza del Popolo during the annual Corpus Christi celebration. Historically, the four streets led from here to the market and the fine palazzo on Piazza del Popolo, the well, the Duomo, and City Hall.

Before heading left down Corso Cavour, side-trip a block farther ahead, behind the tower, for a look at the striking **Palazzo del Popolo.** Built of local *tufo,* this is a textbook example of a fortified medieval public palace: a fortress designed to house the city's lead-

ORVIETO & CIVITA

ership and military, with a market at its base, fancy meeting rooms upstairs, and aristocratic living quarters on the top level.

Return to the tower and head down Corso Cavour (turning right) past classic storefronts to **Piazza della Repubblica** and City Hall. The original vision—though it never came to fruition—was for City Hall to have five arches flanking the main central arch (marked by the flags today). The Church of Sant'Andrea (left of City Hall) sits atop an Etruscan temple that was likely the birthplace of Orvieto centuries before Christ. Inside is an interesting architectural progression: Romanesque (with few frescoes surviving), Gothic (the pointy vaults over the altar), and a Renaissance barrel vault in the apse (behind the altar)—all lit by fine alabaster windows.

From City Hall, you can continue to the far end of town to the **Church of Sant'Agostino,** where you can see the statues of the apostles that once stood in the Duomo (included in the MoDo ticket). From here you can take a left and walk the cliffside ramparts (see "View Walks," later).

Sights in Orvieto

▲▲▲Duomo

Orvieto's cathedral has Italy's liveliest facade. This colorful, prickly Gothic facade, divided by four pillars, has been compared to a medieval altarpiece. The optical-illusion interior features some fine art, including Luca Signorelli's lavishly frescoed Chapel of San Brizio.

Cost and Hours: €3; April-Sept Mon-Sat 9:30-19:00, Sun 13:00-17:30 or until 18:30 July-Sept; March and Oct Mon-Sat 9:30-18:00, Sun 13:00-17:30; Nov-Feb Mon-Sat 9:30-13:00 & 14:30-17:00, Sun 14:30-17:30; sometimes closes for religious services. A €5 combo-ticket includes the Duomo, the chapel, and the Museo dell'Opera del Duomo, called the "MoDo" (available at the chapel; MoDo alone costs €4). Admission is also covered by the €20 Carta Unica combo-ticket.

❍ Self-Guided Tour

Begin by viewing the **exterior facade.** Study this gleaming mass of mosaics, stained glass, and sculpture (c. 1300, by Lorenzo Maitani and others).

At the base of the cathedral, the four broad **marble pillars** carved with biblical scenes tell the history of the world in four acts, from left to right. The relief on the far left shows the Creation (see

Italy Is Made of Tuff Stuff

Tuff (*tufo* in Italian) is a light-colored volcanic rock that is common in Italy. A part of Tuscany is even called the "Tuff Area."

The seven hills of Rome are made of tuff, and quarried blocks of this stone can be seen in the Colosseum, Pantheon, and Castel Sant'Angelo. Just outside of Rome, the catacombs were carved from tuff. Sorrento rises above the sea on a tuff outcrop. Orvieto, Civita di Bagnoregio (pictured), and many other hill towns perch on bluffs of tuff.

Italy's early inhabitants, including the Etruscans and Romans, carved caves, tunnels, burial niches, and even roads out of tuff. Blocks of this rock were quarried to make houses and walls. Tuff is soft and easy to carve when it's first exposed to air, but hardens later, which makes it a good building stone.

Italy's tuff-producing volcanoes resulted from a lot of tectonic-plate bumping and grinding. This violent geologic history is reflected in Italy's volcanoes, like Vesuvius and Etna, and earthquakes such as the 2009 quake in the L'Aquila area northeast of Rome.

Tuff is actually just a big hardened pile of old volcanic ash. When volcanoes hold magma that contains a lot of water, they erupt explosively (think heat + water = steam = POW!). The exploded rock material gets blasted out as hot volcanic ash, which settles on the surrounding landscape, piles up, and over time welds together into the rock called tuff.

So when you're visiting an area in Italy of ancient caves or catacombs built out of this material, you'll know that at least once (and maybe more) upon a time, it was a site of a lot of volcanic activity.

ORVIETO & CIVITA

God creating Eve from Adam's rib, and the snake tempting Eve). Next is the Tree of Jesse (Jesus' family tree—with Mary, then Jesus on top) flanked by Old Testament stories, then the New Testament (look for the unique manger scene, and other events from the life of Christ). On the far right is the Last Judgment (Christ judging on top, with a commotion of sarcophagi popping open and all hell breaking loose at the bottom).

Each pillar is topped by a bronze symbol of one of the Evangelists: angel (Matthew), lion (Mark), eagle (John), and ox (Luke). The bronze doors are modern, by the Sicilian sculptor Emilio Greco. (A gallery devoted to Greco's work is to the immediate

right of the church.) In the mosaic below the rose window, Mary is transported to heaven. In the uppermost mosaic, Mary is crowned.
• *Now step inside.*

The **nave** feels spacious and less cluttered than most Italian churches. Until 1877, it was much busier, with statues of the apostles at each column and fancy chapels. Then the people decided they wanted to "un-Baroque" their church. (The original statues are now on display in the Church of Sant'Agostino, at the west end of town.)

The interior is warmly lit by **alabaster windows,** highlighting the black-and-white striped stonework. Why such a big and impressive church in such a little town? First of all, it's not as big as it looks. The architect created an illusion—with the nave wider at the back and narrower at the altar, the space seems longer than it is. Still, it's a big and rich cathedral—the seat of a bishop. Its historic importance and wealth is thanks to a miracle that happened nearby in 1263. According to the story, a skeptical priest named Peter of Prague passed through Bolsena (12 miles from Orvieto) while on a pilgrimage to Rome. He had doubts that the bread used in communion could really be transformed into the body of Christ. But during Mass, as he held the host aloft and blessed it, the bread began to bleed, running down his arms and dripping onto a linen cloth (a "corporal") on the altar. That miraculously blood-stained cloth is now kept here, in the Chapel of the Corporal.
• *We'll tour the church's interior. First, find the chapel in the north transept, left of the altar.*

Chapel of the Corporal: The bloody cloth from the miracle is displayed in the turquoise frame atop the chapel's altar. It was brought from Bolsena to Orvieto, where Pope Urban IV happened to be visiting. The amazed pope proclaimed a new holiday, Corpus Christi (Body of Christ), and the Orvieto cathedral was built (begun in 1290) to display the miraculous relic. Find the fine reliquary in a glass case on the left. Until the 1970s, this silver-and-blue enamel reliquary—made in the early 1300s, and considered one of the finest medieval jewels in Italy—held the linen relic as if in a frame. Notice how it evokes the facade of this cathedral. For centuries, the precious linen was paraded through the streets of Orvieto in this ornate reliquary.

The room was frescoed in the 14th century with scenes attesting to Christ's presence in the communion wafer (for example,

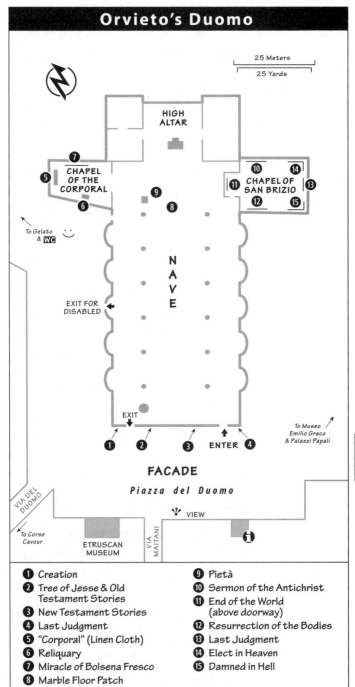

Orvieto's Duomo

25 Meters
25 Yards

HIGH ALTAR

7 CHAPEL OF THE CORPORAL
5
6

To Gelato & WC

9 Pietà
8

N A V E

EXIT FOR DISABLED

10 14
11 CHAPEL OF SAN BRIZIO 13
12 15

EXIT

1 2 3 ENTER 4

To Museo Emilio Greco & Palazzi Papali

FACADE

Piazza del Duomo

VIA DEL DUOMO

To Corso Cavour

ETRUSCAN MUSEUM

VIA MAITANI

VIEW

i

ORVIETO & CIVITA

1 Creation
2 Tree of Jesse & Old Testament Stories
3 New Testament Stories
4 Last Judgment
5 "Corporal" (Linen Cloth)
6 Reliquary
7 Miracle of Bolsena Fresco
8 Marble Floor Patch

9 Pietà
10 Sermon of the Antichrist
11 End of the World (above doorway)
12 Resurrection of the Bodies
13 Last Judgment
14 Elect in Heaven
15 Damned in Hell

the panel above the glass case to the left illustrates how the wafer bleeds if you cook it). You can see the Miracle of Bolsena depicted in the fresco on the chapel's right wall.

• *Leave the Chapel of the Corporal and walk to the middle front of the church, where you'll see a...*

Patch in the Marble Floor Before the High Altar: Stand on the patch, which is a reminder that as the Roman Catholic Church countered the Reformation, it made reforms of its own. For instance, altars were moved back so that the congregation could sit closer to the spectacular frescoes and stained glass. (These decorations were designed to impress commoners by illustrating the glory of heaven—and the Catholic Church needed that propaganda more than ever during the Counter-Reformation.) This confused patching marks where the altar stood prior to the Counter-Reformation.

Enjoy the richness that surrounds you. This cathedral put Orvieto on the map, and with lots of pilgrims came lots of wealth. Two future popes used the town—perched on its easy-to-defend hilltop—as a refuge when their enemies forced them to flee Rome. The brilliant stained glass is the painstakingly restored original, from the 14th century. The fine organ, high on the left, has more than 5,000 pipes. Look high up in the right transept at the alabaster rose window. Then turn and face down the nave, the way you came in. Note how the architect's trick—making the church look bigger from the rear—works in reverse from here. From this angle, the church appears stubbier than it actually is.

• *Still facing down the nave, look a few steps to your right; near the first pillar is a beautiful white-marble statue.*

Pietà: The marble *pietà* (statue of Mary holding Jesus' just-crucified body) was carved in 1579 by local artist Ippolito Scalza. Clearly inspired by Michelangelo's *Pietà,* this exceptional work, with four figures, was sculpted from one piece of marble. Walk around it to notice the texture that Scalza achieved, and how the light plays on the sculpture from every angle.

• *To the right of the main altar is Orvieto's one must-see artistic sight, the...*

Chapel of San Brizio: This chapel features Luca Signorelli's brilliantly lit frescoes of the Day of Judgment and Life after Death (painted 1499-1504). Step into the chapel and you're surrounded by vivid scenes crammed with figures. Although the frescoes refer to themes of resurrection and salvation, they also reflect the turbulent political and religious atmosphere of late 15th-century Italy.

ORVIETO & CIVITA

The chapel is decorated in one big and cohesive story. Start with the wall to your left as you enter, and do a quick counterclockwise spin to get oriented to the basic plot: Antichrist (a false prophet), end of the world (above the arch leading to the nave), Resurrection of the Bodies, hell, Judgment Day (Fra Angelico painted Jesus above the window), and finally heaven.

Now do a slower turn to take in the full story: In the **Sermon of the Antichrist** (left wall), a crowd gathers around a man preaching from a pedestal. It's the Antichrist, who comes posing as Jesus to mislead the faithful. This befuddled Antichrist forgets his lines mid-speech, but the Devil is on hand to whisper what to say next. His words sow wickedness through the world, including executions (upper right). The worried woman in red and white (foreground, left of pedestal) gets money from a man for something she's not proud of (perhaps receiving funds from a Jewish moneylender—notice the Stars of David on his purse).

Most likely, the Antichrist himself is a veiled reference to Savonarola (1452-1498), the charismatic Florentine monk who defied the pope, drove the Medici family from power, and riled the populace with apocalyptic sermons. Many Italians—including the painter Signorelli—viewed Savonarola as a tyrant and heretic, the Antichrist who was ushering in the Last Days.

In the upper left, notice the hardworking angel. He looks as if he's at batting practice, hitting followers of the Antichrist back to earth as they try to get through the pearly gates. In the bottom left is a self-portrait of the artist, **Luca Signorelli** (c. 1450-1523), well-dressed in black with long golden hair. Signorelli, from nearby Cortona, was at the peak of his powers, and this chapel was his masterpiece. He looks out proudly as if to say, "I did all this in just five years, on time and on budget," confirming his reputation as a speedy, businesslike painter. Next to him (also in black) is the artist Fra Angelico, who started the chapel decoration five decades earlier but completed only a small part of it.

Around the arch, opposite the windows, are signs of the **end of the world:** eclipse, tsunami, falling stars, earthquakes, violence in the streets, and a laser-wielding gray angel.

On the right wall (opposite the Antichrist) is the **Resurrection of the Bodies.** Trumpeting angels blow a wake-up call, and the dead climb dreamily out of the earth to be clothed with new bodies. On the same wall (below the action, at eye level) is a gripping *pietà*. Also by Signorelli, this *pietà* gives an insight into

ORVIETO & CIVITA

the artist's genius and personality. Look at the emotion in the faces of the two Marys and consider that Signorelli's son had just died. The Deposition scene (behind Jesus' leg) seems inspired by ancient Greek scenes of a pre-Christian hero's death. In the confident spirit of the Renaissance, the artist incorporates a pagan scene to support a Christian story. This 3-D realism in a 2-D sketch shows the work of a talented master.

The altar wall (with the windows) features the **Last Judgment.** To the left of the altar (and continuing around the corner, filling half the left wall) are the **Elect in Heaven.** They spend eternity posing like bodybuilders while listening to celestial Muzak. To the right (and continuing around the corner on the right wall) are the **Damned in Hell,** in the scariest mosh pit ever. Devils torment sinners in graphic detail, while winged demons control the airspace overhead. In the center, one lusty demon turns to tell the frightened woman on his back exactly what he's got planned for their date. (According to legend, this was Signorelli's lover, who betrayed him...and ended up here.) Signorelli's ability to tell a story through human actions and gestures, rather than symbols, inspired his younger contemporary, Michelangelo, who meticulously studied the elder artist's nudes.

In this chapel, Christian theology sits physically and figuratively upon a foundation of classical logic. Below everything are Greek and Latin philosophers, plus Dante, struggling to reconcile Classical truth with Church doctrine. You can see the intellectual challenge on their faces as they ponder this puzzle. They're immersed in fanciful Grotesque (i.e., grotto-esque) decor. Dating from 1499, this is one of the first uses of the frilly, nubile, and  even sexy "wallpaper pattern" so popular in the Renaissance. (It was inspired by the decorations found in Nero's Golden House in Rome, which had been discovered under street level just a few years earlier and was mistaken for an underground grotto.)

During the Renaissance, nakedness symbolized purity. When attitudes changed during the Counter-Reformation, the male figures in Signorelli's frescoes were given penis-covering sashes. During a 1982 restoration, most—but not all—of the sashes were removed. A little of that prudishness survives to this day, as those in heaven were left with their sashes modestly in place.

• *Our tour is finished. Leaving the church, turn left (passing a small parking lot and WC) to reach a park that affords a fine Umbrian view. Turn left twice, and you'll circle behind the church to reach the cathedral's art collections (part of MoDo, described next).*

ORVIETO & CIVITA

NEAR THE DUOMO: MODO AND OTHER MUSEUMS
▲▲MoDo City Museum (Museo dell'Opera del Duomo)

This museum is an ensemble of three different sights scattered around town: the cathedral art collection behind the cathedral; the Emilio Greco collection (next to the cathedral, in Palazzo Soliano); and, at the far end of town, the Church of Sant'Agostino, which has statues of the 12 apostles that were added to the Duomo in the Baroque Age (c. 1700) and removed in the late 1800s.

Cost and Hours: €4 MoDo ticket covers all MoDo sights (or get the €5 combo-ticket that includes the Duomo); April-Sept daily 9:30-19:00; March and Oct Wed-Mon 10:00-17:00, closed Tue; Nov-Feb Wed-Mon 10:00-13:00 & 14:00-17:00, closed Tue; Piazza Duomo, tel. 0763-343-592, www.opsm.it.

Cathedral Art Collections: Behind the Duomo, a complex of medieval palaces called Palazzi Papali shows off the city's best devotional art. It comes in two parts: the skippable collection of frescoes on the ground floor, and a delightful collection up the metal staircase. The highlight is just inside the upstairs entrance: a marble Mary and Child who sit beneath a bronze canopy, attended by exquisite angels. This proto-Renaissance ensemble, dating from around 1300, once filled the niche in the center of the cathedral's facade (where a replica sits today). In several art-filled rooms on this floor, you'll find Baroque paintings from the late 1500s that decorated the side chapels with a harsh Counter-Reformation message; a *Madonna and Child* from 1322 by the Sienese great Simone Martini, who worked in Orvieto; saintly wooden statues and fine inlaid woodwork from the original choir; a carved 14th-century Crucifixion that shows the dead Christ in gripping detail; Luca Signorelli's *Mary Magdalene* (1504); and more church art surrounded by *sinopias* (preliminary drawings for the frescoes decorating the cathedral's Chapel of the Corporal, with a roughed-up surface so the wet plaster would stick).

Museo Emilio Greco: This fresh little collection shows off the work of Emilio Greco (1913-1995), a Sicilian artist who designed the modern doors of Orvieto's cathedral. His sketches and about 30 of his bronze statues are on display here, showing his absorption with gently twisting and turning nudes. Greco's sketchy outlines of women are simply beautiful. The artful installation of his work in this palazzo, with walkways and a spiral staircase up to the ceiling, is designed to let you view his sculptures from different angles.

National Archaeological Museum of Orvieto (Museo Archeologico Nazionale di Orvieto)

This small five-room collection, immediately behind the cathedral in the ground floor of Palazzi Papali (under MoDo), beautifully shows off a trove of well-preserved Etruscan bronzes, terra-cotta objects, and ceramics—many from the necropolis at the base of Orvieto, and some with painted colors surviving from 500 B.C. To see the treasure of this museum, ask an attendant for the Golini tombs (named after the man who discovered them in 1836). She'll escort you to the reconstructed, fourth-century B.C. tombs, frescoed with scenes from an Etruscan banquet in the afterlife.

Cost and Hours: €3, daily 8:30-19:30, tel. 0763-341-039, www.archeopg.arti.beniculturali.it.

Etruscan Museum (Museo Claudio Faina e Museo Civico)

This 19th-century, Neoclassical nobleman's palace stands on the main square facing the cathedral. Its elegantly frescoed rooms hold an impressive Etruscan collection. The ground floor features the "Museo Civico," with fragments of Etruscan sculpture. On the first floor is the "Collezione Conti Faina," with Etruscan jewelry and an extensive array of Roman coins (push the brass buttons and the coins rotate so you can see both sides). The top floor features the best of the Etruscan and proto-Etruscan (from the ninth century B.C.) vases and bronzes, lots of votives found buried in nearby tombs, and fine views of the Duomo.

Cost and Hours: €4.50; April-Sept daily 9:30-18:00; Oct-March Tue-Sun 10:00-17:00, closed Mon; English descriptions throughout, tel. 0763-341-511, www.museofaina.it.

UNDERGROUND ORVIETO

▲▲St. Patrick's Well (Pozzo di San Patrizio)

Modern engineers are impressed by this deep well—175 feet deep and 45 feet wide—designed in the 16th century with a double-helix pattern. The two spiral stairways allow an efficient one-way traffic flow: intriguing now, but critical then. Imagine if donkeys and people, balancing jugs of water, had to go up and down the same stairway. At the bottom is a bridge that people could walk on to scoop up water.

The well was built because a pope got nervous. After Rome was sacked in 1527 by renegade troops of the Holy Roman Empire, the pope fled to Orvieto. He feared that even this little town (with no water source on top) would be besieged. He commissioned a well, which was started in 1527 and finished 10 years later. It was a huge project. (As it turns out, the town was never besieged, but supporters believe that the well was worth the cost and labor because of its deterrence value—attackers would think twice about besieging a town with a reliable water source.) Even today, when a local is faced with a difficult task, people say, "It's like digging St. Patrick's Well." It's a total of 496 steps up and down—lots of exercise and not much to see other than some amazing 16th-century engineering.

Cost and Hours: €5, interesting €1 audioguide, daily May-Aug 9:00-19:45, shorter hours off-season, to your right as you exit the funicular, Viale Sangallo, tel. 0763-343-768. Bring a sweater if you plan to descend to the chilly depths, and allow about 20 minutes to go down and up.

Well of the Cave (Pozzo della Cava)

While renovating its trattoria, an Orvieto family discovered a vast underground network of Etruscan-era caves, wells, and tunnels. The excavation started in 1984 and continues to this day. It's well-explained in English and makes for a fun subterranean wander.

Cost and Hours: €3, €2 with St. Patrick's Well or funicular ticket, Tue-Sun 9:00-20:00, closed Mon, Via della Cava 28, tel. 0763-342-373, www.pozzodellacava.it.

Underground Orvieto Tours (Parco delle Grotte)

Guides weave archaeological history into a good look at about 100 yards of Etruscan and medieval caves. You'll see the remains of an old olive press, an impressive 130-foot-deep Etruscan well shaft, what's left of a primitive cement quarry, and an extensive dovecote (pigeon coop) where the birds were reared for roasting (pigeon dishes are still featured on many Orvieto menus; look for—or avoid—*piccione*).

Cost and Hours: €6; 45-minute English tours depart at 11:15, 12:30, 16:15, and 17:30; more often with demand, book tour and depart from ticket office at Piazza Duomo 23 (next to main TI); confirm times at TI or by calling 0763-340-688, www.orvietounderground.it.

Etruscan Necropolis
(Necropoli Etrusca di Crocifisso del Tufo)

Below town, at the base of the cliff, is a remarkable "city of the dead" that dates back to the sixth to third century B.C. The tombs, which are laid out in a kind of street grid, are empty, and there's precious little to see here other than the basic stony construction. But it is both eerie and fascinating to wander the streets of an Etruscan cemetery.

Cost and Hours: €3, daily 10:15-15:45; drivers will find it on the ring road below town, hikers can reach it via the Rupe path (see next); tel. 0763-343-611, www.archeopg.arti.beniculturali.it.

View Walks

▲Hike Around the City on the Rupe

Orvieto's Rupe is a peaceful paved path that completely circles the town at the base of the cliff upon which it sits. With the help of the

TI's *Anello delle Rupe* map, you'll see there are five access points from the town for the three-mile walk (allow about two hours round-trip). Once on the trail, it's fairly level and easy to follow. On one side you have the cliff, with the town high above. On the other side you have Umbrian views stretching into the distance. I'd leave Orvieto at Piazza Marconi and walk left (counterclockwise) three-quarters of the way around the town (there's a fine view down onto the Etruscan Necropolis midway), and ride the escalator and elevator back up to the town from the big Campo della Fiera parking lot. If you're ever confused about the path, follow the *la Rupe* signs.

▲Shorter Romantic Rampart Stroll

Thanks to its dramatic hilltop setting, several fine little walks wind around the edges of Orvieto. My favorite after dark, when it's lamp-lit and romantic, is along the ramparts at the far west end of town. Start at the Church of Sant'Agostino. With your back to the church, go a block to the right to the end of town. Then head left along the ramparts, with cypress-dotted Umbria to your right, and follow Vicolo Volsinia to the Church of San Giovanni Evangelista, where you can reenter the old town center near several recommended restaurants.

Near Orvieto

Wine Tasting

Orvieto Classico wine is justly famous. Two inviting wineries sit just outside Orvieto on the scenic Canale route to Bagnoregio; if you're side-tripping to Civita, it's easy to stop at either or both for a tasting (but call ahead for a reservation).

For a short tour of a winery with Etruscan cellars, make an appointment to visit **Tenuta Le Velette,** where English-speaking Corrado and Cecilia (cheh-CHEEL-yah) Bottai will welcome you (€8-24 for tour and tasting, price varies depending on wines, number of people, and if food is requested, Mon-Fri 8:30-12:00 & 14:00-17:00, Sat 8:30-12:00, closed Sun, also has accommodations, tel. 0763-29090, mobile 348-300-2002, www.levelette.it). From their sign (5-minute drive past Orvieto at top of switchbacks just before Canale, on road to Bagnoregio), cruise down a long tree-lined drive, then park at the striped gate (must call ahead; no drop-ins).

Custodi is another respected family-run winery that produces Orvieto Classico, grappa, and olive oil on their 140-acre estate. Helpful Chiara and Laura Custodi speak English. Reserve ahead for a tour of their cantina, an explanation of the winemaking process, and a tasting of four of their wines. An assortment of *salumi* and local cheeses to go with your wine-tasting is possible on request (€7/person for wines only, €16/person with light lunch, daily 8:30-12:30 & 15:30-18:30 except closed Sun afternoons, Viale Venere S.N.C. Loc. Canale; on the road from Orvieto to Civita, a half-mile after Le Velette, it's the first building before Canale; tel. 0763-29053, mobile 392-161-9334, www.cantinacustodi.com).

Sleeping in Orvieto

The prices I've listed are for high season—roughly May to early July and in September and October, as well as during the Umbria Jazz festival in the days before New Year's.

IN THE TOWN CENTER

$$$ Hotel Duomo is centrally located and modern, with splashy art and 17 rooms. Double-paned windows keep the sound of the church bells well-muffled (Sb-€80, Db-€120, Db suite-€140, Tb-€150, extra bed-€10, 10 percent discount with this book in 2016 if you pay cash and book direct, air-con, elevator, private parking-€10/day, sunny terrace, a block from the Duomo at Vicolo di Maurizio 7, tel. 0763-341-887, www.orvietohotelduomo.com, info@orvietohotelduomo.com, Gianni and Maura Massaccesi don't speak English, daughter Elisa does). The Massaccesi family also owns a three-room B&B 50 yards from the hotel (Sb-€70, Db-€90, Tb-€110, breakfast at the main hotel).

$$$ Grand Hotel Italia feels businesslike, bringing predictable modern amenities to this small town. The 46 rooms are well-located in the heart of Orvieto (Sb-€80, Db-€120, Db with terrace-€140, extra bed-€20, air-con, elevator, stay-awhile lobby and terrace, parking-€10/day—reserve ahead, Via di Piazza del Popolo 13, tel. 0763-342-065, www.grandhotelitalia.it, hotelita@libero.it).

$$ Hotel Corso is friendly, with 18 frilly and flowery rooms—a few with balconies and views. Their sunlit little terrace is enjoyable, but the location—halfway between the center of town and the

Sleep Code

Abbreviations   (€1=about $1.10, country code: 39)
S=Single, **D**=Double/Twin, **T**=Triple, **Q**=Quad, **b**=bathroom
Price Rankings
  $$$ Higher Priced—Most rooms €100 or more
   $$ Moderately Priced—Most rooms €70-100
    $ Lower Priced—Most rooms €70 or less
Unless otherwise noted, credit cards are accepted, English is spoken, free Wi-Fi and/or a guest computer is generally available, and breakfast is included (but usually optional). Many towns in Italy levy a hotel tax of €1.50-5 per person, per night (often collected in cash; usually not included in the rates I've quoted). Prices change without notice; verify current rates online or by email. For the best prices, always book directly with the hotel.

funicular—feels less convenient than others (Sb-€65, Db-€95, Tb-€120, 10 percent discount for my readers if you book directly with hotel, buffet breakfast-€6.50, ask for quieter room off street, air-con, elevator, reserved parking-€8/day, up from funicular toward Duomo at Corso Cavour 343, tel. 0763-342-020, www.hotelcorso.net, info@hotelcorso.net, Carla).

$ La Magnolia B&B has lots of fancy terra-cotta tiles, a couple of rooms with frescoed ceilings, terraces, and other welcoming touches. Its seven unique rooms, some like mini apartments with kitchens, are cheerfully decorated and on the town's main drag. The three units facing the busy street are air-conditioned and have good double-paned windows (Db-€68, plush Db apartment-€78, extra person-€15, family deals; book directly with hotel, pay cash, and stay at least 2 nights to get a 10 percent Rick Steves discount; no elevator, use of washer-€3.50; Via Duomo 29, tel. 0763-342-808, mobile 349-462-0733, www.bblamagnolia.it, info@bblamagnolia.it, Serena and Loredana).

$ Affittacamere Valentina rents six clean, airy, well-appointed rooms, all with big beds and antique furniture. Her place is located in the heart of Orvieto, behind the palace on Piazza del Popolo (Db-€58/€65, Tb-€75/€85, studio with kitchen-€80/€90, lower rates are cash only and good with this book for stays of 2 or more nights; breakfast at nearby cafe-€5, air-con-€5, parking-€10/day, Via Vivaria 7, tel. 0763-341-607, mobile 393-970-5868, www.bandbvalentina.com, valentina.z@tiscalinet.it). Valentina also rents three rooms across the square (D-€58, shared bath and kitchen, no air-con) and three offsite apartments (€170/night with 3-night minimum).

$ Hotel Posta is a centrally located, long-ago-elegant palazzo renting 20 quirky and clean rooms with vintage furniture. The rooms without private bath are among the cheapest in town (S-€31, Sb-€37, D-€44, Db-€57, T-€60, Tb-€75, breakfast-€6, elevator, Via Luca Signorelli 18, tel. 0763-341-909, www.orvietohotels.it, hotelposta@orvietohotels.it, Alessia).

$ Villa Mercede, a good value, is owned by a religious institution and offers 23 cheap, simple, mostly twin-bedded rooms, each with a big modern bathroom and many with glorious Umbrian views (Sb-€50, Db-€70, Tb-€90, elevator, free parking, a half-block from Duomo at Via Soliana 2, reception upstairs, tel. 0763-341-766, www.villamercede.it, info@villamercede.it).

$ Istituto S.S. Salvatore rents nine spotless twin rooms and five singles in their convent, which comes with a peaceful terrace and garden, great views, and a 22:30 curfew. Though the nuns don't speak English, tech-savvy Sister Maria Stella has mastered Google Translate, and will happily use it to answer your questions (Sb-€40, Db-€60, €5 less/person Oct-March, cash only, no breakfast, elevator, Wi-Fi in common areas only, free parking, just off Piazza del Popolo at Via del Popolo 1, tel. 0763-342-910, www.istitutosansalvatore.it, istitutosansalvatore@tiscali.it).

$ B&B Michelangeli offers two comfortable and well-appointed apartments hiding along a residential lane a few blocks from the tourist scene. It's run by eager-to-please Francesca, who speaks limited English but provides homey touches and free tea, coffee, and breakfast supplies. This is a good choice for families (Db-€70, kids-€10 extra, fully equipped kitchen, washing machine, private parking-€5/day, Via dei Saracinelli 20—ring bell labeled *M. Michelangeli*, tel. 0763-393-862, mobile 347-089-0349, www.bbmichelangeli.com).

Just Outside the Town Center: **$$ Casa Sèlita B&B,** a peaceful country house, offers easy access to Orvieto (best for drivers, but workable for adventurous train travelers). It's nestled in an orchard just below the town cliffs; to get to town, you'll climb an uphill path through their olive orchard (with a view terrace along the way) to reach the big Campo della Fiera parking lot, with its handy escalator taking you the rest of the way up into Orvieto. Its five rooms with terraces are airy and fresh, with dark hardwood floors, fluffy down comforters, and modern baths. Enjoy the views from the relaxing garden. Conscientious Sèlita, her husband Ennio, and daughter Elena are gracious hosts (Sb-€55, Db-€80, Tb-€90, €5 less with stays of two or more nights, €5 more off-season for heat, air-con-€5, these prices promised to my readers through 2016 if you book directly with hotel, cash preferred, free parking, Strada di Porta Romana 8, don't use GPS—sends you to the wrong location, mobile 339-225-4000 or 328-611-2052, tel. 0763-344-218, www. casaselita.com, info@casaselita.com).

ORVIETO & CIVITA

NEAR ORVIETO

All of these (except the last one) are within a 20-minute drive of Orvieto, in different directions, and require a car.

$$$ Alta Rocca Wine Resort, run by Emiliano and Sabrina, is a fancy spa-type "country resort," located 15 minutes north of Orvieto by car. They produce their own olive oil and wine and have 17 rooms and 10 apartments—all with air-conditioning (Db-€90-160, pool, panoramic view restaurant, wellness center with Jacuzzi and steam room, gym, mountain bikes, bocce court, hiking paths, tel. 0763-344-210 or 0763-393-437, www.altaroccawineresort.com, info@altaroccawineresort.com).

At **$$$ Agriturismo Locanda Rosati** you'll be greeted by friendly hosts Giampiero Rosati and niece Cristiana, who rent 10 tastefully decorated rooms in a pleasant, homey atmosphere (Db-€110-140, Tb-€140-160, full traditional dinners for €35 on request with this book, air-con, swimming pool, 5 miles from Orvieto on the road to Viterbo, tel. 0763-217-314, www.locandarosati.it, info@locandarosati.it).

$$$ Agriturismo Poggio della Volara, located between Todi and Orvieto (12 miles from either), has seven apartments (sleeping from two to five people) and five rooms in two buildings overlooking a swimming pool. Along with keeping rabbits, geese, dogs, and ducks, Marco produces wine and olive oil and offers dinner on request (Db-€110, smaller apartment-€120, larger apartment-€170, room rates include breakfast but costs €8 extra in apartments, dinner-€30-35, air-con, mobile 347-335-2523, www.poggiodellavolara.it, info@poggiodellavolara.it).

$$ Borgo Fontanile is a vacation home with a swimming pool, terrace, and kids' play area. Its five new apartments with rustic wood beams and terra-cotta tile floors sleep up to four people each (Db-€60-90, discounts for longer stays, €400-800/apartment per week, air-con-€8, Vocabolo Fornace 159, Loc. Baschi, tel. 0744-957-452, www.borgofontanile.com, info@borgofontanile.com).

$$ Tenuta le Velette is a sprawling, family-run farmhouse. Cecilia and Corrado Bottai rent six fully furnished apartments and villas scattered over their family's expansive and scenic grounds. Rooms range wildly in size—accommodating from 2 to 14 people—but they all nestle in perfect Umbrian rural peace and tranquility (Db apartment-€80-110, see website or email for details on various villas—not all are listed online, 2-night minimum, 10 percent discount for weekly stay, pool, bocce court, 10 minutes from Orvieto—drive toward Bagnoregio-Canale and follow *Tenuta le Velette* signs, tel. 0763-29090, mobile 348-300-2002, www.levelette.it, cecilialevelette@libero.it). They also offer wine tastings.

$$ **Agriturismo Cioccoleta** ("Little Stone") has eight rooms with cozy country decor, each named after one of the grapes grown in the *agriturismo*'s vineyards. It's family-run and offers sweeping views of Orvieto and the pastoral countryside (Db-€85, Tb-€105, Qb-€115, 10 percent discount with this book—mention when you reserve, fans, 3 miles north of Orvieto at Località Bardano 34 in Bardano, tel. 0763-316-011, mobile 349-860-9780, www.cioccoleta.it, info@cioccoleta.it, Angela Zucconi).

Farther Out, Northwest of Todi: $$$ **Agriturismo Fattoria di Vibio** produces olive oil and honey, sells organic products, and offers classes and spa services. In August, its 14 rooms rent at peak prices (and for one week during the month they require a minimum seven-night stay, with arrivals and departures on Saturdays). The rest of the year, no minimum stay is required, although rates drop dramatically for longer visits. Its three cottages sleep from four to six people and rent only by the week (Db-€120-200, cottages-€1,260-2,100/week depending on amenities, see complicated rate table on website, farthest cottage is 20 miles northeast of Orvieto, tel. 075-874-9607, www.fattoriadivibio.com, info@fattoriadivibio.com).

Eating in Orvieto

TRATTORIAS IN THE CENTER

Trattoria La Palomba features game and truffle specialties in a wood-paneled dining room. Giampiero, Enrica, and the Cinti family enthusiastically take care of their regulars and visiting travelers, offering both a fine value and a classy conviviality. Truffles are shaved right at your table—try the *ombricelli al tartufo* (homemade pasta with truffles) or *spaghetti dell'Ascaro* (with truffles), then perhaps follow that with *piccione* (pigeon). As firm believers in the slow-food movement, they use ingredients that are mostly organic and locally sourced (€10 pastas, €9-15 *secondi*, Thu-Tue 12:30-14:15 & 19:30-22:00, closed Wed and July, reservations smart, just off Piazza della Repubblica at Via Cipriano Manente 16, tel. 0763-343-395).

L'Antica Trattoria dell'Orso offers well-prepared Umbrian cuisine paired with fine wines in a homey, bohemian-chic, peaceful atmosphere. Ciro and chef Gabriele enjoy getting to know their diners, and will steer you toward the freshest seasonal plates of their famous pastas and passionately prepared vegetables. Gabriele—who loves to put together a "trust your chef" multicourse tasting *menu*—offers an amazing value for my readers: €30 for two people, including their fine house wine and water—my vote for the best dining value in town (€10-12 pastas, €12-16 *secondi*, Wed-Sat 12:00-14:00 & 19:30-22:00, Sun 12:00-14:00, closed Mon-Tue and Feb, just off Piazza della Repubblica at Via della Misericordia 18, tel. 0763-341-642).

Trattoria del Moro Aronne is a long-established family bistro run by Cristian and his mother Rolanda, who lovingly prepare homemade pasta and market-fresh meats and produce for their typical Umbrian specialties. Be sure to sample the *nidi*—folds of fresh pasta enveloping warm, gooey pecorino cheese sweetened with honey. The crème brûlée is a winner for dessert. Three small and separate dining areas make the interior feel intimate. It's touristy and not particularly atmospheric, but this place is known locally as an excellent value (€8-10 pastas, €10-14 *secondi,* Wed-Mon 12:30-14:30 & 19:30-22:00, closed Tue, Via San Leonardo 7, tel. 0763-342-763).

Trattoria la Grotta prides itself on serving only the freshest food and finest wine. The decor is Signorelli-mod, and the ambience is quiet, with courteous service. Owner-chef Franco has been at it for 50 years, and promises diners a free coffee, grappa, *limoncello,* or *vin santo* with this book (€8 pastas, €14-18 *secondi,* Wed-Mon opens at 12:00 for lunch and at 19:00 for dinner, closed Tue, Via Luca Signorelli 5, tel. 0763-341-348).

Trattoria da Carlo, hiding on its own little *piazzetta* between Via Corso Cavour and Piazza del Popolo, is a cozy spot with a charming interior and inviting tables outside. Animated and opinionated Carlo—a likeable loudmouth—holds court, chatting up his diners as much as he cooks, while his mama scuttles about taking orders, bussing dishes, and lovingly rolling her eyes at her son's big personality. They put an unpretentious modern twist on traditional dishes such as pasta with *guanciale* (pork cheeks—like bacon), fennel seeds, and pecorino cheese (€9 pastas, €12-16 *secondi,* daily 12:00-15:00 & 19:00-24:00, Vicolo del Popolo 1, tel. 0763-343-916).

Trattoria Antico Bucchero, elegant under a big white vault, makes for a nice memory with its candlelit ambience and delicious food (€8 pastas, €12 *secondi,* daily 12:00-15:00 & 19:00-23:00 except closed Wed Nov-March, seating indoors and on a peaceful square in summer, air-con, a half-block south of Corso Cavour, between Torre del Moro and Piazza della Repubblica at Via de Cartari 4, tel. 0763-341-725; Piero and Silvana, plus sons Fabio and Pericle).

Pizzeria & Ristorante Charlie is a local favorite. Its noisy dining hall and stony courtyard are popular with families and students for casual dinners of wood-fired €6-8 pizzas, big salads, homemade €7-9 pastas, or €12-15 *secondi.* In a quiet courtyard guarded by a medieval tower, it's centrally located a block southwest of Piazza della Repubblica (Wed-Mon 19:00-12:30 & 14:30-23:00 except no midday closure in summer, closed Tue year-round, Via Loggia dei Mercanti 14, tel. 0763-344-766).

Enoteca al Duomo, to the left of the Duomo with pleasant outdoor seating, is run by Roman transplants Emilano and Ilaria. They serve rustic *panini* (€7 to eat in, €5 to go), wines by the glass, and a full menu of local dishes in a wine-bar atmosphere (€10 pastas and meal-size salads, €10-15 *secondi,* daily 10:00-24:00, closed Feb, Piazza del Duomo 13, tel. 0763-344-607).

FAST AND CHEAP EATS

L'Oste del Re is a simple trattoria on Corso Cavour, with hearty sandwiches and focaccia to go. They serve a two-course lunch-of-the-day (a pasta and a *secondo*) for about €15, and €7.50 focaccia in the evenings (no cover, daily 11:00-15:30 & 19:00-22:00 but closed weekday evenings Nov-April, Corso Cavour 58, tel. 0763-343-846).

For lunch each day, **Caffè Montanucci,** along the main street, lays out an appetizing display of pastas (€7) and main courses (€10) behind the counter. Choose one (or mix—called a *bis*), find a seat in the modern interior, and they'll bring it out on a tray. You'll eat among newspaper-reading locals on lunch break. They also serve dinner with regular table service, as well as good *caffè,* simple sandwiches, and tasty sweets all day (no cover, daily 7:00-24:00, Corso Cavour 21, tel. 0763-341-261).

Panini and a Picnic: Scattered around town you'll find many *alimentari* (grocers) selling cured meats, cheese, and other staples. If you're feeling adventurous, order prosciutto or salami made from *cinghiale* (cheen-gee-AH-lay; wild boar), a surprisingly mild-tasting local favorite. They're usually willing to make you a simple sandwich of bread, cold cuts, and/or cheese for a few euros.

Sample high-quality cold cuts or *porchetta* (roast pork with herbs) on a basic *panino* for around €3 at **Roticiani,** a third-generation butcher shop, where Paolo and his sister Fausta cure meats according to their grandfather's recipes (Mon-Sat 8:00-13:00 & 17:00-20:00, closed Wed afternoon and all day Sun, on Corso Cavour halfway between Via Duomo and the funicular at Piazza S. Angelo 1, tel. 0763-341-776).

Closer to the Via Duomo, **Enoteca La Loggia** has a nice selection of quality wine and spirits (Mon-Fri 9:00-13:00 & 14:30-20:00, Sat 10:00-13:00 & 16:30-20:00, closed Sun, ask them for plastic cups and to uncork your bottle, Corso Cavour 129, tel. 0763-341-657).

Elsewhere along the Corso Cavour, you'll find places selling fruit, vegetables, and other picnic items. The fortress/garden, to the right as you face the funicular, is a great spot to enjoy it.

Groceries: While the small *alimentari* might have what you need for a picnic, two slightly larger markets are tucked away two minutes from the Duomo: **Metà** (Mon-Sat 8:30-20:00, Sun 8:30-13:00, Corso Cavour 100, opposite Piazza Cesare Fracassini) and **Sigma** (Mon-Sat 8:00-20:00, Sun 9:00-13:00, just past recommended Trattoria la Grotta at Via Luca Signorelli 23).

Gelato: For dessert, try the deservedly popular *gelateria* **Pasqualetti** (daily 12:00-21:00, open later June-Aug, closed Dec-Feb, next to left transept of church, Piazza del Duomo 14; another branch is at Via Duomo 10, open daily 11:00-23:00, closes at 20:00 in winter).

CORSO CAVOUR CAFÉ SCENE

Orvieto has a charming, traffic-free, pedestrian-friendly vibe. To enjoy it, be sure to spend a little time savoring *la dolce far niente* while sitting at a café. There are inviting places all over town. The first three listed below are along Corso Cavour, the main strolling drag, and offer the very best people-watching.

Caffè ClanDestino is the town hot spot, with a youthful energy. It's well-located, with plenty of streetside seating and endless little bites served with your drink (Corso Cavour 40). **Café Barrique** is less crowded, less trendy, and quieter, with nice outdoor tables and good free snacks with your drink (Corso Cavour 111). **Caffè Montanucci,** where locals go to read their newspaper, is the town's venerable place for a coffee and pastry, but it has no on-street seating (Corso Cavour 21, described earlier). **Bar Palace,** on Piazza del Popolo, is a sunny, relaxed perch facing a big square that's generally quiet (except on market day), with free Wi-Fi and quality coffee and pastries.

Cafés Facing the Cathedral: Several cafés on Piazza del Duomo invite you to linger over a drink with a view of Orvieto's amazing cathedral.

Orvieto Connections

From Orvieto by Train to: Rome (roughly hourly, 1-1.5 hours), **Florence** (hourly, 2 hours, use Firenze S.M.N. train station), **Siena** (12/day, 2.5 hours, change in Chiusi, all Florence-bound trains stop in Chiusi), **Assisi** (roughly hourly, 2-3 hours, 1 or 2 transfers), **Milan** (2/day direct, 5.5 hours; otherwise about hourly with a transfer in Florence, Bologna, or Rome, 4.5-5 hours). The train station's Buffet della Stazione is surprisingly good if you need a quick focaccia sandwich or pizza picnic for the train ride.

Tip for Drivers: If you're thinking of driving to Rome, consider stashing your car in Orvieto instead. You can easily park the car, safe and free, in the big lot below the Orvieto train station (for up to a week or more), and zip effortlessly into Rome by train (1-1.5 hours).

Civita di Bagnoregio

Perched on a pinnacle in a grand canyon, the 2,500-year-old, traffic-free village of Civita di Bagnoregio is Italy's ultimate hill town. In the last decade, the old, self-sufficient Civita (chee-VEE-tah) has died—the last of its lifelong residents have passed on, and the only work here is in serving visitors. But relatives and newcomers are moving in and revitalizing the village, and it remains an amazing place to visit. (It's even become popular as a backdrop for movies, soap operas, and advertising campaigns.) Civita's only connection to the world and the town of Bagnoregio is a long pedestrian bridge.

Civita's history goes back to Etruscan and ancient Roman times. In the early Middle Ages, Bagnoregio was a suburb of Civita, which had a population of about 4,000. Later, Bagnoregio surpassed Civita in size—especially following a 1695 earthquake, after which many residents fled Civita to live in Bagnoregio, fearing their houses would be shaken off the edge into the valley below. You'll notice Bagnoregio is dominated by Renaissance-style buildings while, architecturally, Civita remains stuck in the Middle Ages.

While Bagnoregio lacks the pinnacle-town romance of Civita, it's actually a healthy, vibrant community (unlike Civita, the suburb now nicknamed "the dead city"). In Bagnoregio, get a haircut, sip a coffee on the square, and walk down to the old laundry (ask, *"Dov'è la lavanderia vecchia?"*).

GETTING TO CIVITA DI BAGNOREGIO

To reach Civita, you'll first head for the adjacent town of Bagnoregio. From there, it's a 30-minute walk or 5-minute drive to the base of Civita's pedestrian bridge. Then you'll have a fairly steep 10-minute walk up to the town's main square.

By Bus from Orvieto to Bagnoregio: The trip from Orvieto to Bagnoregio takes about 45 minutes (€2.20 one-way if bought in advance at a bar or tobacco shop, €7 one-way if purchased from driver—this includes a fine for not buying your ticket in advance).

Here are likely departure times (but confirm at the TI) from Orvieto's Piazza Cahen on the blue Cotral bus, Monday to Saturday only (no buses on Sundays or holidays): 6:20, *7:25, 7:50, 12:45, 13:55, *14:00, 15:45, 17:40, and 18:20. Departures marked with an asterisk (*) run only during the school year (roughly Sept-June). It's

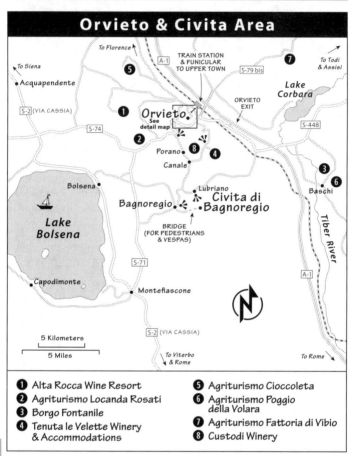

Orvieto & Civita Area

To Florence
To Siena
Acquapendente
TRAIN STATION & FUNICULAR TO UPPER TOWN
5
S-79 bis
7
To Todi & Assisi
Lake Corbara
S-2 (VIA CASSIA)
ORVIETO EXIT
1 Orvieto
See detail map
S-74
2
S-448
Porano **8** **4**
Canale
3
6
Bolsena
Lubriano
Bagnoregio Civita di Bagnoregio
Baschi
Lake Bolsena
BRIDGE (FOR PEDESTRIANS & VESPAS)
S-71
Tiber River
A-1
Capodimonte
Montefiascone
N
5 Kilometers
5 Miles
S-2 (VIA CASSIA)
To Viterbo & Rome
To Rome

1 Alta Rocca Wine Resort
2 Agriturismo Locanda Rosati
3 Borgo Fontanile
4 Tenuta le Velette Winery & Accommodations
5 Agriturismo Cioccoleta
6 Agriturismo Poggio della Volara
7 Agriturismo Fattoria di Vibio
8 Custodi Winery

nice to get up early, take the 7:50 bus, and see Civita in the cool morning calm. If you take the 12:45 bus, you can make the last (17:25) bus back, but your time in Civita may feel a little rushed.

Buy your ticket from Silvia at the tobacco shop at Corso Cavour 306, a block up from the funicular (daily 8:00-13:00 & 16:00-20:00)—otherwise you'll pay the premium ticket price on board the bus. If you'll be returning to Orvieto by bus, it's simpler to get a return ticket now rather than in Bagnoregio.

Officially, the bus stop is at Piazza Cahen's far left end (as you face the funicular, it's across the street from the bus section of the parking lot. The schedule is posted at the stop—look for the *A.co.tra.l. Capolinea* sign. The bus you want says *Bagnoregio* in the window and will stop in the bus spaces in the parking lot (yellow lines). You'll see lots of buses marked *Umbria Mobilità* stopping in front of the funicular; but because Civita is in Lazio, it's served by a different bus company (Cotral).

Buses departing Piazza Cahen stop five minutes later at Orvieto's train station—to catch the bus there, wait to the left of the funicular station (as you're facing it); schedule and tickets are available in the tobacco shop/bar in the train station. For more information, call 06-7205-7205 or 800-174-471 (press 7 for English), or see www.cotralspa.it (click "Orari," then fill in "Orvieto" and "Bagnoregio" in the trip planner—Italian only).

For information on buses returning to Orvieto see "Bagnoregio Connections," later.

Getting from Bagnoregio Bus Stop to Civita: Walking is the simplest way to get from the Bagnoregio bus stop in Piazzale Battaglini to the base of Civita's pedestrian bridge (20-30 minutes, slightly uphill at first, but downhill overall). The walk through Bagnoregio also offers a delightful look at a workaday Italian town. Take the road going uphill, Via Garibaldi (over-

looking the big parking lot). Once on the road, take the first right, and then an immediate left, to cut over onto the main drag, Via Roma. Follow this straight out to the belvedere for a superb viewpoint. From there, backtrack a few steps (staircase at end of viewpoint is a dead end) and take the stairs down to the road leading to the bridge.

A **shuttle bus** runs to the Civita bridge from a stop just 20 yards from the bus stop in Piazzale Battaglini. However, the shuttle departs from Piazzale Battaglini only from July through March. From April through June, you can board the shuttle only at another stop, which is halfway along the walking route to Civita (Piazza Sant'Agostino). Locals say this is to make visitors more likely to shop along the main street in Bagnoregio. Skip the shuttle bus unless it's pouring rain, but take it on the uphill return; it will drop you at the Orvieto-bound bus stop. Note the return times on the schedule posted by the bridge or ask at the recommended Trattoria Antico Forno in Civita (usually 1-2/hour, 5 minutes, 7:30-18:15 but no buses 13:15-15:30 or on Sun Oct-March, €0.70 one-way, €1 round-trip, pay driver).

By Taxi or Shared Taxi from Orvieto to Civita: If you can share the cost, a 30-minute taxi ride from Orvieto to Civita is a good deal. Giulio taxi service can take groups by car (€90) or mini-bus (€120) from Orvieto to Civita's pedestrian bridge, wait an hour, and then bring you back to Orvieto.

ORVIETO & CIVITA

By Car from Orvieto to Bagnoregio and Civita: Driving from Orvieto to Civita takes about 30 minutes. Orvieto overlooks the autostrada (and has its own exit). From the Orvieto exit, the shortest way to Civita is to turn left (below Orvieto), and then simply follow the signs to *Lubriano* and *Bagnoregio*.

A more winding and scenic route takes about 10-15 minutes longer: From the Orvieto exit on the autostrada, go right (toward *Orvieto*), then at the first big roundabout, follow signs to *Bolsena* (passing under hill-capping Orvieto on your right). Take the first left (direction: Bagnoregio), winding up past great Orvieto views and the recommended Tenuta Le Velette and Custodi wineries (reservations required) en route to Canale, and through farms and fields of giant shredded wheat to Bagnoregio.

Whichever route you take, just before Bagnoregio, follow the signs left to *Lubriano*, head into that village, turn right as you enter town, and pull into the first little square by the yellow church (on the left) for a breathtaking view of Civita. You'll find an even better view farther inside the town, from the tiny square at the next church (San Giovanni Battista). Then return to the Bagnoregio road.

Drive through the town of Bagnoregio (following yellow *civita* signs) and park in the lot at the base of the steep pedestrian bridge. If the parking lot by the bridge is full, you can park at the belvedere overlook (above the lot) and take the stairs down to the bridge. Pay for parking at the ticket machine under the bridge entrance (€2/first hour, €1/each additional hour, maximum €6/day, free 20:00-8:00, public WC at parking lot). Warning: The time limit on your parking ticket is strictly enforced.

Orientation to Civita

Civita charges an **admission fee** of €1.50 to enter the old town (waived for overnight guests). The revenue helps with its extensive maintenance expenses. Buy your ticket from the brown kiosk, just before the bridge, on the left. On summer weekends, tours may be offered from here—ask.

HELPFUL HINTS

Market Day: A lively market fills the Bagnoregio bus-station parking lot each Monday.

Baggage Storage: While there's no official baggage-check service in Bagnoregio, I've arranged with Mauro Laurenti, who runs the **Bar/Enoteca/Caffè Gianfu** and **Cinema Alberto Sordi**, to let you leave your bags there for a small fee (Thu-Tue 6:00-13:00 & 13:30-24:00, closed Wed, tel. 0761-792-580). As you get off the bus, go back 50 yards or so in the direction that the Orvieto bus just came from, and go right around corner.

Food near Bagnoregio Bus Stop: Across the street from Mauro's bar/cinema and baggage storage is **L'Arte del Pane,** with fresh pizza by the slice (Via Matteotti 5). Thirty yards down the road, Mauro runs a small eatery, **Il Ripi&Go** (Via Giacomo Matteotti 35). On the other side of the old-town gate (Porta Albana), in the roundabout, is a small grocery store.

Orvieto Bus Tickets: To save money on bus fare to Orvieto, buy a ticket before boarding from the newsstand across from the gas station near the Bagnoregio bus stop—look for white awning at #47 (€2.20 one-way in advance; €7 from driver).

Civita Walk

Civita was once connected to Bagnoregio, before the saddle between the separate towns eroded away. Photographs around town show the old donkey path, the original bridge. It was bombed in World War II and replaced in 1966 with the new footbridge that you're climbing today.

• *Entering the town, you'll pass through Porta Santa Maria, a 12th-century Romanesque arch. This stone passageway was cut by the Etruscans 2,500 years ago, when this town was a stop on an ancient trading route. Inside the archway, you enter a garden of stones. Stand in the little square—the town's antechamber—facing the Bar La Piazzetta. To your right are the remains of a...*

Renaissance Palace

The wooden door and windows (above the door) lead only to thin air. They were part of the facade of one of five palaces that once

graced Civita. Much of the palace fell into the valley, riding a chunk of the ever-eroding rock pinnacle. Today, the door leads to a remaining section of the palace—complete with Civita's first hot tub. It was once owned by the "Marchesa," a countess who married into Italy's biggest industrialist family.

• *A few steps uphill, farther into town (on your left, beyond the Bottega souvenir store), notice the two shed-like buildings.*

Old WC and Laundry

In the nearer building (covered with ivy), you'll see the town's old laundry, which dates from just after World War II, when water was

ORVIETO & CIVITA

Civita di Bagnoregio

Note: Map not to scale; a walk across Civita takes approx. 5 minutes—but don't rush it!

To Lubriano Town

Cliffs

Cliffs

OSTERIA AL FORNO DI AGNESE

ANTICO FORNO TRATTORIA & CIVITA B&B

CAMPANILE (BELL TOWER)

LOCANDA DELLA BUONA VENTURA

ANTICO FRANTOIO OLIVE PRESS & BRUSCHETTERIA

WC

Piazza

CHURCH

OLD LAUNDRY

ETRUSCAN COLUMNS

ALMA CIVITA

ARCH

MAIN   STRADA

ANTICA CIVITA MUSEUM

FOOTBRIDGE

To Bagnoregio

SNACK BAR

TRATTORIA LA CANTINA DE ARIANNA

WINE BAR DA PEPPONE & GEOLOGICAL MUSEUM

CAVES & CHAPEL CARVED IN ROCK

PALACE (PRIVATE)

Cliffs

RUINS OF HOUSE OF ST. BONAVENTURE

Trail to Etruscan tunnel under Civita

finally piped into the town. Until a few years ago, this was a lively village gossip center. Now, locals park their mopeds here. Just behind that is another stone shed, which houses a poorly marked and less-than-pristine WC.

• *The main square is just a few steps farther along, but we'll take the scenic circular route to get there, detouring around to the right. Belly up to the...*

ORVIETO & CIVITA

Canyon Viewpoint

Lean over the banister and listen to the sounds of the birds and the bees. Survey old family farms, noticing how evenly they're spaced. Historically, each one owned just enough land to stay in business. Turn left along the belvedere and walk a few steps to the site of the long-gone home of Civita's one famous son, St. Bonaventure, known as the "second founder of the Franciscans" (look for the small plaque on the wall).

• *From here, a lane leads past delightful old homes and gardens, and then to...*

Civita's Main Square

The town church faces Civita's main piazza. Grab a stone seat along the biggest building fronting the square (or a drink at Peppone's bar) and observe the scene. They say that in a big city you can see a lot, but in a small

town like this you can feel a lot. The generous bench is built into the long side of the square, reminding me of how, when I first discovered Civita back in the 1970s and 1980s, the town's old folks would gather here every night. The piazza has been integral to Italian culture since ancient Roman times. While Civita is humble today, imagine the town's former wealth, when mansions of the leading families faced this square, along with the former city hall (opposite the church, to your left). The town's history includes a devastating earthquake in 1695. Notice how stone walls were reinforced with thick bases, and how old stones and marble slabs were recycled and built into walls.

Here in the town square, you'll find Bar Da Peppone (open daily, local wines and microbrews, inviting fire in the winter) and two restaurants. There are wild donkey races on the first Sunday of June and the second Sunday of September. At Christmastime, a living Nativity scene is enacted in this square, and if you're visiting at the end of July or beginning of August, you might catch a play here. The pillars that stand like giants' bar stools are ancient Etruscan. The church, with its *campanile* (bell tower), marks the spot where an Etruscan temple, and then a Roman temple, once stood. Across from Peppone's, on the side of the former city hall, is a small, square stone counter. Old-timers remember when this was a meat shop, and how one day a week the counter was stacked with fish for sale.

The humble **Geological Museum,** next to Peppone's, tells the story of how erosion is constantly shaping the surrounding "Bad Lands" valley, how landslides have shaped (and continue to threaten) Civita, and how the town plans to stabilize things (€3, June-Sept Tue-Sun 9:30-13:30 & 14:00-18:30, closed Mon, Fri-Sun only off-season, closed Jan-Feb, mobile 328-665-7205).
• *Now step inside...*

Civita's Church

A cathedral until 1699, the church houses records of about 60 bishops that date back to the seventh century (church open daily 10:00-13:00 & 15:00-17:00, often closed Feb). Inside you'll see Romanesque columns and arches with faint Renaissance frescoes peeking through Baroque-era whitewash. The central altar is built upon the relics of the Roman martyr St. Victoria, who once was the patron saint of the town. St. Marlonbrando served as a bishop here in the ninth century; an altar dedicated to him is on the right. The fine crucifix over this altar, carved out of pear wood in the 15th century, is from the school of Donatello. It's remarkably expressive and greatly venerated by locals. Jesus' gaze is almost haunting. Some say his appearance changes based on what angle you view him from: looking alive from the front, in agony from the left, and dead from the right. Regardless, his eyes follow you from side to side. On Good Friday, this crucifix goes out and is the focus of the midnight procession.

On the left side, midway up the nave above an altar, is an intimate fresco of the *Madonna of the Earthquake,* given this name because—in the great shake of 1695—the whitewash fell off and revealed this tender fresco of Mary and her child. (During the Baroque era, a white-and-bright interior was in vogue, and churches such as these—which were covered with precious and historic frescoes—were simply whitewashed over. Look around to see examples.) On the same wall—just toward the front from the *Madonna*—find the faded portrait of Santa Apollonia, the patron saint of your teeth; notice the scary-looking pincers.

• *From the square, you can follow...*

The Main Street

A short walk takes you from the church to the end of the town. Along the way, you'll pass a couple of little eateries (described later, under "Eating in Civita"), olive presses, gardens, a rustic town museum, and valley views. The rock below Civita is honeycombed with ancient tunnels, caverns (housing olive presses), cellars (for keeping wine at a constant temperature all year), and cisterns (for collecting rainwater, since there was no well in town). Many date from Etruscan times.

Wherever you choose to eat (or just grab a bruschetta snack), be sure to take advantage of the opportunity to poke around—every place has a historic cellar. At the trendy **Alma Civita,** notice the

damaged house facing the main street—broken since the 1695 earthquake and scarred to this day. Just beyond, the rustic **Antico Frantoio Bruschetteria** serves bruschetta in an amazing old space. Whether or not you buy food, venture into their back room to see an interesting collection of old olive presses (if you're not eating here, a €1 donation is requested). The huge olive press in the entry is about 1,500 years old. Until the 1960s, blindfolded donkeys trudged in the circle here, crushing olives and creating paste that filled the circular filters and was put into a second press. Notice the 2,500-year-old sarcophagus niche. The hole in the floor (with the glass top) was a garbage hole. In ancient times, residents would toss their jewels down when under attack; excavations uncovered a windfall of treasures.

In front is the well head of an ancient cistern—designed to

collect rainwater from neighboring rooftops—carved out of *tufo* and covered with clay to be waterproof.

• *Across the street and down a tiny lane, find...*

Antica Civita

This is the closest thing the town has to a history museum. The humble collection is the brainchild of Felice, the old farmer who's hung black-and-white photos, farm tools, olive presses, and local artifacts in a series of old caves. Climb down to the "warm blood machine" (another donkey-powered grinding wheel) and a viewpoint. You'll see rooms where a mill worker lived until the 1930s. Felice wants to give visitors a feeling for life in Civita when its traditional economy was strong (€1, daily 10:00-19:00, until 17:00 in winter, some English explanations).

• *Another few steps along the main street take you to...*

The End of Civita

Here the road is literally cut out of the stone, with a dramatic view of the Bad Lands opening up. Pop in to the cute "Garden of Poets" (immediately on the left just outside town, with the tiny local crafts shop) to savor the view. Then, look back up at the end of town and ponder the precarious future of Civita. There's a certain stillness here, far from the modern world and high above the valley.

Continue along the path a few steps toward the valley below the town, and you come to some shallow caves used as stables until a few years ago. The third cave, cut deeper into the rock, with a barred door, is the **Chapel of the Incarcerated** (Cappella del Carcere). In Etruscan times, the chapel—with a painted tile depicting the Madonna and child—may have been a tomb, and in medieval times, it was used as a jail (which collapsed in 1695).

Although it's closed to the public now, an Etruscan tunnel just beyond the Chapel of the Incarcerated cuts completely through the hill. Tall enough for a woman with a jug on her head to pass through, it may have served as a shortcut to the river below. It was widened in the 1930s so that farmers could get between their scattered fields more easily. Later, it served as a refuge for frightened villagers who huddled here during WWII bombing raids.

• *Hike back into town. Make a point to take some time to explore the peaceful back lanes before returning to the modern world.*

Sleeping in Civita or Bagnoregio

Civita has nine B&B rooms up for grabs. Bagnoregio has larger lodgings, and there are plenty of *agriturismi* nearby; otherwise, there's always Orvieto. Off-season, when Civita and Bagnoregio are deadly quiet—and cold—I'd side-trip in from Orvieto rather

ORVIETO & CIVITA

than spend the night here. Those staying overnight in Civita don't pay the admission charge and may be able to get a discount on parking at the base of the bridge—ask when you reserve.

IN CIVITA

$$$ Alma Civita is a classic old stone house that was recently renovated by a sister-and-brother team, Alessandra and Maurizio (hence the name: Al-Ma). These are Civita's two most comfortable, modern, and warmly run rooms (Db-€140, Wi-Fi in their restaurant downstairs—listed later, tel. 0761-792-415, mobile 347-449-8892, www.almacivita.com, prenotazione@almacivita.com).

$$$ Locanda della Buona Ventura rents four overpriced rooms with tiny bathrooms, up narrow stairs, decorated in medieval rustic-chic, and overlooking Civita's piazza. You're not likely to see the owner—the La Cisterna Etrusca shop across the square functions as the reception (Db-€120, or €100 in Oct-May, extra bed-€20, skimpy breakfast at nearby restaurant, no Wi-Fi, tel. 0761-792-025, mobile 347-627-5628, www.locandabuonaventura. it, info@locandabuonaventura.it).

$$ Civita B&B, run by gregarious Franco Sala, has three little rooms above Trattoria Antico Forno, each overlooking Civita's main square. Two are doubles with private bath. The third is a triple (with one double and one kid-size bed), which has its own bathroom across the hall (D-€80, Db-€85, T-€100, continental breakfast, Piazza del Duomo Vecchio, tel. 076-176-0016, mobile 347-611-5426, www.civitadibagnoregio.it, fsala@pelagus.it). Franco also rents two apartments, one in Civita and one in Bagnoregio.

IN BAGNOREGIO

$$ Romantica Pucci B&B is a haven for city-weary travelers. Its five spacious rooms are indeed romantic, with canopied beds and flowing veils (Db-€80, extra bed-€25, air-con, free parking, Piazza Cavour 1, tel. 0761-792-121, www.hotelromanticapucci.it, hotelromanticapucci@gmail.com). It's just above the public parking lot you see when you arrive in Bagnoregio: From the bus stop, take Via Garibaldi uphill above the parking lot, and then turn right, before the *Forno* sign onto Via Roma. The B&B is just to the left.

$ Hotel Divino Amore has 23 bright, modern rooms, four with perfect views of a miniature Civita. These view rooms, and the ones with air-conditioning, do not cost extra—but are booked first (Sb-€50, Db-€70, Tb-€80, Qb-€90, air-con in seven rooms, closed Jan-March, Via Fidanza 25-27, tel. 076-178-0882, mobile 329-344-8950, www.hoteldivinoamore.com, info@hoteldivinoamore. com, Silvia). From the bus stop, passing the *Forno* sign where the street becomes Via Fidanza, follow Via Garibaldi uphill above the parking lot for 200 yards.

Eating in Civita or Bagnoregio

IN CIVITA

Osteria Al Forno di Agnese is a delightful spot where Manuela and her friends serve visitors simple yet delicious meals on a covered patio just off Civita's main square or in a little dining room when the weather isn't fine (nice €7 salads, €9 pastas—including gluten-free options, €7-12 *secondi,* good selection of local wines, opens daily at 12:00 for lunch, June-Sept also at 19:00 for dinner, closed Tue in winter and sometimes in bad weather, tel. 0761-792-571, mobile 340-1259-721).

Trattoria Antico Forno serves up rustic dishes, homemade pasta, and salads at affordable prices. Try their homemade pasta with truffles (€7 pastas, €7-12 *secondi,* €15 fixed-price meal, daily for lunch 12:30-15:30 and dinner 19:00-22:00, on main square, also rents rooms—see Civita B&B listing earlier, tel. 076-176-0016, Franco, daughter Elisabetta, and assistants Nina and Fiorella).

Trattoria La Cantina de Arianna is a family affair, with a busy open fire specializing in grilled meat and wonderful bruschetta. It's run by Arianna, her sister Antonella, and their parents, Rossana and Antonio. After eating, wander down to their cellar, where you'll see traditional winemaking gear and provisions for rolling huge kegs up the stairs. Tap on the kegs in the bottom level to see which are full (€10 pastas, €8-14 *secondi,* daily 11:00-16:30, tel. 0761-793-270).

Alma Civita feels like a fresh, new take on old Civita. It's owned by two of its longtime residents: Alessandra (an architect) and her brother Maurizio (who runs the restaurant). Choose from one of three seating areas: outside on a stony lane, in the modern and trendy-feeling main-floor dining room, or in the equally modern but atmospheric cellar. Even deeper is an old Etruscan tomb that's now a wine cellar (€4 *bruschette* and *antipasti,* €7 pastas, €7-10 *secondi,* May-Oct lunch Wed-Mon 12:00-16:00, dinner Fri-Sat only 19:00-21:30, closed Tue; Nov-April Fri-Sun only for lunch, tel. 0761-792-415).

Antico Frantoio Bruschetteria, the last place in town, is a rustic, super-atmospheric spot for a bite to eat. The specialty here: delicious bruschetta toasted over hot coals. Peruse the menu, choose your toppings (chopped tomato is super), and get a glass of wine for a fun, affordable snack or meal (roughly 10:00-18:00 in summer, off-season weekends only 10:00-17:00, mobile 328-689-9375, Fabrizio).

ORVIETO & CIVITA

AT THE FOOT OF THE BRIDGE

Hostaria del Ponte is a more serious restaurant than anything in Civita itself. It offers creative and traditional cuisine with a great view terrace at the parking lot at the base of the bridge to Civita. Big space heaters make it comfortable to enjoy the wonderful view as you dine from their rooftop terrace, even in spring and fall (€9 pastas, €12-13 *secondi*, reservations often essential, Tue-Sun 12:30-14:30 & 19:30-21:30, closed Mon, Nov-April also closed Sun eve, tel. 076-179-3565, www.hostariadelponte.it, Lorena).

IN BAGNOREGIO

The recommended **Romantica Pucci B&B** offers a small restaurant with tables in its private garden (€25-30 meals, closed Mon, see contact details earlier).

Bagnoregio Connections

From Bagnoregio to Orvieto: Public Cotral buses (45 minutes, €2.20 one-way if purchased in advance, €7 one-way from driver) connect Bagnoregio to Orvieto. Departures from Bagnoregio—Monday to Saturday only (no buses on Sunday or holidays)—are likely to be at the following times (but confirm): 5:30, *6:35, 6:50, 9:55, 10:25, 13:00, *13:35, 14:40, and 17:25. Departures marked with an asterisk (*) operate only during the school year (roughly Sept-June). For more information, call 06-7205-7205 or 800-174-471 (press 7 for English), or see www.cotralspa.it (click "Orari," then fill in "Bagnoregio" and "Orvieto" in the trip planner—Italian only).

Remember to save money by buying your ticket in Bagnoregio before boarding the bus—purchase one from the newsstand near the bus stop, across from the gas station. Better yet, if you're side-tripping from Orvieto, buy two tickets in Orvieto so you already have one when you're ready to come back.

From Bagnoregio to Points South: Cotral buses also run to **Viterbo,** which has a good train connection to Rome (buses go weekdays at 5:10, 6:30, 7:15, 7:40, 10:00, 13:00, 13:45, and 14:50; less frequent Sat-Sun, 35 minutes, see phone number and website earlier).

PRACTICALITIES

This section covers just the basics on traveling in Italy (for much more information, see Rick Steves Italy). You'll find free advice on specific topics at www.ricksteves.com/tips.

MONEY

Italy uses the euro currency: 1 euro (€) = about $1.10. To convert prices in euros to dollars, add about 10 percent: €20 = about $22, €50 = about $55. (Check www.oanda.com for the latest exchange rates.)

The standard way for travelers to get euros is to withdraw money from ATMs (which locals call a *bancomat*) using a debit or credit card, ideally with a Visa or MasterCard logo. Before departing, call your bank or credit-card company: Confirm that your card(s) will work overseas, ask about international transaction fees, and alert them that you'll be making withdrawals in Europe. Also ask for the PIN number for your credit card in case it'll help you use Europe's "chip-and-PIN" payment machines (see below); allow time for your bank to mail your PIN to you. To keep your valuables safe while traveling, wear a money belt.

Dealing with "Chip and PIN": Much of Europe (including Italy) is adopting a "chip-and-PIN" system for credit cards, and some merchants rely on it exclusively. European chip-and-PIN cards are embedded with an electronic chip, in addition to the magnetic stripe used on our American-style cards. This means that your credit (and debit) card might not work at payment machines, such as those at train and subway stations, toll roads, parking garages, luggage lockers, and gas pumps. Major US banks are beginning to offer credit cards with chips, but many of these are chip-and-signature cards, for which your signature (not your PIN) verifies your identity. In Europe, these cards should work for live transactions and at most payment machines, but probably won't work for offline transactions such as at unattended gas pumps. If a payment machine won't take your card, look for a machine that takes cash or see if there's a cashier nearby who can manually process your transaction. Often the easiest solution is to pay for your purchases with cash you've withdrawn from an ATM using your debit card (Europe's ATMs still accept magnetic-stripe cards).

Dynamic Currency Conversion: If merchants or hoteliers offer to convert your purchase price into dollars (called dynamic currency conversion, or DCC), refuse this "service." You'll pay more in fees for the expensive convenience of seeing your charge in dollars. If an ATM offers to "lock in" or "guarantee" your conversion rate, choose "proceed without conversion." Other prompts might state, "You can be charged in dollars: Press YES for dollars, NO for euros." Always choose the local currency.

STAYING CONNECTED

Smart travelers call ahead or go online to double-check tourist information, learn the latest on sights (special events, tour schedules, and so on), book tickets and tours, make reservations, reconfirm hotels, and research transportation connections.

To call Italy from the US or Canada: Dial 011-39 and then the local number. (The 011 is our international access code, and 39 is Italy's country code.)

To call Italy from a European country: Dial 00-39 followed by the local number. (The 00 is Europe's international access code.)

To call within Italy: Just dial the local number.

To call from Italy to another country: Dial 00 followed by the country code (for example, 1 for the US or Canada), then the area code and number. If you're calling European countries whose phone numbers begin with 0, you'll usually omit that 0 when you dial.

Tips: Traveling with a mobile phone—whether an American one that works in Italy, or a European one you buy when you arrive—is handy, but can be pricey. Consider getting an international plan; most providers offer a global calling plan that cuts the per-minute cost of phone calls and texts, and a flat-fee data plan.

Use Wi-Fi whenever possible. Most hotels and many cafés offer free Wi-Fi, and you'll likely also find it at tourist information offices, major museums, and public-transit hubs. With Wi-Fi you can use your smartphone to make free or inexpensive domestic and international calls by taking advantage of a calling app such as Skype, FaceTime, or Google+ Hangouts. When you can't find Wi-Fi, you can use your cellular network to connect to the Internet, text, or make voice calls. When you're done, avoid further charges by manually switching off "data roaming" or "cellular data."

It's possible to stay connected without a mobile phone. To make cheap international calls from any phone (even your hotel-room

From:	rick@ricksteves.com
Sent:	Today
To:	info@hotelcentral.com
Subject:	Reservation request for 19-22 July

Dear Hotel Central,

I would like to reserve a double room for 2 people for 3 nights, arriving 19 July and departing 22 July. If possible, I would like a quiet room with a bathroom inside the room.

Please let me know if you have a room available and the price.

Thank you!
Rick Steves

phone), you can buy an international phone card in Italy. These work with a scratch-to-reveal PIN code, allow you to call home to the US for pennies a minute, and also work for domestic calls. Calling from your hotel-room phone without using an international phone card is usually expensive. Though they are disappearing in Italy, you can still find public pay phones in post offices and train stations. For more on phoning, see www.ricksteves.com/phoning.

MAKING HOTEL RESERVATIONS

I recommend reserving rooms in advance, particularly during peak season. For the best rates, book directly with the hotel using their official website (not a booking agency's site). If there's no secure reservation form, or for complicated requests, send an email with the following information: number and type of rooms; number of nights; arrival date; departure date; and any special requests. (For a sample email, see the sidebar.) Use the European style for writing dates: day/month/year. Hoteliers typically ask for your credit-card number as a deposit.

Some hotels are willing to deal to attract guests—try emailing several to ask their best price. In general, hotel prices can soften if you do any of the following: offer to pay cash, stay at least three nights, or travel off-season. You can also try asking for a cheaper room or a discount.

While most taxes are included in the price, a variable city tax of €1.50-5/person per night is often added to hotel bills in Italy (and is not included in the prices in this book). Some hoteliers will ask to collect the city tax in cash to make their bookkeeping and accounting simpler.

EATING

Italy offers a wide array of eateries. A *ristorante* is a formal restaurant, while a *trattoria* or *osteria* is usually more traditional and simpler (but can still be pricey). Italian "bars" are not taverns, but small cafés selling sandwiches, coffee, and other drinks. An *enoteca* is a wine bar with snacks and light meals. Take-away food from pizza shops and delis (*rosticcería*) makes an easy picnic.

Italians eat dinner a bit later than we do; better restaurants start serving around 19:00. A full meal consists of an appetizer (antipasto), a first course (*primo piatto,* pasta, rice, or soup), and a second course (*secondo piatto,* expensive meat and fish/seafood dishes). Vegetables *(verdure)* may come with the *secondo*, but more often must be ordered separately as a side dish (*contorno*). Desserts (*dolci*) can be very tempting. The euros can add up in a hurry, but you don't have to order each course. My approach is to mix anti-pasti and *primi piatti* family-style with my dinner partners (skipping *secondi*). Or, for a basic value, look for a *menù del giorno*, a three- or four-course, fixed-price meal deal (avoid the cheapest ones, often called a *menù turistico*).

Good service is relaxed (slow to an American). You won't get the bill until you ask for it: *"Il conto?"* Most restaurants include a service charge in their prices (check the menu for *servizio incluso*— generally around 10 percent). You can add on a tip, if you choose, by including a euro or two for each person in your party. If you order at a counter rather than from waitstaff, there's no need to tip. Many (but not all) restaurants in Italy add a cover charge *(coperto)* of €1-3.50 per person to your bill.

At bars and cafés, getting a drink while standing at the bar (*banco)* is cheaper than drinking it at a table *(tavolo)* or sitting outside *(terrazza)*. This tiered pricing system is clearly posted on the wall. Sometimes you'll pay at a cash register, then take the receipt to another counter to claim your drink.

TRANSPORTATION

By Train: In Italy, most travelers find it's cheapest simply to buy train tickets as they go. To see if a railpass could save you money, check www.ricksteves.com/rail. To research train schedules, visit Germany's excellent all-Europe website, www.bahn.com, or Italy's www.trenitalia.com. A private company called Italo also runs fast trains on major routes in Italy; see www.italotreno.it.

You can buy tickets at train stations (at the ticket window or at machines with English instructions) or from travel agencies. Before boarding the train, you must validate your train documents by stamping them in the machine near the platform (usually marked *convalida biglietti* or *vidimazione*). Strikes *(sciopero)* are common and generally announced in advance (but a few sporadic trains still run—ask around).

By Car: It's cheaper to arrange most car rentals from the US. For tips on your insurance options, see www.ricksteves.com/

cdw, and for route planning, consult www.viamichelin.com. Theft insurance is mandatory in Italy ($15-20/day). In Italy, most car-rental companies' rates automatically include Collision Damage Waiver (CDW) coverage. Even if you try to decline CDW when you reserve your Italian car, you may find when you show up at the counter that you must buy it after all.

Bring your driver's license. You're also technically required to have an International Driving Permit (sold at your local AAA office for $15 plus the cost of two passport-type photos; see www.aaa.com).

Italy's superhighway *(autostrada)* system is slick and speedy, but you'll pay a toll. Be warned that car traffic is restricted in many city centers—don't drive or park in any area that has a sign reading *Zona Traffico Limitato* (*ZTL*, often shown above a red circle)...or you might be mailed a ticket later.

Italians love to tailgate; otherwise, local road etiquette is similar to that in the US. Ask your car-rental company for details, or check the US State Department website (www.travel.state.gov, click on "International Travel," then specify your country of choice and click "Traffic Safety and Road Conditions").

A car is a worthless headache in cities—park it safely (get tips from your hotelier). As break-ins are common, be sure all of your valuables are out of sight and locked in the trunk, or even better, with you or in your hotel room.

HELPFUL HINTS

Emergency Help: For English-speaking **police** help, dial 113. To summon an **ambulance**, call 118. For passport problems, call the **US Embassy** (in Rome, 24-hour line—tel. 06-46741) or **US Consulates** (Milan—tel. 02-290-351, Florence—tel. 055-266-951, Naples—tel. 081-583-8111); or the **Canadian Embassy** (in Rome, tel. 06-854-442-911). If you have a minor illness, do as the locals do and go to a pharmacist for advice. Or ask at your hotel for help—they'll know of the nearest medical and emergency services. For other concerns, get advice from your hotelier.

Theft or Loss: Italy has particularly hardworking pickpockets—wear a money belt. Assume beggars are pickpockets and any scuffle is simply a distraction by a team of thieves. If you stop for any commotion or show, put your hands in your pockets before someone else does.

To replace a passport, you'll need to go in person to an embassy or consulate (see above). Cancel and replace your credit and debit cards by calling these 24-hour US numbers collect: Visa—tel. 303/967-1096, MasterCard—tel. 636/722-7111, American Express—tel. 336/393-1111. In Italy, to make a collect call to the US, dial 800-172-444; press zero or stay on the line for an operator.

File a police report either on the spot or within a day or two; you'll need it to submit an insurance claim for lost or stolen railpasses or electronics, and it can help with replacing your passport or credit and debit cards. Precautionary measures can minimize the effects of loss—back up your digital photos and other files frequently. For more information, see www.ricksteves.com/help.

Time: Italy uses the 24-hour clock. It's the same through 12:00 noon, then keep going: 13:00, 14:00, and so on. Italy, like most of continental Europe, is six/nine hours ahead of the East/West Coasts of the US.

Business Hours: Many businesses have now adopted the government's recommended 8:00 to 14:00 workday (although in tourist areas, shops are open longer). Still, expect small towns and villages to be more or less shut tight during the midafternoon. Stores are also usually closed on Sunday, and often on Monday.

Sights: Opening and closing hours of sights can change unexpectedly; confirm the latest times with the local tourist information office or its website. Some major churches enforce a modest dress code (no bare shoulders or shorts) for everyone, even children.

Holidays and Festivals: Italy celebrates many holidays, which can close sights and attract crowds (book hotel rooms ahead). For information on holidays and festivals, check Italy's website: www.italia.it. For a simple list showing major—though not all—events, see www.ricksteves.com/festivals.

Numbers and Stumblers: What Americans call the second floor of a building is the first floor in Europe. Europeans write dates as day/month/year, so Christmas 2016 is 25/12/16. Commas are decimal points and vice versa—a dollar and a half is 1,50, and there are 5.280 feet in a mile. Italy uses the metric system: A kilogram is 2.2 pounds; a liter is about a quart; and a kilometer is six-tenths of a mile.

RESOURCES FROM RICK STEVES

This Snapshot guide is excerpted from my latest edition of *Rick Steves Italy*, which is one of more than 30 titles in my series of guidebooks on European travel. I also produce a public television series, *Rick Steves' Europe*, and a public radio show, *Travel with Rick Steves*. My website, www.ricksteves.com, offers free travel information, a forum for travelers' comments, guidebook updates, my travel blog, an online travel store, and information on European railpasses and our tours of Europe. If you're bringing a mobile device on your trip, you can download my free Rick Steves Audio Europe app, featuring podcasts of my radio shows, audio tours of major sights in Europe, and travel interviews about Italy. You can get Rick Steves Audio Europe via Apple's App Store, Google

Play, or the Amazon Appstore. For more information, see www.
ricksteves.com/audioeurope. You can also follow me on Facebook
and Twitter.

ADDITIONAL RESOURCES
Tourist Information: www.italia.it
Passports and Red Tape: www.travel.state.gov
Packing List: www.ricksteves.com/packing
Travel Insurance: www.ricksteves.com/insurance
Cheap Flights: www.kayak.com
Airplane Carry-on Restrictions: www.tsa.gov
Updates for This Book: www.ricksteves.com/update

How Was Your Trip?
If you'd like to share your tips, concerns, and discoveries after
using this book, please fill out the survey at www.ricksteves.com/
feedback. Thanks in advance—it helps a lot.

Italian Survival Phrases

English	Italian	Pronunciation
Good day.	*Buon giorno.*	bwohn **jor**-noh
Do you speak English?	*Parla inglese?*	**par**-lah een-**glay**-zay
Yes. / No.	*Sì. / No.*	see / noh
I (don't) understand.	*(Non) capisco.*	(nohn) kah-**pees**-koh
Please.	*Per favore.*	pehr fah-**voh**-ray
Thank you.	*Grazie.*	**graht**-seeay
You're welcome.	*Prego.*	**pray**-go
I'm sorry.	*Mi dispiace.*	mee dee-speeah-chay
Excuse me.	*Mi scusi.*	mee **skoo**-zee
(No) problem.	*(Non) c'è un problema.*	(nohn) cheh oon proh-**blay**-mah
Good.	*Va bene.*	vah **behn**-ay
Goodbye.	*Arrivederci.*	ah-ree-vay-**dehr**-chee
one / two	*uno / due*	**oo**-noh / **doo**-ay
three / four	*tre / quattro*	tray / **kwah**-troh
five / six	*cinque / sei*	**cheeng**-kway / **seh**ee
seven / eight	*sette / otto*	**seht**-tay / **ot**-toh
nine / ten	*nove / dieci*	**nov**-ay / dee**eay**-chee
How much is it?	*Quanto costa?*	**kwahn**-toh **kos**-tah
Write it?	*Me lo scrive?*	may loh **skree**-vay
Is it free?	*È gratis?*	eh **grah**-tees
Is it included?	*È incluso?*	eh een-**kloo**-zoh
Where can I buy / find...?	*Dove posso comprare / trovare...?*	**doh**-vay **pos**-soh kohm-**prah**-ray / troh-**vah**-ray
I'd like / We'd like...	*Vorrei / Vorremmo...*	vor-**reh**ee / vor-**ray**-moh
...a room.	*...una camera.*	**oo**-nah **kah**-meh-rah
...a ticket to ____.	*...un biglietto per ____.*	oon beel-**yeht**-toh pehr
Is it possible?	*È possibile?*	eh poh-**see**-bee-lay
Where is...?	*Dov'è...?*	**doh**-veh
...the train station	*...la stazione*	lah staht-see**oh**-nay
...the bus station	*...la stazione degli autobus*	lah staht-see**oh**-nay **dayl**-yee **ow**-toh-boos
...tourist information	*...informazioni per turisti*	een-for-maht-see**oh**-nee pehr too-**ree**-stee
...the toilet	*...la toilette*	lah twah-**leht**-tay
men	*uomini, signori*	**woh**-mee-nee, seen-**yoh**-ree
women	*donne, signore*	**don**-nay, seen-**yoh**-ray
left / right	*sinistra / destra*	see-**nee**-strah / **dehs**-trah
straight	*sempre diritto*	**sehm**-pray dee-**ree**-toh
When do you open / close?	*A che ora aprite / chiudete?*	ah kay **oh**-rah ah-**pree**-tay / keeoo-**day**-tay
At what time?	*A che ora?*	ah kay **oh**-rah
Just a moment.	*Un momento.*	oon moh-**mayn**-toh
now / soon / later	*adesso / presto / tardi*	ah-**dehs**-soh / **prehs**-toh / **tar**-dee
today / tomorrow	*oggi / domani*	**oh**-jee / doh-**mah**-nee

PRACTICALITIES

In an Italian-speaking Restaurant

English	Italian	Pronunciation
I'd like...	Vorrei...	vor-**rehee**
We'd like...	Vorremmo...	vor-**ray**-moh
...to reserve...	...prenotare...	pray-noh-**tah**-ray
...a table for one / two.	...un tavolo per uno / due.	oon **tah**-voh-loh pehr **oo**-noh / **doo**-ay
Non-smoking.	Non fumare.	nohn foo-**mah**-ray
Is this seat free?	È libero questo posto?	eh **lee**-bay-roh **kwehs**-toh **poh**-stoh
The menu (in English), please.	Il menù (in inglese), per favore.	eel may-**noo** (een een-**glay**-zay) pehr fah-**voh**-ray
service (not) included	servizio (non) incluso	sehr-**veet**-seeoh (nohn) een-**kloo**-zoh
cover charge	pane e coperto	**pah**-nay ay koh-**pehr**-toh
to go	da portar via	dah **por**-tar **vee**-ah
with / without	con / senza	kohn / **sehn**-sah
and / or	e / o	ay / oh
menu (of the day)	menù (del giorno)	may-**noo** (dayl **jor**-noh)
specialty of the house	specialità della casa	spay-chah-lee-**tah dehl**-lah **kah**-zah
first course (pasta, soup)	primo piatto	**pree**-moh pee**ah**-toh
main course (meat, fish)	secondo piatto	say-**kohn**-doh pee**ah**-toh
side dishes	contorni	kohn-**tor**-nee
bread	pane	**pah**-nay
cheese	formaggio	for-**mah**-joh
sandwich	panino	pah-**nee**-noh
soup	minestra, zuppa	mee-**nehs**-trah, **tsoo**-pah
salad	insalata	een-sah-**lah**-tah
meat	carne	**kar**-nay
chicken	pollo	**poh**-loh
fish	pesce	**peh**-shay
seafood	frutti di mare	**froo**-tee dee **mah**-ray
fruit / vegetables	frutta / legumi	**froo**-tah / lay-**goo**-mee
dessert	dolci	**dohl**-chee
tap water	acqua del rubinetto	**ah**-kwah dayl roo-bee-**nay**-toh
mineral water	acqua minerale	**ah**-kwah mee-nay-**rah**-lay
milk	latte	**lah**-tay
(orange) juice	succo (d'arancia)	**soo**-koh (dah-**rahn**-chah)
coffee / tea	caffè / tè	kah-**feh** / teh
wine	vino	**vee**-noh
red / white	rosso / bianco	**roh**-soh / bee**ahn**-koh
glass / bottle	bicchiere / bottiglia	bee-kee**ay**-ray / boh-**teel**-yah
beer	birra	**bee**-rah
Cheers!	Cin cin!	cheen cheen
More. / Another.	Ancora un po'. / Un altro.	ahn-**koh**-rah oon poh / oon **ahl**-troh
The same.	Lo stesso.	loh **stehs**-soh
The bill, please.	Il conto, per favore.	eel **kohn**-toh pehr fah-**voh**-ray
tip	mancia	**mahn**-chah
Delicious!	Delizioso!	day-leet-see**oh**-zoh

For more user-friendly Italian phrases, check out *Rick Steves' Italian Phrase Book & Dictionary* or *Rick Steves' French, Italian, and German Phrase Book*.

PRACTICALITIES

INDEX

Explore Europe

At ricksteves.com you can browse through thousands of articles, videos, photos and radio interviews, plus find a wealth of money-saving travel tips for planning your dream trip. And with our mobile-friendly website, you can easily access all this great travel information anywhere you go.

TV Shows

Preview the places you'll visit by watching entire half-hour episodes of Rick Steves' Europe (choose from all 100 shows) on-demand, for free.

ricksteves.com

your travel dreams into affordable reality

Radio Interviews

Enjoy ready access to Rick's vast library of radio interviews covering travel

tips and cultural insights that relate specifically to your Europe travel plans.

Travel Forums

Learn, ask, share! Our online community of savvy travelers is a great resource for first-time travelers to Europe, as well as seasoned pros. You'll find forums on each country, plus travel tips and restaurant/hotel reviews. You can even ask one of our well-traveled staff to chime in with an opinion.

Travel News

Subscribe to our free Travel News e-newsletter, and get monthly updates from Rick on what's happening in Europe.

Audio Europe™

Rick's Free Travel App

Get your FREE **Rick Steves Audio Europe**™ app to enjoy…

- Dozens of self-guided tours of Europe's top museums, sights and historic walks
- Hundreds of tracks filled with cultural insights and sightseeing tips from Rick's radio interviews
- All organized into handy geographic playlists
- For iPhone, iPad, iPod Touch, Android

With Rick whispering in your ear, Europe gets even better.

Find out more at ricksteves.com

Pack Light and Right

Gear up for your next adventure at ricksteves.com

Light Luggage

Pack light and right with Rick Steves' affordable, custom-designed rolling carry-on bags, backpacks, day packs and shoulder bags.

Accessories

From packing cubes to moneybelts and beyond, Rick has personally selected the travel goodies that will help your trip go smoother.

Shop at ricksteves.com

Experience maximum Europe

Save time and energy

This guidebook is your independent-travel toolkit. But for all it delivers, it's still up to you to devote the time and energy it takes to manage the preparation and logistics that are essential for a happy trip. If that's a hassle, there's a solution.

Rick Steves Tours

A Rick Steves tour takes you to Europe's most interesting places with great

with minimum stress

guides and small groups of 28 or less. We follow Rick's favorite itineraries, ride in comfy buses, stay in family-run hotels, and bring you intimately close to the Europe you've traveled so far to see. Most importantly, we take away the logistical headaches so you can focus on the fun.

customers—along with us on 40 different itineraries, from Ireland to Italy to Istanbul. Is a Rick Steves tour the right fit for your travel dreams? Find out at ricksteves.com, where you can also get Rick's latest tour catalog and free Tour Experience DVD.

Join the fun

This year we'll take 18,000 free-spirited travelers— nearly half of them repeat

Europe is best experienced with happy travel partners. We hope you can join us.

See our itineraries at ricksteves.com

EUROPE GUIDES

COUNTRY GUIDES

CITY & REGIONAL GUIDES

SNAPSHOT GUIDES

POCKET GUIDES

Maximize your travel skills
with a good guidebook.

TRAVEL CULTURE

Europe 101
European Christmas
Postcards from Europe
Travel as a Political Act

eBOOKS

Nearly all Rick Steves guides are available as ebooks. Check with your favorite bookseller.

RICK STEVES' EUROPE DVDs

12 New Shows 2015–2016
Austria & the Alps
The Complete Collection 2000-2016
Eastern Europe
England & Wales
European Christmas
European Travel Skills & Specials
France
Germany, BeNeLux & More
Greece, Turkey & Portugal
The Holy Land: Israelis & Palestinians Today
Iran
Ireland & Scotland
Italy's Cities
Italy's Countryside
Scandinavia
Spain
Travel Extras

PHRASE BOOKS & DICTIONARIES

French
French, Italian & German
German
Italian
Portuguese
Spanish

PLANNING MAPS

Britain, Ireland & London
Europe
France & Paris
Germany, Austria & Switzerland
Ireland
Italy
Spain & Portugal

Photo © Patricia Feaster

Avalon Travel
a member of the Perseus Books Group
1700 Fourth Street
Berkeley, CA 94710

Printed in Canada by Friesens
First printing December 2015

ISBN 978-1-63121-203-1

For the latest on Rick's lectures, guidebooks, tours, public radio show, and public television series, contact Rick Steves' Europe, Inc., 130 Fourth Avenue North, Edmonds, WA 98020, tel. 425/771-8303, www.ricksteves.com, rick@ricksteves.com.

Rick Steves' Europe

Special Publications Manager: Risa Laib
Managing Editor: Jennifer Madison Davis
Editors: Glenn Eriksen, Tom Griffin, Katherine Gustafson, Suzanne Kotz, Cathy Lu, John Pierce, Carrie Shepherd
Editorial & Production Assistant: Jessica Shaw
Editorial Intern: Shirley Qiu
Researchers: Virginia Agostinelli, Ben Cameron, Trish Feaster, Cameron Hewitt, Suzanne Kotz
Contributor: Gene Openshaw
Maps & Graphics: David C. Hoerlein, Sandra Hundacker, Lauren Mills, Mary Rostad

Avalon Travel

Senior Editor and Series Manager: Madhu Prasher
Editor: Jamie Andrade
Associate Editor: Maggie Ryan
Copy Editors: Judith Brown and Suzie Nasol
Proofreader: Denise Silva
Indexer: Stephen Callahan
Production and Typesetting: Rue Flaherty, Tabitha Lahr
Cover Design: Kimberly Glyder Design
Maps & Graphics: Kat Bennett, Mike Morgenfeld

Photo Credits

Front Cover: View over the Tuscan countryside and the town of Montepulciano at sunset© Jennifer Barrow | Dreamstime.com
Front Cover Photo: Montepulciano © Jenifoto406/Dreamstime.com
Additional Photography: Dominic Bonuccelli, Ben Cameron, Jennifer Hauseman, Cameron Hewitt, David C. Hoerlein, Anne Jenkins, Gene Openshaw, Michael Potter, Robyn Stencil, Rick Steves, Bruce VanDeventer, Laura VanDeventer, Les Wahlstrom, Ian Watson, Wikimedia Commons

ABOUT THE AUTHOR

RICK STEVES

 Since 1973, Rick Steves has spent 100 days every year exploring Europe. Along with writing and researching a bestselling series of guidebooks, Rick produces a public television series *(Rick Steves' Europe)*, a public radio show *(Travel with Rick Steves)*, a blog (on Facebook), and an app and podcast *(Rick Steves Audio Europe);* writes a nationally syndicated newspaper column; organizes guided tours that take over 20,000 travelers to Europe annually; and offers an information-packed website (www.ricksteves.com). With the help of his hardworking staff of 100 at Rick Steves' Europe—in Edmonds, Washington, just north of Seattle—Rick's mission is to make European travel fun, affordable, and culturally enlightening for Americans.

Connect with Rick:

 facebook.com/RickSteves   twitter: @RickSteves
 instagram: ricksteveseurope